MODELLING INCOME DISTRIBUTION

Modelling Income Distribution

John Creedy

New Zealand Treasury

Edward Elgar
Cheltenham, UK • Northampton, MA, USA

Published by
Edward Elgar Publishing Limited
Glensanda House
Montpellier Parade
Cheltenham
Glos GL50 1UA
UK

Edward Elgar Publishing, Inc.
136 West Street
Suite 202
Northampton
Massachusetts 01060
USA

A catalogue record for this book
is available from the British Library

Library of Congress Cataloguing in Publication Data

Creedy, John, 1949-
     Modelling income distribution / John Creedy.
          p. cm.
     Includes bibliographical references and index.
     1. Income distribution—Mathematical models. I. Title.

HB523 .C736 2002
339.2'01'51—dc21   2002020227

ISBN 1-84376-009-6

Printed and bound in Great Britain by MPG Books Ltd, Bodmin, Cornwall

Contents

Preface

This book collects a number of recent papers, produced during the late 1990s and early 2000s, concerned with modelling income distribution and redistribution. The material divides naturally into three parts.

Part I is concerned with modelling the functional form of the income distribution using the generalised exponential family of distributions. It involves collaborations with Alex Bakker, Jenny Lye and especially Vance Martin. This family of distributions has several advantages. In particular, the distribution can be derived explicitly from the combination of a structural economic model with a stochastic error-correction process. This distinguishes the approach from many models of the genesis of the income distribution, which rely purely on stochastic processes or very simple economic assumptions, or simply use a functional form for its tractability or ability to describe specific datasets. The exponential family is highly flexible and is able to describe a wide range of forms of unimodal and, importantly, multimodal distributions. The modes of the distribution correspond to stable equilibrium positions in the economic model, while antimodes correspond to unstable equilibria. Furthermore the parameters can be expressed as functions of a range of relevant (exogenous) economic variables.

Chapter 1, written with Vance Martin, provides a broad introduction to the generalised exponential family. In chapter 2, written with Jenny Lye and Vance Martin, the income distribution is derived from a model of demand and supply in the labour market. In the case of price distributions, the functional form again arises from an explicit model of demand and supply in the relevant market. In chapter 3, written with Vance Martin, a general model of prices is considered and in chapter 4, written with Jenny Lye and Vance Martin, the foreign exchange market is examined. The estimation of the generalised exponential family requires iterative methods involving repeated numerical integration. The empirical applications in these chapters use individual observations. However, chapter 5, written with Alex Bakker, applies the exponential family to grouped data.

Part II, involving collaboration with Alex Bakker, is concerned with the influence on the personal income distribution of macroeconomic variables. Given the complexity of the relationship between macroeconomic variables and the personal distribution, involving a mapping from just a few variables to a very large number of incomes, it is perhaps not surprising that statistical approaches have usually been taken. These have involved relating summary measures of the income distribution to selected macroeconomic variables using regression analysis. One broad strategy has been to use a measure of inequality as the dependent variable, while others have carried out several regressions, using the income share of a specified percentile of the distribution as dependent variable. In contrast, the approach in part II uses conditional distribution modelling in which the parameters of the distribution depend on macroeconomic variables. Chapter 6 uses the exponential family while chapter 7 involves mixture distributions.

Part III is concerned with several aspects of income redistribution modelling. Chapter 8, written with Justin van de Ven and Peter Lambert, examines the problem of decomposing the redistributive effect of taxation, measured in terms of the difference between the Gini measures of pre-tax and post-tax income, into vertical, horizontal and reranking effects. A practical problem arises in view of the fact that sample data rarely contain individuals having identical incomes, yet horizontal equity is defined in terms of 'equal treatment of equals'. The choice of a class width for combining individuals into groups containing near-equals in terms of pre-tax incomes is examined. The method proposed is to select the class width that maximises the estimated vertical effect. Chapter 9, written with Justin van de Ven, applies the method in the context of the redistributive effect on annual and lifetime incomes in Australia of direct taxes and a range of transfer payments. This is achieved using a cohort lifetime income simulation model allowing for a certain amount of demographic and labour market heterogeneity.

In measuring redistribution where households differ in their composition, a crucial role is played by the choice of equivalence scales. Chapter 10, written with Justin van de Ven, examines this issue in detail. In particular the question arises of whether the scales that minimise estimated reranking can be taken as an implicit set of scales used by decision makers in designing the tax and transfer system. In chapter 11, the decomposition method developed in chapter 8 is applied to indirect taxes in Australia. Comparisons are made between the indirect tax structure before and after the introduction of the Goods and Services Tax. Chapter 12 considers the question of the extent to which redistribution can be achieved by the use of differential consumption taxes, often described as a blunt instrument. The final two chapters, involving collaboration with Duangkamon Chotikapanich, turn to an examination of the statistical properties of a range of inequality, social welfare and progressivity measures. In each case, a Bayesian approach is used to generate posterior distributions of the various measures.

I should like to thank my co-authors, from whom I have learnt so much.

PART I

GENERALISED EXPONENTIAL DISTRIBUTIONS

[1]

Bulletin of Economic Research 50:3, 1998, 0307-3378

NONLINEAR MODELLING USING THE GENERALIZED EXPONENTIAL FAMILY OF DISTRIBUTIONS*

John Creedy and Vance L. Martin

ABSTRACT

This paper introduces an approach to nonlinear modelling which is based on the use of the generalized exponential family of distributions. The flexibility of the approach is illustrated using hypothetical data based on an economic model which exhibits multiple equilibria for certain periods of time and a unique equilibrium for other periods. The distributional analogue of multiple equilibria is multimodality. An advantage of this framework is that discrete jumps can be modelled without the need for identifying the timing of jumps *ex post*. The framework also has the advantage of explaining how smooth changes in market fundamentals can give rise to large and sudden changes in prices. The introduction of economic assumptions into nonlinear models is explained, and it is shown how an explicit form for the distribution of the dependent variable can be derived. It is suggested that the approach has considerable potential in a wide variety of economic contexts.

I. INTRODUCTION

The purpose of this paper is to provide an introduction to nonlinear economic modelling using the generalized exponential family of distributions. The approach is very flexible and extremely powerful, but it is not yet widely used by economists. The development of this type of nonlinear modelling is enhanced by advances in computers which have made possible the use of computationally intensive numerical iterative procedures. However, the paper does not emphasize the technical

*We are grateful to two referees and the Editors for helpful comments on an earlier version of this paper.

details involved, particularly concerning methods of estimation, but instead provides appropriate references to the growing literature. The aim of the paper is rather to illustrate the power of the approach and show how it can be used in a variety of economic contexts. The method is illustrated by examining a time series of hypothetical data and comparing nonlinear and linear approaches. It is suggested that there are contexts in which the assumptions of linear models are not appropriate, even though they may sometimes appear to produce quite good results.

An economic model to be estimated is characterized by a specification in which an endogenous variable is related in some way to a set of exogenous variables. In linear models it is possible to express the model, using a transformation of variables if necessary, so that the conditional value of the endogenous variable is expressed as a linear function of the exogenous variables. The conditional distribution of the endogenous variable is usually regarded as following the normal distribution or one of the other standard unimodal distributions. This paper discusses the advantages of using, instead of a given form of unimodal distribution, the family of distributions known as the generalized exponential family; examples of the application of this family can be found in Cobb *et al.* (1983), Cobb and Zachs (1985), Creedy and Martin (1994), Creedy *et al.* (1996a, b), Fischer and Jammernegg (1986), Lye and Martin (1993a), and Martin (1990).

Nonlinear modelling using the generalized exponential family is particularly useful because it can handle phenomena such as large discrete 'jumps' in the endogenous variable that cannot easily be modelled using modifications of the linear model, such as the addition of dummy variables which require the investigator to specify precisely when the jump takes place. An important feature is that the approach is able to provide a link between simple economic models and the distributional forms of economic variables. This link can be derived directly from the structural form of the model rather than involving the more or less arbitrary imposition of a form of distribution at the estimation stage. The flexibility of the approach means that a wide range of models can be 'nested' and therefore more easily compared. Importantly, it also allows for the possibility that the form of the conditional distributions may themselves change over time, and indeed may sometimes be multimodal.

In order to illustrate alternative approaches, a hypothetical time series of prices is used. The prices are regarded as being influenced by two fundamental variables that are treated as exogenous. Results using a standard linear approach are obtained in Section II. This section also presents an alternative way of specifying the linear model, which facilitates an immediate comparison with the nonlinear approach. The extension of the linear model is presented in Section III, where the generalized exponential family of distributions is introduced. The results of estimating a nonlinear model are contrasted with the use of the linear model. A further valuable feature of the approach is that, starting from a simple economic model, it is possible explicitly to generate the distributional implications of a stochastic process imposed on the model. The way in which the distributions can be generated is described in Section IV. Some examples showing how the general result can easily be applied in special cases are provided in Section V. Brief conclusions are given in Section VI. As mentioned above, the emphasis of this paper is on illustrating the great potential of the approach, not on presenting the technical details in full. However, references are made to more technical studies.

II. LINEAR MODELS

Basic courses in econometrics stress the idea that in a standard regression analysis each observed value of an endogenous or dependent variable is usually regarded as being an observation selected at random from a conditional distribution, for a given set of values of exogenous or independent variables. The estimation and testing of models proceeds by specifying an assumed form for the conditional distributions, and this is combined with the idea of random independent selection. In practice, only one observation from each conditional distribution is available, so the form of the conditional distribution cannot be observed directly. The assumptions that the conditional means are given by a linear combination of the exogenous variables while the conditional variances are homoskedastic are therefore very convenient. With the additional assumption of normality of the conditional distributions, it is easy to show that maximum likelihood estimation reduces to ordinary least squares and has other desirable properties such as efficiency.

Within the context of this type of linear model, it is of course possible to allow for additional complexities, arising for example if the selection process is not random, so that the probability of observing a value from one conditional distribution depends in some way on the values drawn from other conditional distributions, or if the conditional variances are not all the same. When such modifications to the basic model are made, such as assuming that the data generation process involves some serial correlation or introducing heteroskedasticity, the assumption is retained that all the conditional distributions take the same fundamental form, that is the unimodal normal distribution. Even where nonnormal distributions are specified, it is typically assumed that they are unimodal.

This assumption of unimodality often appears to be supported by the available evidence. For example, in the context of the analysis of a stationary time series of relative prices, it is possible to produce an unconditional distribution by a simple process of temporal aggregation, whereby all the relative prices are treated as coming from the same distribution. Such empirical distributions obtained in this way are typically unimodal, although they tend to exhibit sharper peaks and fatter tails than a normal distribution with the same mean and variance. For example in the context of exchange rate returns, see Boothe and Glassman (1987), Friedman and Vandersteel (1982), Hsieh (1989), Mandelbrot (1963), and Tucker and Pond (1988).

II.1. Estimation and prediction

Suppose that an economist has a set of data consisting of a time series of 200 observations on a variable, p_t, that will for convenience be called a price. The price is thought to be influenced by two exogenous variables, x_t and y_t. The price series and the two exogenous variables are shown in Figure 1 The precise model used to generate these hypothetical time series is described in the Appendix; in practice the 'true' model must of course remain unknown.

Linear regression analysis proceeds by specifying an equation in which the price, or a simple transformation such as its logarithm, is a linear function of the exogenous variables, x_t and y_t, or transformed values, and an additive stochastic term, u_t. Faced with the data in Figure 1, alternative specifications or functional forms within the context of linear regression analysis would be estimated and a range of tests applied, starting with the simplest assumptions about the stochastic term, u_t.

Suppose that the linear model is specified as

$$p_t = \alpha_0 + \alpha_1 x_t + \alpha_2 y_t + u_t \tag{1}$$

with the u_ts assumed to be independently distributed as $N(0, \sigma_u^2)$. Each value of u_t is regarded as being independently drawn from a distribution which is assumed to have the same form, $N(0, \sigma_u^2)$, irrespective of the values of x_t and y_t. This implies that prices are also normally distributed, although around a time-varying conditional mean which is a function of both x_t and y_t. Estimation by ordinary least squares produces the following results, where absolute values of t-statistics are given in brackets:

$$\hat{p}_t = -1.746 + 0.185x_t - 0.020y_t \tag{2}$$
$$(5.068)\ (59.166)\quad (0.663)$$

with $\hat{\sigma}_u = 0.462$; $\bar{R}^2 = 0.947$; $DW = 1.327$; $BP(2) = 69.142$; $ARCH(1) = 45.018$; $RESET(1) = 68.213$.[1]

Using conventional criteria of goodness of fit, the linear model

---

[1]The reported diagnostics are: $\hat{\sigma}_u$, the standard error of estimate; $\bar{R}^2$, the degrees of freedom adjusted coefficient of determination; DW, the Durbin–Watson statistic for first-order autocorrelation; $BP(2)$, the Breusch–Pagan statistic for heteroskedasticity which is distributed as χ_2^2; $ARCH(1)$, Engle's statistic for testing for first-order autoregressive conditinal heteroskedasticity which is distributed as χ_1^2; $RESET(1)$, statistic to test for nonlinearities which is distributed as χ_1^2.

performs well. The value for $\bar{R}^2$ shows that a high proportion of variation in p_t is explained by a linear relationship between the dependent
variable and the independent variables x_t and y_t, as well as the intercept
term. A comparison of the actual and the predicted price series, $\hat{p}_t$, that
is the conditional mean in each period, is shown in Figure 2. This shows
that the linear model is able to predict very well the general swings in p_t
over most of the sample. However, closer inspection of Figure 2 reveals
some evidence of misspecification as the linear model fails to capture
the large swings in prices at the start, middle and end of the sample
period. Evidence of misspecification is also highlighted by the *DW* and
BP statistics which both suggest significant serial correlation and heteroskedasticity respectively. These results suggest that there is some underlying characteristic which is not being captured by this linear model. This

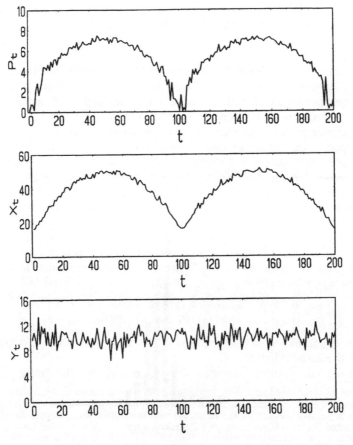

Fig. 1. Data series

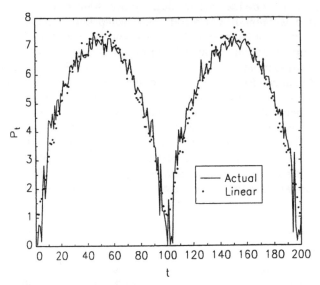

Fig. 2. Actual and predicted p_t based on the linear model

is supported by the *ARCH* and *RESET* test statistics which suggest that there is strong evidence of nonlinearities in the residuals.

One way to test the normality assumption of u_t, and hence p_t, is to construct a histogram of the ordinary least squares residuals. This is presented in Figure 3 and shows that there is no evidence to reject the hypothesis that the distribution of u_t is unimodal. A more formal test of

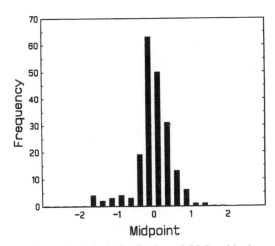

Fig. 3. Empirical distribution of OLS residuals

normality is given by the Jarque–Bera test. The computed value of the test statistic is 114.071. Comparing this value with a χ_2^2 critical value shows that the null hypothesis that the disturbance term u_t is normally distributed is rejected at standard significance levels.

A standard approach to solve the problems of autocorrelation, heteroskedasticity and *ARCH*, are to re-estimate (1) by generalized least squares. It is important to stress at this stage that these solutions are based, implicitly at least, on the assumption that the underlying distribution of p_t is unimodal. There is no sign of multimodality. In fact, as is highlighted by the nonlinear modelling framework developed in Section III below, the rejection of normality using the Jarque–Bera test potentially provides the most illuminating information of all of the diagnostics reported so far, concerning the presence of multimodality.

II.2. A structural form

The linear approach described above began, as do many empirical studies, by writing a linear regression model relating the relevant variables; it was not derived directly from an economic theory of price determination. The specification in (1) may, however, be regarded as the reduced form of a model which is based on a structural form consisting of linear demand and supply functions. The price changes are assumed to be generated by shifts over time in these structural equations. Thus, suppose the demand, q_t^d, and supply, q_t^s, of the good in question can be written respectively as

$$q_t^d = a_t - bp_t \tag{3}$$

$$q_t^s = c_t + dp_t. \tag{4}$$

The intercepts, a_t and c_t, are assumed to be linear functions of the 'fundamental' exogenous variables x_t and y_t respectively, while the slope coefficients, b and d, are assumed to be constant, reflecting the idea that the price changes are produced by shifts in the curves rather than changes in their slopes, although this assumption can be easily relaxed. In equilibrium, $q_t^d = q_t^s$, so the equilibrium price in period t is given by the root of the equation:

$$p_t - \frac{a_t - c_t}{d + b} = 0. \tag{5}$$

II.3. A distributional specification

One way to introduce stochastics into the structural model in (3) and (4) is to include additive shocks in the intercept terms in the supply and demand functions. This has the effect of forcing p_t to deviate from its equilibrium price h_t. Assuming that the shock, v_t, is distributed as $N(0, 1)$, equation (5) generalizes to

$$p_t = h_t + \sigma_u v_t \qquad (6)$$

where h_t is given by

$$h_t = \frac{a_t - c_t}{d + b} \qquad (7)$$

and is the equilibrium price. A comparison between (1) and (6) shows that the equilibrium price, h_t, is also the conditional mean $\alpha_0 + \alpha_1 x_t + \alpha_2 y_t$. It also shows that the linear equation given in (1) can be interpreted as the reduced form of this model.

The conditional price distribution, $f(p_t)$, which follows immediately from (6) and by use of the additive property of the normal distribution, is given by

$$f(p_t) = N(h_t, \sigma_u^2). \qquad (8)$$

The observed prices are treated as being random drawings from a conditional normal distribution whose mean in period t is given by the root of equation (5), which is of course $h_t = (a_t - c_t)/(d + b)$.

The form of the density function for the normal distribution is given by

$$f(p_t) = \frac{1}{\sqrt{2\pi\sigma_u^2}} \exp\left[-\frac{1}{2\sigma_u^2}(p_t - h_t)^2 \right]. \qquad (9)$$

It is useful to consider an alternative way of specifying this density which helps to make the contrast between linear models and the class of nonlinear models developed below more clearly. First, noting that $1/\sqrt{(2\pi\sigma^2)}$ can be expressed as $\exp\left[-\frac{1}{2}\log(2\pi\sigma^2)\right]$, $f(p_t)$ can be rearranged in the form of a second-order polynomial in p_t given by

$$f(p_t) = \exp\left(\theta_{1,t} p_t + \theta_{2,t} p_t^2/2 - \eta_t^*\right) \qquad (10)$$

where the coefficients on p_t and $p_t^2/2$ are respectively given by

$$\theta_{1,t} = \frac{h_t}{\sigma_u^2} \qquad (11)$$

$$\theta_{2,t} = -\frac{1}{\sigma_u^2} \qquad (12)$$

and η_t^* is

$$\eta_t^* = \frac{1}{2}\left[\frac{h_t^2}{\sigma_u^2} + \log\left(2\pi\sigma_u^2\right)\right]. \tag{13}$$

This term varies with t because h_t contains x_t and y_t. Essentially its role is to ensure that $f(p_t)$ qualifies as a density function; that is, it is required to have $\int_{-\infty}^{+\infty} f(p_t)\, dp_t = 1$. For this reason η_t^* is known as the 'normalizing constant'. The term $\theta_{2,t}$ in (10) involves only the variance σ_u^2, which in the present model is assumed to be constant over time. The first term $\theta_{1,t}$ is a function of the exogenous variables and the variance term. This approach to the linear model, involving rewriting the standard expression for the normal distribution as a second-order polynomial, may at first sight appear cumbersome, but it provides the clearest way to see how it can be extended.

III. A NONLINEAR APPROACH

III.1. The generalized exponential family

A nonlinear approach can be developed as a natural extension of the above linear model by the simple addition of terms in the expression for the price distribution in equation (10). These terms may be powers of prices or transformations of prices such as reciprocals or logarithms. This is all that is required to produce the generalized exponential family of distributions. In the case where only additional powers are used, the price distribution, $f(p_t)$, takes the form

$$f(p_t) = \exp\left(\theta_{1,t}p_t + \theta_{2,t}p_t^2/2 + \theta_{3,t}p_t^3/3 + \ldots + \theta_{k,t}p_t^k/k - \eta_t\right) \tag{14}$$

where η_t is a normalizing constant defined as

$$\eta_t = \log \int \exp\left(\theta_{1,t}p_t + \theta_{2,y}p_t^2/2 + \theta_{3,t}p_t^3/3 + \ldots \theta_{k,t}p_t^k/k\right) dp_t. \tag{15}$$

This corresponds to η_t^* above for the normal distribution and ensures that $f(p_t)$ qualifies as a density function. There is thus a direct comparison between equations (14) and (10).

The term in brackets in (14) may contain any number of terms in the polynomial, and as noted above may also contain terms involving transformed values of p, such as its logarithm. If only terms in p_t and p_t^2 appear in (14), then the price distribution reduces to the normal distribution by comparison with (10). If only terms in $\log(p_t)$, where p_t is strictly positive, and p_t appear, the distribution follows the unimodal gamma distribution; whereas if only p_t appears in (14), then it is a simple exponential distribution. Other forms contained within the generalized exponential family include the generalized gamma and generalized Student's t distributions; see Cobb *et al.* (1983), and Lye and Martin (1993a).

The terms $\theta_{j,t}$ in equation (14) are in general assumed to be functions of the fundamental or exogenous variables, x_t and y_t. For example, they could be written as linear functions such as

$$\theta_{j,t} = \alpha_{j,0} + \alpha_{j,1} x_t + \alpha_{j,2} y_t \qquad (16)$$

for $j = 1, 2, \ldots, k$. This means that over time the θs can change. This has the far-reaching implication that the form of the conditional price distribution can change over time. This occurs not necessarily as a result of a changing conditional mean, as in the case of the linear model, or a changing conditional variance, as in the case where there is hetero-skedasticity, but as a result of changes in higher-order conditional moments such as skewness and kurtosis. More interestingly, there is also a possibility that the distribution can change over time from being unimodal to being multimodal. In practice, the precise relationship between the θs and the exogenous variables is not known. However, a significant advantage of the approach is that a form of (14) can be derived from an economic model, as described in the following section. First, the remainder of this section examines the condition under which the distribution has more than one mode and then considers the performance of the nonlinear approach when faced with the hypothetical data used earlier.

III.2. Bimodality and the generalized exponential

It is important to be able to identify whether or not the generalized exponential distribution displays multimodality in any time period. This information is particularly valuable because multimodality may be associated with large discrete jumps in the price, where a movement takes place from one mode to another. Such a jump in the price need not be associated with large changes in the fundamental, or exogenous variable, of interest. This type of phenomenon is observed during stock market crashes where smooth changes in the economic fundamentals, as represented by dividends, are associated with relatively larger movements in the share price; see for example Barskey and De Long (1993), Genotte and Leland (1990), and Lim *et al.* (1998). This phenomenon is also typical of foreign exchange markets where large swings in exchange rates are associated with relatively smaller movements in the economic fundamentals; see Creedy *et al.* (1996b).

For the purpose of identifying bimodality, it is convenient to transform the model. This alternative form exhibits the same qualitative properties as the original model. To show this, consider (14) with $k = 4$, whereby

$$f(p_t) = \exp \left(\theta_{1,t} p_t + \theta_{2,t} p_t^2/2 + \theta_{3,t} p_t^3/3 + \theta_{4,t} p_t^4/4 - \eta_t \right). \qquad (17)$$

This can be transformed to a distribution in the variable w_t by using

$$w_t = p_t(-\theta_{4,t})^{0.25} + \theta_{3,t}(-\theta_{4,t})^{-0.75}/3. \tag{18}$$

After some tedious algebra it can be shown that

$$f(w_t) = \exp\left(\tau_{0,t} w_t + \tau_{1,t} w_t^2/2 - w_t^4/4 - \eta_t^{**}\right) \tag{19}$$

where the terms $\theta_{0,t}$ and $\tau_{1,t}$, are expressed as functions of the θs, and η_t^{**} is the normalizing constant. Notice that the coefficient on $w_t^3/3$ is zero, so that the cubed term is eliminated and the coefficient on $w_t^4/4$ is minus unity. This type of variate transformation is known as a 'diffeomorphism'; in general, in a polynomial of order k, the $(k-1)$th term can be eliminated. For further discussion of this type of transformation see Gilmore (1981).

The importance of the transformation in (18) is that the transformed distribution in (19) exhibits the same characteristics as the untransformed distribution in (17); in particular, if (17) exhibits bimodality then so will (19). The advantage of eliminating the cubic term is that it is easier to examine the conditions for multimodality. It is possible to show, as in Cobb *et al.* (1983, p. 128), that a necessary and sufficient condition for (19) to exhibit bimodality involves the term, δ_t, defined by

$$\delta_t = \frac{\tau_{0,t}^2}{4} - \frac{\tau_{1,t}^3}{27}. \tag{20}$$

This is known as Cardan's discriminant, and it needs to be negative for (19) to have two modes and one antimode. As $\tau_{0,t}$ and $\tau_{1,t}$ are functions of the exogenous variables x_t and y_t, which vary over time, then δ_t also varies over time. Hence δ_t can change sign, say from positive to negative over the sample period, which means that the conditional distribution changes from being unimodal to being multimodal. Inspection of (20) also shows that a necessary condition for bimodality is that $\tau_{1,t}$ needs to be positive; for a discussion in the context of multiple equilibria, see Creedy and Martin (1993, pp. 343–5).

III.3. *Estimation and prediction*

The generalized exponential family, such as the model described in equations (14) and (16), or the simplified transformed version in equation (19), can be estimated using maximum likelihood methods. For a time series consisting of observations on $t = 1, 2, \ldots T$ periods, the log-likelihood is

$$L(\Psi) = \sum_{t=1}^{T} \log f(p_t; \Psi) \tag{21}$$

where Ψ represents the set of parameters that need to be estimated. The maximum likelihood point estimates, given by $\hat{\Psi}$, are those values which maximize $L(\Psi)$. Quasi maximum-likelihood standard errors can be computed in the usual way from the hessian and outer-product of the log-likelihood when evaluated at the maximum-likelihood estimates. Asymptotic t-statistics can be constructed which are asymptotically distributed as $N(0, 1)$ under the usual regularity conditions.

The log-likelihood in (21) is maximized using standard iterative gradient algorithms. This contrasts with the linear model where the first-order conditions for maximum likelihood are solved explicitly for the coefficients. While the use of an iterative algorithm to compute maximum-likelihood estimates is standard, what is not standard for the model developed in this paper is that special attention has to be given to the normalizing constant, η_t. This is because, as inspection of (15) shows, in general η_t is different for each time period, and numerical methods of integration have to be used. Further, as the normalizing constant is a function of the parameters, the first-order conditions for maximum-likelihood estimation also contain the derivatives of η_t with respect to the parameters in Ψ. However, as mentioned earlier, the aim of the present paper is to introduce the approach, so that the more technical aspects of estimation are not discussed here; see Cobb *et al.* (1983) and Lye and Martin (1993a). Computer software for alternative specifications has been developed using GAUSS routines which are available from the authors.

It has been mentioned that a standard approach to prediction with the linear model is simply to take the conditional mean of the dependent variable, for given values of x_t and y_t. With a normal distribution, this conditional mean corresponds to the single model. With the nonlinear model, however, it is necessary to devise an appropriate convention for obtaining predictions because of the possible multimodality of the distribution. One approach, called the 'global' convention, is based on choosing that value corresponding to the highest mode; see Creedy and Martin (1994) for a discussion of other conventions.

As when using the linear model, the true data-generating model cannot be known to the investigator, and it is necessary to specify a form for the distribution. If there is no *a priori* information concerning its form (for example, using the type of model discussed in the following section), one approach is to adopt a general specification whereby the θ terms in (17) are regarded as being functions of both x_t and y_t. An appropriate order for the polynomial in p_t must also be chosen.

The results of estimating one of many potential nonlinear model specifications are as follows, where absolute values of t-statistics, as based on the quasi maximum-likelihood standard errors, are given in brackets:

$$f(p_t) = \exp\left(\hat{\theta}_{1,t}p_t + \hat{\theta}_{2,t}p_t^2/2 + \hat{\theta}_{3,t}p_t^3/3 + \hat{\theta}_{4,t}p_t^4/4 - \hat{\eta}_t\right) \qquad (22)$$

where

$\hat{\theta}_{1,t} = 3.437$
$\quad\quad (3.333)$

$\hat{\theta}_{2,t} = -5.663 - 0.174y_t - 0.220x_t$
$\quad\quad (2.160)\,(0.803)\quad(1.805)$

$\hat{\theta}_{3,t} = 3.805 + 0.304x_t - 0.043y_t$
$\quad\quad (4.945)\,(6.684)\quad(1.073)$

$\hat{\theta}_{4,t} = -2.261$
$\quad\quad (7.343)$

$\hat{\eta}_t$ is the normalizing constant which is written with a circumflex to signify that it is a function of the estimated parameters, and $\hat{\sigma}_u = 0.328$; $\bar{R}^2 = 0.973$; $DW = 2.051$; $BP(2) = 24.844$; $ARCH(1) = 0.946$; $RESET(1) = 6.609$, with the residuals defined as the difference between p_t and the predictions based on the global mode of (22) at each t.[2] In this specification, a fourth-order polynomial is chosen, and the terms $\theta_{1,t}$ and $\theta_{4,t}$ are treated as constant. As explained in the next section, this specification is motivated by a supply and demand model where the slopes of the respective curves are assumed to be constant. A comparison of the adjusted coefficient of determination shows some marginal improvement in goodness of fit with $\bar{R}^2$ increasing from 0.947 for the linear model to 0.973 for the nonlinear model.

Inspection of the t-statistics in (22) suggests that the coefficient on the variable y_t in the function $\theta_{3,t}$ is insignificant. However, the coefficients on both x_t and y_t in the function $\theta_{2,t}$ appear to be insignificant. Faced with these results, a sensible approach is to re-estimate the model deleting only the variable y_t in $\theta_{3,t}$. This gives the following results:

$\hat{\theta}_{1,t} = 3.374$
$\quad\quad (3.192)$

$\hat{\theta}_{2,t} = -4.013 - 0.367y_t - 0.186x_t$
$\quad\quad (1.861)\,(3.812)\quad(1.357)$ $\hfill (23)$

$\hat{\theta}_{3,t} = 3.260 + 0.294x_t$
$\quad\quad (4.307)\,(6.083)$

$\hat{\theta}_{4,t} = -2.203$
$\quad\quad (6.746)$

It can be seen that the coefficient on y_t in $\theta_{2,t}$ has become significant,

[2]The degrees of freedom used in computing $\bar{R}^2$ equals the total number of parameters estimated. For the estimated non-linear model in equation (22), the number of estimated parameters is 8. The diagnostics reported for the estimated non-linear model in (22), as well as subsequent estimated nonlinear models, are the same diagnostics reported for the linear model. For the present purposes, these diagnostics are used as portmanteau tests for identifying the presence of nonlinearity by identifying if there is any additional information in the residuals. On testing for $ARCH$ where the conditional distribution is from the generalized exponential family, see Lim et al. (1998).

while that on x_t clearly remains insignificant. Dropping this last term leads to the following estimated model, where as before absolute values of t-statistics are given in brackets:

$$\hat{\theta}_{1,t} = 2.819$$
$$(3.260)$$
$$\hat{\theta}_{2,t} = -5.563 - 0.380y_t$$
$$(3.622)\,(3.878)$$

(24)

$$\hat{\theta}_{3,t} = 2.633 + 0.254x_t$$
$$(5.251)\,(7.940)$$
$$\hat{\theta}_{4,t} = -1.982$$
$$(8.117)$$

with $\hat{\sigma}_u = 0.379$; $\bar{R}^2 = 0.965$; $DW = 2.022$; $BP(2) = 26.572$; $ARCH(1) = 0.657$; $RESET(1) = 3.744$. The coefficients are now all significantly different from zero.

In terms of standard criteria, the adjusted coefficient of determination shows that there is a marginal improvement in goodness of fit over the linear model, while the DW statistic shows no evidence of autocorrelation. The $ARCH$ and $RESET$ test statistics show no evidence of nonlinearities, and while the BP statistic still points to some evidence of heteroskedasticity the degree of significance of heteroskedasticity has been dramatically decreased from the result reported for the linear model. Comparing the predictions of this model, shown in Figure 4, with

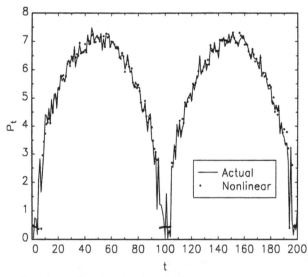

Fig. 4. Actual and predicted p_t based on the estimated nonlinear model in equation (24)

the predictions of the linear model given in Figure 2, shows that the nonlinear model performs better in predicting the price in those periods where prices are relatively low.

More importantly, by using Cardan's discriminant as given in equation (20), the nonlinear model is able to identify periods of bimodality. This is shown by the negative values of Cardan's discriminant, displayed in Figure 5. The bimodal properties of the model are further demonstrated in Figure 6, which gives snapshots of the distribution of prices conditional on specific values of x_t and y_t. Hence, it is concluded that the prices observed for the relevant periods shown in Figure 4 have been selected from an underlying distribution that is multimodal. This has been revealed by the nonlinear approach, in contrast with the linear approach which, at best, suggests only that the tails of the homoskedastic price distribution are somewhat fatter than the normal distribution and that it is a little more peaked.[3] The distribution obtained by temporal aggregation may not, as in the case here, reveal the informa-

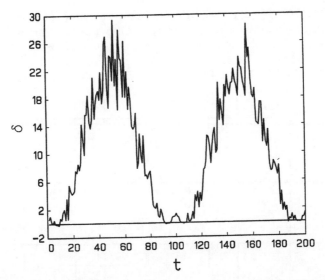

Fig. 5. Cardan's discriminant: $\delta_t < 0$ ($\delta_t > 0$) implies bimodality (unimodality)

[3] In particular, Lye and Martin (1993b) show that a Lagrange multiplier test of the joint restrictions $\theta_3 = \theta_4 = 0$, in the density

$$f(p_t) = \exp\left(\theta_1 p_t + \theta_2 p_t^2/2 + \theta_3 p_t^3/3 + \theta_4 p_t^4/4 - \eta\right)$$

is equivalent to the Jarque–Bera test of normality. The implication of this result for empirical research is that when the normality assumption is rejected, this could be the result that the underlying distribution comes from the generalized exponential family which can exhibit multimodality.

tion that multimodality is present in some of the periods, particularly if there are relatively few periods of such multimodality.

It is shown later, and in the Appendix, that this is in fact the model used to generate the hypothetical data. The parameter estimates are close to those used to generate the data, and the three periods of multimodality identified in Figure 5, namely at the start, middle and end of the sample, are the correct periods. In particular, the number of

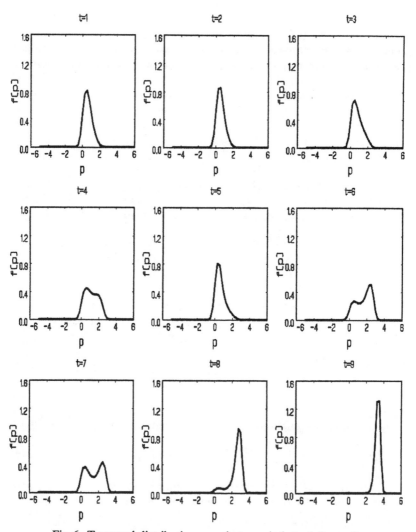

Fig. 6. Temporal distribution snapshots: periods $t = 1, 2, \ldots, 9$

points in time where the actual distribution is bimodal is 24, of which the estimated model predicts 17 correctly. The estimated model does not predict any periods of bimodality when the true distribution is unimodal. In comparison with the linear model, the nonlinear model is able to capture a great deal more of the properties of the data generation process. The investigator does not need to know *ex ante* which periods display multimodality and involve jumps from one mode to another.

IV. DATA GENERATING PROCESSES

The procedure followed in Section III is one in which the price distribution at any time is specified as a generalized exponential distribution which is conditional on the exogenous variables. Without knowing any thing about the true data generation process, it was shown how an investigator might select various specifications. The purpose of this section is to show how it is possible to start from an *a priori* specification of a model and generate the implied form of the distribution. Instead of the linear structural form of the model where the equilibrium priced is the unique root of the linear equation (5), it is possible to start with a nonlinear structure whereby the equation giving the equilibrium price may have more than one root. In addition, as shown in the following subsection, the stochastics can be introduced into the structure in a more complex manner.

IV.1. The stochastic differential equation

Suppose an economic model of price determination generates the equilibrium price as the root, or an appropriate root, of the equation

$$\mu(p_t) = 0. \tag{25}$$

The function $\mu(p_t)$ may, for example, be a polynomial in p_t, where the coefficients on p_t are time-varying as they depend in some way on exogenous economic variables. This represents the deterministic form of the price model. For example, in the partial equilibrium supply and demand model discussed in Section II, $\mu(p_t)$ is a linear function, $p_t - h_t$, with the equilibrium price given as a linear function of the exogenous variables. In that linear context, the observed price in each period is regarded as a random drawing from a normal distribution with the equilibrium price as the arithmetic mean. Examples of alternative models which give rise to nonlinear forms of $\mu(p_t)$ are given below, but at this stage it is useful to concentrate on the stochastics of the general form of the model.

Stochastics can be introduced into the deterministic model in various ways. One approach is to assume that (25) represents the mean of a stochastic process and that deviations from the mean are regarded as arising from continuous additive stochastic shocks. The stochastic representation of the model is then given by

$$\frac{dp_t}{dt} = -\mu(p_t) + \sigma_t v_t \tag{26}$$

where the stochastic term, v_t, is assumed to follow a normal distribution with zero mean and unit variance. This differential equation can be interpreted as an 'error correction' model whereby the price adjusts continuously from its mean as a result of short-run stochastic shocks, v_t; see Creedy *et al.* (1996b). The negative sign means that on average the price adjusts over time back to the long-run equilibrium position, that is it 'error corrects'. Indeed, (25) can be regarded as a special case of (26) since in the absence of random shocks, $v_t = 0$, prices are in equilibrium and $dp_t/dt = 0$. The formulation in (26) may usefully be compared with the linear model as expressed in (6). The latter introduces stochastics simply by adding a normally distributed 'disturbance' term to the equilibrium price.

Since it is assumed that p_t and v_t are continuous random variables, it is convenient to express (26) in its stochastic continuous time form, which produces what is known as an Ito process (see Kamien and Schwartz, 1981, pp. 243–4). This can be written as follows:

$$dp_t = -\mu(p_t)\,dt + \sigma(p_t)\,dW_t. \tag{27}$$

In this formulation, $\mu(p_t)$ is the (instantaneous) mean given by (27) and $\sigma^2(p_t)$ is the (instantaneous) variance; the latter is in general also a function of p_t. The term dW_t is equal to $(v_t/\sigma(p_t))\,dt$, where W_t is known as a Wiener process, such that dW_t is distributed as $N(0, dt)$. This represents the continuous time analogue of the normal distribution. For a more formal discussion of the relationship between (26) and (27), see Brock and Malliaris (1982, pp. 67–8).

IV.2. Transitional and stationary distributions

For a given set of structural parameters, the imposition of the above stochastic process implies that p_t is a random variable with density function $f(p_t)$. In view of the fact that the structural parameters themselves may change as a result of changes in any exogenous variables of which the structural parameters are functions, it is necessary to distinguish two types of distribution. First, if in the deterministic form of the model, adjustment of prices towards equilibrium is instantaneous, then the continuous stochastic process described in (27) results in a stable distribution. This can be referred to as a stationary distribution. Secondly, when adjustment is not instantaneous, the process can be regarded as moving through a sequence of transitional distributions before converging to the stationary distribution. It is important to stress that the stationary distribution is in general a function of exogenous variables. By changing the values of the exogenous variables this gives rise to a sequence of transitional distributions which converges to a stationary distribution. If the values of the exogenous variables do not change thereafter, realized observations on p_t will come from this stationary distribution.

This transitional distribution can be examined by considering a shock to the system resulting from an exogenous change in the structural parameters in $\mu(p_t)$. If adjustment is not instantaneous, then over time the process moves through a sequence of temporary equilibria. Associated with each temporary equilibrium is the transitional density of p_t. The dynamics of the process given by (27) are summarized by the Kolmogorov forward equation (see, for example, Cox and Miller, 1984, p. 208):

$$\frac{\partial f_t(p_t)}{\partial t} = \frac{\partial}{\partial p_t}[\mu(p_t)f_t(p_t)] + \frac{1}{2}\frac{\partial^2}{\partial p_t^2}[\sigma^2(p_t)f_t(p_t)]. \tag{28}$$

This is a partial differential equation which defines the transitional density, $f_t(p_t)$, at each point in time. Unfortunately, except for very simple expressions for both the mean and the variance, $\mu(p_t)$ and $\sigma^2(p_t)$, no analytical solution for this partial differential equation exists. The complexity of apparently simple processes is highlighted in Soong (1973). One procedure to overcome this problem is the concept of the stationary density mentioned above, and discussed by Soong (1973, pp. 197–9).

The stationary density represents the stochastic analogue of long-run equilibrium in the deterministic model; see Brock and Malliaris (1982, pp. 106–8). It is possible to derive analytical expressions for the stationary density using general expressions for the mean and the variance. From (28), the stationary density, $f(p_t)$, is found by setting

$$\frac{\partial f(p_t)}{\partial t} = 0. \tag{29}$$

This converts the partial differential equation in (28) to an ordinary differential equation in the stationary density $f(p_t)$ which is independent of time. The general expression for the stationary density is derived as follows. First combine (28) and (29) to get

$$0 = \frac{d}{dp_t}[\mu(p_t)f(p_t)] + \frac{1}{2}\frac{d^2}{dp_t^2}[\sigma^2(p_t)f(p_t)]. \tag{30}$$

Expanding the second term using the product rule, (30) can be rewritten as

$$0 = \frac{d}{dp_t}[\mu(p_t)f(p_t)] + \frac{1}{2}\frac{d}{dp_t}\left[f(p_t)\frac{d\sigma^2(p_t)}{dp_t} + \sigma^2(p_t)\frac{df(p_t)}{dp_t}\right]. \tag{31}$$

Integrating both sides with respect to p_t gives a first-order linear differential equation

$$k = \mu(p_t)f(p_t) + \frac{1}{2}\left[f(p_t)\frac{d\sigma^2(p_t)}{dp_t} + \sigma^2(p_t)\frac{df(p_t)}{dp_t}\right] \tag{32}$$

where k is a constant of integration. Solving for $df(p_t)/dp_t$ gives

$$\frac{df(p_t)}{dp_t} = \frac{2k}{\sigma^2(p_t)} - \left[\frac{2\mu(p) + d\sigma^2(p_t)/dp_t}{\sigma^2(p_t)}\right]f(p_t). \tag{33}$$

Finally, the stationary density is given as the solution of this differential equation:

$$f(p_t) = \exp\left[-\int_0^{p_t}\left(\frac{2\mu(s) + d\sigma^2(s)/ds}{\sigma^2(s)}\right)ds - \eta_t\right] \tag{34}$$

where η_t denotes the appropriate normalizing constant to ensure that $f(p_t)$ qualifies as a density. This density represents the generalized exponential distribution discussed in Section III.

It is also possible to show that the number of modes and antimodes of the density is given by the number of roots of

$$2\mu(p_t) + d\sigma^2(p_t)/dp_t = 0. \tag{35}$$

For the case where the variance is constant, $d\sigma^2(p_t)/dp_t = 0$, the modes and antimodes equal the stable and unstable equilibrium values respectively. In the general case where the variance is not constant, the modes and antimodes are displaced from the equilibrium points by the factor $d\sigma(p_t)/dp_t$. The variance of the process, $\sigma^2(p_t)$, plays an important part in determining the form of the stationary density; see Cobb *et al.* (1983).

The result shown in equation (34) is extremely useful. It can be applied directly to a wide variety of contexts, where the forms of $\mu(p_t)$ and $\sigma^2(p_t)$ are given from basic economic arguments. The way in which it can be applied is perhaps best illustrated by considering a number of examples, and several special cases are therefore discussed in the following section.

V. EXAMPLES OF NONLINEAR MODELS

V.1. Partial equilibrium analysis

In order to illustrate how the above results can be used, consider again the special case where the equilibrium price in a partial equilibrium model is given by the root of equation (5). This can be written as $\mu(p_t) = p_t - h_t$, where the variable h_t is understood to be a function of the exogenous variables. Suppose also that the variance is constant, so that $\sigma^2(p_t) = \gamma$. Substituting these assumptions into (34) gives the stationary distribution

$$f(p_t) = \exp\left[-\int_0^{p_t}\left(\frac{2(s - h_t)}{\gamma}\right)ds - \eta_t\right]. \tag{36}$$

Integrating and collecting terms gives the result that

$$f(p_t) = \exp\left(\theta_{1,t} p_t + \theta_{2,t} p_t^2 - \eta_t\right) \tag{37}$$

with

$$\theta_{1,t} = 2h_t/\gamma \tag{38}$$

$$\theta_{2,t} = -1/\gamma. \tag{39}$$

Comparison with (10) shows that this stationary distribution corresponds to the familiar normal distribution. Substitution of these assumptions into (35) shows, not surprisingly, that this distribution has just one mode. This example serves to illustrate the link between the linear and nonlinear models: the former is just a special case of the latter.

V.2. Variance proportional to price

A modification of the model of the previous subsection is obtained by allowing the variance, $\sigma^2(p_t)$, to be proportional to the price instead of being constant, so that $\sigma^2(p_t) = \gamma p_t$. Substitution into (34) gives

$$f(p_t) = \exp\left[-\int_0^{p_t}\left(\frac{2(s - h_t) + \gamma}{\gamma s}\right)ds - \eta_t\right]. \tag{40}$$

The integration of the term in $1/s$ introduces $\log(p_t)$, so that the stationary distribution becomes

$$f(p_t) = \exp\left(\theta_{1,t}\log(p_t) + \theta_{2,t} p_t - \eta_t\right) \tag{41}$$

with

$$\theta_{1,t} = -(1 - 2h_t/\gamma) \tag{42}$$

$$\theta_{2,t} = -2/\gamma. \tag{43}$$

This is the unimodal gamma distribution. The term $\theta_{1,t}$ is a function of the exogenous variables which produce the shifts in the structural equations, while the term $\theta_{2,t}$ depends only on the variance term γ.

V.3. A structural model with multiple equilibria

The previous two examples have involved the linear reduced form of a partial equilibrium structural model. Consider next an exchange model involving two goods, where the demands for these goods at time t, $q^d_{i,t}$ ($i=1, 2$) are assumed to be linear functions of the relative price, where now $p_t = p_{1,t}/p_{2,t}$, such that

$$q^d_{1,t} = a_t - b_t p_t \tag{44}$$

$$q^d_{2,t} = c_t - d_t p_t^{-1}. \tag{45}$$

In this formulation, the intercepts and slopes of the two demand curves, $a_t, \ldots, d_t$, are given t subscripts to indicate that they can change over time. Each parameter may be specified as a function of a set of exogenous variables. The fundamental reciprocal demand and supply concept means that only the two demand curves need to be specified. This is in fact a special case of an exchange model which has a long pedigree; see Creedy (1992, 1996). If $q^s_{2,t}$ denotes the supply of good 2 in period t, then

$$p_{1,t}/p_{2,t} = q^s_{2,t}/q^d_{1,t} \tag{46}$$

so that the supply of good 2 in period t is given by $p_t q^d_{1,t}$. Equating this with the demand for good 2, $q^d_{2,t}$, gives the equilibrium price as the root or roots of

$$b_t p_t^3 - a_t p_t^2 + c_t p_t - d_t = 0. \tag{47}$$

The reduced form of the model in (47) is thus a cubic, which can have up to three distinct roots. Substitution into (34), with the additional assumption that the variance, $\sigma^2(p_t)$, is constant at γ, gives the result that the equilibrum distribution of the relative price is

$$f(p_t) = \exp\left[-\frac{2}{\gamma} \int_0^{p_t} (b_t s^3 - a_t s^2 + c_t s - d_t)\, ds - \eta_t \right]. \tag{48}$$

The integration of this expression gives

$$f(p_t) = \exp\left(\theta_{1,t} p_t + \theta_{2,t} p_t^2/2 + \theta_{3,t} p_t^3/3 + \theta_{4,t} p_t^4/4 - \eta_t \right) \tag{49}$$

where

$$\theta_{1,t} = 2d_t/\gamma \tag{50}$$

$$\theta_{2,t} = -2c_t/\gamma \tag{51}$$

$$\theta_{3,t} = 2a_t/\gamma \tag{52}$$

$$\theta_{4,t} = -2b_t/\gamma. \tag{53}$$

In this model, shifts in the two demand curves are produced solely by variations over time in the intercepts, a_t and c_t, resulting from changes in the exogenous variables which influence them. Hence the two terms $\theta_{2,t}$ and $\theta_{3,t}$ can also be expressed as the same types of function of the exogenous variables. If the slope coefficients, b_t and d_t, are constant over time, so that $b_t = b$ and $d_t = d$ for all t, then inspection of (50) and (53) shows that the terms $\theta_{1,t}$ and $\theta_{4,t}$ are also constant over time. This is indeed the basic model used to generate the hypothetical data used above, as explained in the Appendix.

It can also be seen by comparison with the previous example that the alternative assumption that the variance term is proportional to the price, so that $\sigma^2(p_t) = \gamma p_t$, leads to what is referred to as a generalized gamma distribution because of the introduction of the term in $\log(p_t)$; see Cobb *et al.* (1983). The number of modes and antimodes of the distribution of relative prices given in (49) is given by the number of roots of (35). It can be shown that the antimode corresponds to the root of (47) which is unstable: see Creedy and Martin (1993).

The fundamental result in (34) can therefore be applied to a large variety of economic models. So far, the discussion has been in terms of time series models, but the approach can also be used in a cross-sectional context; for an application to modelling the distribution of income, see Creedy *et al.* (1996a). If the economic model does not give rise to a convenient polynomial for $\mu(p_t)$, it is usually possible to convert it to a polynomial of appropriate order using an appropriate Taylor series expansion; see Creedy and Martin (1993, pp. 346–7).

VI. CONCLUSIONS

This paper has introduced an approach to nonlinear modelling which is based on the use of the generalized exponential family of distributions. The considerable flexibility of the approach has been illustrated using hypothetical data based on an economic model which exhibits multiple equilibria for certain periods of time and a unique equilibrium for other periods. It was shown that the distributional analogue of multiple equilibria is multimodality.

An important advantage of this framework is that discrete jumps can be modelled in a natural way without the need for identifying the timing of jumps *ex post*. This is particularly valuable for policy analysis. For example, one of the fundamental exogenous variables of the model may be a policy variable that can be controlled by the government. It is possible that a very small change in such a variable can in some time periods lead to a very large jump in the dependent variable, depending on the values of other exogenous variables. The same type of change in the policy variable may at other times have only a small effect on the dependent variable. Such jumps can be predicted even if they have never been observed during the sample period.

The framework developed in the paper also has the advantage of explaining how smooth changes in market fundamentals can give rise to large and sudden changes in prices, as is characteristic of foreign exchange and stock markets. This result is important as it suggests that when standard economic models break down during stock market crashes, for example, this need not be the result of a misspecification of the variables used to model the market fundamentals, but it may represent the adoption of an incorrect functional form.

The introduction of economic assumptions into nonlinear models has been explained, and it was shown, with the addition of stochastics, how an explicit form for the distribution of the dependent variable can be derived. It is suggested that the approach has considerable potential in a wide variety of economic contexts.

Department of Economics   *Received February 1995*
University of Melbourne   *Final version accepted October 1997*

REFERENCES

Barsky, R. B. and De Long, J. B. (1993). 'Why does the stock market fluctuate?' *Quarterly Journal of Economics*, vol. CVIII, pp. 291–311.
Boothe, P. and Glassman, D. (1987). 'The statistical distribution of exchange rates: empirical evidence and economic implications', *Journal of International Economics*, vol. 22, pp. 297–319.
Brock, W. A. and Malliaris, A. G. (1982). *Stochastic Methods in Economics and Finance*. North-Holland, New York.
Cobb, L., Koppstein, P. and Chen, N. H. (1983). 'Estimation and moment recursion relations for multimodal distributions of the exponential family', *Journal of the American Statistical Association*, vol. 78, pp. 124–30.
Cobb, L. and Zacks, S. (1985). 'Applications of catastrophe theory for statistical modelling in the biosciences', *Journal of the American Statistical Association*, vol. 80, pp. 793–802.
Cox, D. R. and Miller, H. D. (1984). *The Theory of Stochastic Processes*. Chapman & Hall, London.
Creedy, J. (1992). *Demand and Exchange in Economic Analysis*. Edward Elgar, Aldershot.
Creedy, J. (1996). *General Equilibrium and Welfare*. Edward Elgar, Aldershot.
Creedy, J., Lye, J. N. and Martin, V. L. (1996a). 'A labour market equilibrium model of the personal distribution of earnings', *Journal of Income Distribution*, vol. 6, pp. 127–44.
Creedy, J., Lye, J. N. and Martin, V. L. (1996b). 'A nonlinear model of the real US/UK exchange rate', *Journal of Applied Econometrics*, vol. 11, pp. 669–89.

Creedy, J. and Martin, V. L. (1993). 'Multiple equilibria and hysteresis in simple exchange models', *Economic Modelling*, vol. 10, pp. 339–47.

Creedy, J. and Martin, V. L. (eds) (1994). *Chaos and Nonlinear Models in Economics*. Edward Elgar, Aldershot.

Fischer, E. O. and Jammernegg, W. (1986). 'Empirical investigation of a catastrophe theory extension of the Phillips curve', *Review of Economics and Statistics*, vol. 68, pp. 9–17.

Friedman, D. and Vandersteel, S. (1982). 'Short-run fluctuations in foreign exchange rates: evidence from the data 1973–79', *Journal of International Economics*, vol. 13, pp. 171–86.

Gennotte, G. and Leland, H. (1990). 'Market liquidity, hedging, and crashes', *American Economic Review*, vol. 80, pp. 999–1021.

Gilmore, R. (1981). *Catastrophe Theory for Scientists and Engineers*. John Wiley, New York.

Hsieh, D. A. (1989). 'Modeling heteroskedasticity in daily foreign-exchange rates', *Journal of Business and Economic Statistics*, vol. 7, pp. 307–17.

Kamien, M. I. and Schwartz, N. L. (1981). *Dynamic Optimization: The Calculus of Variations and Optimal Control in Economics and Management*. North-Holland, New York.

Lim, G. C., Martin, V. L. and Teo, L. (1998). 'Endogenous jumping and asset price dynamics', *Macroeconomic Dynamics*, forthcoming.

Lim, G. C., Lye, J. N., Martin, G. M. and Martin, V. L. (1998). 'The distribution of exchange rate returns and the pricing of currency options', *Journal of International Economics*, forthcoming.

Lye, J. and Martin, V. L. (1993a). 'Robust estimation, non-normalities and generalized exponential distributions', *Journal of the American Statistical Association*, vol. 88, pp. 253–9.

Lye, J. N. and Martin, V. L. (1993b). 'Non-linear time series modelling and distributional flexibility', *Journal of Time Series Analysis*, vol. 15, pp. 65–84.

Mandelbrot, B. B. (1963). 'The variation of certain speculative prices', *Journal of Business*, vol. 36, pp. 394–419.

Martin, V. L. (1990). *Properties and Applications of Distributions from the Generalized Exponential Family*, PhD thesis, Monash University.

Soong, T. T. (1973). *Random Differential Equations in Science and Engineering*. Academic Press, New York.

Tucker, A. L. and Pond, L. (1988). 'The probability distribution of foreign exchange price changes: tests of candidate processes', *Review of Economics and Statistics*, vol. LXX, pp. 638–47.

APPENDIX: GENERATING THE HYPOTHETICAL TIME SERIES

A.1. The model

The basic model used is the exchange model introduced in Section V.3, involving two goods in a general equilibrium context. The feature of the model is that the demands are linear functions of the relative price, p_t, and the reduced form is the cubic equation in (47). It is assumed that the intercepts, a_t and c_t, of the demand curves in equations (44) and

(45), are functions respectively of the exogenous variables x_t and y_t, such that

$$a(x_t)=3+0.25x_t \tag{A1}$$

$$c(y_t)=5+0.5y_t. \tag{A2}$$

The slope terms in equations (44) and (45) are, however, assumed to be constant at

$$b=2 \tag{A3}$$

$$d=3. \tag{A4}$$

It is also assumed that the variance $\sigma^2(p_t)$ in (48) is constant, where

$$\sigma^2(p_t)=\gamma=2. \tag{A5}$$

It is also necessary to specify the processes used to generate hypothetical values of the exogenous variables x_t and y_t. The series x_t is generated as

$$x_t=15+1.4t-0.014t^2+u_{x,t} \tag{A6}$$

for $1\le t\le100$. For $100<t\le200$, t and t^2 on the right-hand side of (A6) are simply replaced by $t-100$ and $(t-100)^2$. The error term $u_{x,t}$ is distributed as $N(0, 1)$. The series y_t is generated as

$$y_t=10+u_{y,t} \tag{A7}$$

where $u_{y,t}$ is $N(0, 1)$.

The choice of parameters and specifications of the exogenous variables in the simulation experiment give rise to 24 points in time where the price distribution is bimodal. This results in an unconditional distribution of p_t through temporal aggregation of the data which is unimodal. It has been seen that such an approach can give a misleading indication of the form of the appropriate conditional distributions. The simulation experiments could also be run where the number of points of time for which the conditional distribution is bimodal is increased. This, however, would raise the possibility that the unconditional distribution is also bimodal, which is not typical of actual data.

A.2. Simulation procedure

The above model can be used to provide a simulated price series using an approach known as the 'the inverse cumulative density method'. This involves constructing the cumulative density and using a uniform random number generator. The approach consists of the following steps. First, using the expressions for (A1)–(A5) in (50)–(53), the density function in (49) for the random variable p_t is

$$f(p_t) = \exp\left[3p_t - (5 + 0.5y_t)p_t^2/2 + (3 + 0.25x_t)p_t^3/3 - 2p_t^4/4 - \eta_t\right] \qquad \text{(A8)}$$

where as before the normalizing constant for each period, η_t, is chosen to ensure that the condition $\int f(p_t)\, dp_t = 1$ is satisfied. Second, a cumulative density is constructed:

$$F(u) = \int_{-\infty}^{u} f(p_t)\, dp_t. \qquad \text{(A9)}$$

As there is no explicit expression for the cumulative density, it is computed numerically by replacing the integral sign with a summation sign and choosing small steps for dp_t. Third, using the property that the cumulative density is monotonic and starts at zero and ends at unity, a uniform random number generator can be used to generate random numbers for u in (A9) on the interval $[0, 1]$. Associated with each random number u in (A9) is a value for p, which acts as the random price used.

To obtain a time series of p_t for the periods $t = 1, 2, \ldots, 200$, the approach consists of initially setting $t = 1$ in (A8). This amounts to substituting in the realized values of x_1 and y_1 in (A8). By using (A9) with $t = 1$, the realized price p_1 is generated. The time step is incremented to $t = 2$, and the process repeated until the last time step, $t = 200$. Hence at each t the density used to generate the realization of p_t varies as a result of the variation in the values of x_t and y_t when substituted in (A8).

[2]
A LABOR MARKET EQUILIBRIUM MODEL OF THE PERSONAL DISTRIBUTION OF EARNINGS

John Creedy, J.N. Lye, and V.L. Martin

Univrsity of Melbourne

A model of the distribution of income is derived from a two market general equilibrium model consisting of a goods market and a labor market. The dynamics of income distributional changes as well as their stationary counterparts are also derived.

I. INTRODUCTION

There is a substantial literature seeking to explain the form of the distribution of earnings in terms of the outcome of some kind of random process. Approaches involve the application of a form of the central limit theorum to the sum of random variables, or the analysis of the results of applying a transition matrix to an arbitrary initial distribution, in terms of the characteristic vector corresponding to the unit root of the matrix. In each case the "final" distribution is independent of the initial distribution. These include the famous "law of proportiate effect" of Gibrat, discussed by Aitchison and Brown (1957) and Brown (1976) as a possible genesis of the lognormal form, and the alternative model of Champernowne (1953) which produces the Pareto distribution; see also Mandelbrot (1960), Klein (1962), Hart (1973), and Shorrocks (1975). For a useful nontechnical discussion see Phelps Brown (1977, pp. 290–294).

These models have, perhaps not surprisingly, been criticized on the grounds that they are "purely statistical" and thereby have a negligible degree of economic content; see in particular Mincer (1970) and Lydall (1979, pp. 233-236). Lydall (1976, p. 19) has argued, for example, that "this type of stochastic theory is ... not scientific in the usual sense. The "explanation" which it offers is at a very superficial

---

Direct all correspondence to: **John Creedy**, Department of Economics, University of Melbourne, Parkville 3052, Australia.

Journal of Income Distribution, 6(1), 127–144
ISSN: 0926-6437

---

level and does not explain any of the real factors—economic or other—which are responsible for the shape of the distribution."

The purpose of the present paper is to explore an approach to modelling the earnings distribution which involves both stochastic and economic components. Individuals' earnings are seen as resulting from a simple market supply and demand model in which individual earnings are deterministic, though the model can have multiple solutions. A stochastic error correction mechanism is then imposed and the resulting form of the distribution of earnings is derived, where the distributional analogue of multiple equilibria in the deterministic form is multimodality. In particular the model generates a flexible functional form described as the generalized gamma distribution. Special cases of this general distribution include the gamma, exponential and Weibull distributions as well as the power distribution. An advantage of the approach is that changes in the form of the distribution over time can be modelled explicitly in terms of changes in commodity and labour market conditions since the parameters governing the characteristics of the distribution are shown to be functions of the underlying economic parameters of the model. This makes it possible to give a clearer economic interpretation of the distribution of personal income and the reasons for changes in inequality over time.

The basic model is introduced in Section II, which describes the labor demand and supply components and the stochastic specification. In view of the exploratory nature of the analysis, the model is very simple; however it is rich enough to generate a distribution of personal earnings from first principles which is sufficiently flexible to capture a range of observed distributional characteristics. Section III describes the method of estimation, where both least squares and maximum likelihood methods are discussed. The generalized gamma distribution is applied in Section IV to estimating the distribution of alternative earnings models. Conclusions are drawn in Section V.

II. THE MODEL

A. Labor Demand and Supply

Consider a market in which all individuals are assumed to be in the labor force. Individual i's real earnings are denoted y_i, which are by definition the product of the wage rate per hour which the individual can obtain, w_i, and the number of hours worked, n_i. Thus:

$$y_i = w_i n_i \qquad (1)$$

The individual's labor supply may of course be derived using a standard utility maximising approach in which the arguments of the utility function are consumption and leisure. For present purposes it is convenient to adopt the approach discussed by Robbins (1930) which exploited the reciprocal nature of labor supply in terms of the demand for goods, or real income. Suppose that the individual's demand for goods can be expressed as the following simple function of the real wage, the reciprocal of which represents the price of goods in terms of labor:

$$x_i^d = \alpha_i - \beta_i w_i^{-1} \qquad (2)$$

The associated labor supply function is therefore given by:

$$n_i^s = x_i^d / w_i \qquad (3)$$

The labor demand function facing the individual can be viewed as resulting from profit maximizing, such that the optimal solution involves the demand for labor being expressed as a function of the real wage. For a linear labor demand schedule, the relationship is represented as:

$$n_i^d = \delta_i - \gamma_i w_i \qquad (4)$$

It is required to solve these equations for the individual's real income, y_i. This can be done as follows. Use the demand function in Equation (2) to express w_i in terms of x_i^d, so that $w_i = \beta_i/(\alpha_i - x_i^d)$, and substitute the result into Equation (3) to give:

$$n_i^s = x_i^d(\alpha_i - x_i^d)/\beta_i \qquad (5)$$

This is in fact the "offer curve" of the individual, since it expresses the supply of labor directly in terms of the demand for goods: this has the typical "backward bending" shape of standard offer curves. In equilibrium, the supply of labor given by Equation (5) must equal the demand as in Equation (4), where in the latter, w_i is also expressed in terms of x_i^d. This equilibrium condition gives, after some rearrangement, the following cubic, writing $x_i = x_i^d$:

$$x_i^3 - 2\alpha_i x_i^2 + (\alpha_i^2 + \beta_i \delta_i) x_i - (\beta_i \delta_i \alpha_i - \gamma_i \beta_i^2) = 0 \qquad (6)$$

In this model real consumption is equivalent to real earnings since there is no role for savings, so it is only necessary to subsitute for $y_i = x_i$ in Equation (6) to obtain the equation for earnings. Hence:

$$y_i^3 - 2\alpha_i y_i^2 + (\alpha_i^2 + \beta_i \delta_i) y_i - (\beta_i \delta_i \alpha_i - \gamma_i \beta_i^2) = 0 \qquad (7)$$

This summarizes the equilibrium properties for the *i*th individual in the market. There may be a unique equilibrium when Equation (7) has a single real root, or multiple equilibria when it exhibits two or three real roots. In cases where there are three real roots, two of the equilibria can be shown to be stable; and if there are two real roots, only one is stable.

It can also be shown that the equilibrium wage rate corresponds to the root or roots of a cubic equation: substitute for x_i^d in Equation (3) using Equation (2), and equate the result to the labor demand given by Equation (4). The equilibrium properties of the determination of a price, in this case the price of labor per hour, rather than the product of price and quantity, in this case real earnings, have been examined in detail in Creedy and Martin (1993, 1994).

The above supply and demand model is obviously very simple, but for present purposes it is sufficient for demonstrating how such an economic model can be used as the basic component of a distributional model. Further complications may provide a more detailed foundation for the functions used, and may even change the order of the polynomial in Equation (7). A further possibility is that the equilibrium real wage may not be expressed as the root (or roots) of a polynomial, but it would be possible to rewrite the condition as a polynomial using a Taylor series expansion. The major elements of the approach followed below would thus remain unchanged, and examples of alternative specifications are discussed in Section II.C.

B.   The Stochastic Specification

The analysis so far is deterministic and describes the equilibrium properties of the level of earnings of an individual, with a specified demand function for goods (real earnings) and facing a demand function for labor. If some joint distribution of the parameters α_i, β_i, δ_i, γ_i, were specified, it would in principle be possible to examine the implied distribution of real earnings, though this would be extremely complex and some method of handling the multiple equilibria would be required. It is most unlikely that any analytical expression for the distribution could be obtained following such an approach. Furthermore, it would in some sense simply be "pushing back" the explanation of the form of the distribution one stage, in that some rationale for the joint distribution of the parameters among individuals would be required.

The present approach is quite different and is based on the view that the parameters of each individual's demand and supply functions are subject to random or stochastic "shocks" which lead to movements of earnings away from their equilibrium values. However, earnings are subsequently assumed to return or "error correct" to their values which held before the shocks. Given the possibility of multiple equilibria, even small shocks can lead to large jumps in the value of real earnings over time. A standard representation of such a stochastic process involves the following expression, written in terms of the proportionate change in the individual's real earnings:

$$\frac{dy_i}{y_i} = -[y_i^3 - 2\alpha_i y_i^2 + (\alpha_i^2 + \beta_i \delta_i)y_i - (\beta_i \delta_i \alpha_i - \gamma_i \beta_i^2)]dt + \sigma_i dZ_i \qquad (8)$$

Here Z_i is a Wiener process with the property that dZ_i is normally distributed as $N(0, dt)$ and σ_i is the standard deviation of dy_i/y_i which for simplicity is assumed to be constant; however, more elaborate specifications can be accommodated. For further details of this type of process, see Cox and Miller (1984).

The formulation in Equation (8) applies to each individual in the market. Its continued application, following the approach described below, would generate the form of the probability density of each individual's earnings resulting from changes over time in response to the stochastic shocks. The informational requirements of such an approach are of course enormous, and ultimately it is required to generate the distribution of real earnings defined over all individuals. Thus to continue to allow for such a large degree of heterogeneity would not be helpful.

This Gordian knot may, however, be cut by introducing an assumption of population homogeneity. Thus the random shocks applying to individuals are assumed to be drawn from essentially the same distribution: this assumption is of course precisely the same as that used by all the stochastic process models mentioned above. Furthermore, the individuals are homogeneous to the extent that they have the same demand and supply functions. However, it will be shown below that some heterogeneity can be introduced by allowing some of the structural parameters to be functions of various characteristics such as labor market experience and education. At any moment in time, individuals are affected by quite different shocks; they are simply assumed to originate from the same distribution. This simplification makes it possible to drop the individual subscripts from Equation (8) and to regard the resulting distribution as applying over all individuals in the market. The form of the distribution will be seen to depend on the precise nature of the demand and supply schedules and the characteristics of the Wiener process. The only distributional assumption made in the model is that of the normality of dZ.

If the density function of real income is written as $f(y)$, then Equation (8) gives rise to the following Kolgomorov forward equation (see Cox and Miller, 1984):

$$\frac{\partial f}{\partial t} = \frac{\partial}{\partial y}[y^4 - 2\alpha y^3 + (\alpha^2 + \beta\delta)y^2 - (\beta\delta\alpha - \gamma\beta^2)y] + \frac{1}{2}\frac{\partial^2}{\partial y^2}[\sigma^2 y^2] \qquad (9)$$

This is a partial differential equation which has the solution:

$$f(y) = \exp[h(y, t; \theta) - \eta(t;\theta)], 0 < y < \infty \qquad (10)$$

where θ is a vector of parameters which, in turn, are functions of the structural parameters α, β, δ, γ, and $\eta(t; \theta)$ is the normalizing constant given by:

$$\eta(t;\theta) = \ln \int \exp[h(y, t;\theta)]dy \qquad (11)$$

The function $h(y, t; \theta)$ is a general expression which unfortunately has no closed form solution. This means that it is not possible to derive an analytical solution of the transitional density $f(y)$ except for some very special cases of the model given above. It is possible, however, to compute it numerically, but this approach and associated estimation problems are very cumbersome. For a general discussion of the problems, see Soong (1973). This form of $f(y)$ in Equation (10) is known as a transitional distribution since it describes the evolution over time of the distribution of earnings from an initial equilibrium distribution after a change in the parameters of the demand and supply functions caused by some shock.

This process will converge to what is called the "stationary" distribution, which is obtained by setting $\partial f/\partial t = 0$ in Equation (9). This is the approach followed below. Thus, it must be acknowledged that the same type of issue arises here as with all the other types of stochastic process models, namely that of the speed of adjustment. Critics of the stochastic models have argued that any observed distribution is unlikely to be an equilibrium distribution, so that the results of such processes cannot strictly be applied. In addition, Shorrocks (1975) has used numerical simulation methods, finding that the "half life" of such processes is typically many "periods."

A substantial advantage of the stationary distribution is that, unlike the transitional distribution, the stationary distribution can in general be derived analytically. By setting $\partial f/\partial t = 0$ in Equation (9), this converts the partial differential equation into an ordinary first order differential equation which can be solved by standard integration methods to yield a closed form solution. For a general solution of the stationary distribution for general specifications corresponding to Equation (8), see Creedy and Martin (1994, pp. 70–72). For the stochastic differential equation in Equation (8), the stationary density, $f^*(y)$, is:

$$f^*(y) = \exp\left[-\int^y \left(\frac{2s^2 - 4\alpha s + 2(\alpha^2 + \beta\delta) - 2(\beta\delta\alpha - \gamma\beta^2 + 2\sigma^2)s^{-1}}{\sigma^2}\right)d(s - \eta^*)\right]$$

After integration this becomes:

$$f^*(y) = \exp\left(\left[-\left(\frac{2y^3/3 - 2\alpha y^2 + 2(\alpha^2 + \beta\delta)y - 2(\beta\delta\alpha - \gamma\beta^2 + 2\sigma^2)\ln(y)}{\sigma^2}\right)\right] - \eta^*\right) \quad (12)$$

or, more compactly:

$$f^*(y) = \exp[\theta_1\ln(y) + \theta_2 y + \theta_3 y^2 + \theta_4 y^3 - \eta^*], \quad 0 < y < \infty \quad (13)$$

where the θs are functions of the structural form parameters, obtained by comparing coefficients in Equations (12) and (13), and:

$$\eta^* = \ln\int_0^\infty \exp[\theta_1\ln(s) + \theta_2 s + \theta_3 s^2 + \theta_4 s^3]ds \quad (14)$$

The distribution given by Equation (13) is in fact the generalized gamma. This type of distribution was first derived by Cobb, Koppstein and Chen (1983). Creedy and Martin (1994) have shown that the same form applies in the context of price distribution models, using a simple general equilibrium model similar to that used here. It can be unimodal which corresponds to the situation where the economic model given by Equations (1)-(4) contains a unique equilibrium. Unlike the standard gamma distribution proposed by Salem and Mount (1974) to describe income distributions, this generalized gamma can also be multimodal. This situation arises when the model has multiple equilibria whereby the modes of the density correspond to the stable equilibria and the antimode corresponds to the unstable equilibrium. The flexibility of the generalized gamma distribution to model alternative empirical earnings distributions arises from the inclusion of the higher order terms, which enable such properties as skewness and kurtosis to be modelled adequately. Marron and Schmitz (1992) give an example of a distribution displaying multimodality.

The above approach can be applied to a single cross section of earnings, or to a time series of cross sections. In the latter case the parameters may be regarded as functions of exogenous variables which change over time. An advantage of this framework is that it provides a method of modelling the influence of macroeconomic variables on the personal distribution of earnings. This also introduces the interesting possibility that the form of the distribution of earnings could change in distinct ways, while the underlying generating process is unchanged. This represents a potentially fruitful area of future research.

A comparison of Equations (12) and (13) shows that the five structural parameters σ, α, β, γ, δ cannot all be recovered from the θ_is. The emphasis in the present paper is on the form of the distribution and hence the distributional parameters θ, so the lack of identifiability of the structural parameters is not considered to be a problem. However, as shown below, it is possible to discriminate between alternative classes of structural models through tests on the form of the distribution.

C.   Alternative Specifications

The theoretical model discussed in Section II.A involves linear demand and supply functions. However, alternative specifications can be explored. For example, suppose that the goods demand function is rewritten as:

$$w_i = \alpha_i + \beta_i \ln(x_i^d) \tag{15}$$

Notice that when using a nonlinear specification of Equation (2), it is simpler to write w as a function of x^d. This provides a tractable formulation in view of the need to solve the model for y. Combining Equation (15) with Equations (1), (3) and (4) gives real earnings as the root or roots of:

$$y_i + \gamma_i\beta_i^2(\ln(y_i))^2 + \beta_i(2\gamma_i\alpha_i - \delta_i)\ln(y_i) + (\gamma_i\alpha_i - \delta_i)\alpha_i = 0 \qquad (16)$$

which corresponds to Equation (7). This gives rise to a stationary distribution of the form:

$$f^*(y) = \exp[\theta_1(\ln(y))^3 + \theta_2(\ln(y))^2 + \theta_3\ln(y) + \theta_4 y - \eta^*], 0 < y < \infty \qquad (17)$$

where the θ_is are functions of the structural parameters. This is a generalized lognormal distribution.

Another example consists of specifying the labor demand function in reciprocal form as

$$n_i^d = \delta + \frac{\gamma}{w_i} \qquad (18)$$

When combined with Equations (1)-(3), this gives rise to a quadratic of the form

$$y_i^2 - y_i(\gamma + \alpha) + (\delta\beta + \gamma\alpha) = 0 \qquad (19)$$

Alternatively, if Equation (2) is replaced by

$$x_i^d = \alpha + \beta w_i \qquad (20)$$

and is combined with Equation (4), the following quadratic results

$$\gamma y_i^2 - y_i(\delta\beta - \beta^2 + 2\alpha\gamma) + \alpha(\delta\beta + \gamma\alpha) = 0 \qquad (21)$$

Finally, the combination of Equations (18) and (2) leads to the linear form

$$y_i(\beta - \delta) + (\alpha\delta - \beta\gamma) = 0 \qquad (22)$$

An interesting feature of this equation is that the resulting distribution is the standard gamma distribution which is a special case of Equation (13) with $\theta_3 = \theta_4 = 0$. The generalized gamma distribution also contains as special cases a number of other distributions which have been used in the empirical modelling of earnings distributions: the exponential distribution ($\theta_1 = \theta_3 = \theta_4 = 0$), the Weibull distribution ($\theta_2 = \theta_4 = 0$), and the power distribution ($\theta_2 = \theta_3 = \theta_4 = 0$). Where each distribution has been used in the past, a special estimation method has been devised, as in Salem and Mount (1974). The present approach thus has the substantial advantage of nesting several distributions which can therefore be consistently estimated and compared. In the case of the generalized lognormal distribution, as with the generalized gamma distribution, it is possible to devise theoretical models which give rise to special cases. For example the standard lognormal distribution arises in Equation (17) when $\theta_1 = \theta_4 = 0$, and the gamma distribution when $\theta_1 = \theta_2 = 0$.

III.   ESTIMATION METHODS

This section presents procedures for estimating the theoretical income distributions derived above. Two cases need to be distinguished depending upon whether the structural form parameters α, β, δ, γ, are constant or are functions of individual characteristics. In the former case, the derived earnings distribution is referred to as an unconditional distribution, while for the latter, a set of conditional distributions are estimated. These cases are discussed in turn below. The generalized gamma distribution given by Equation (13) represents a special case of a more general family of distributions known as the generalized exponential family. The estimation strategies of this family have been explored in detail by Cobb, Koppstein and Chen (1983) and Lye and Martin (1993, 1994) on which the following is based. For those cases when the data are truncated, the methods devised by Lye and Martin (1994) may be used.

A.   The Unconditional Distribution

From the discussion above, a general form of the density for y is

$$f^{*}(y) = \exp\left[\sum_{i=1}^{M} \theta_i \psi_i(y) - \eta\right] \tag{23}$$

where $\psi_i(.)$ is some general function depending on the density type, M is the number of terms in the density depending on the specification of the model, and η is the normalizing constant which is given by:

$$\eta = \ln\int\exp\left[\sum_{i=1}^{M} \theta_i \psi_i(y)\right]dy \tag{24}$$

The $\psi_i(.)$ in the case of the generalized gamma income distribution are $\psi_1(y) = \ln(y)$, $\psi_2(y) = y$, $\psi_3(y) = y^2$, and $\psi_4(y) = y^3$, by comparison with Equation (13). In the case of the generalized lognormal distribution, the $\psi_i(.)$ are $\psi_1(y) = (\ln(y))^3$, $\psi_2(y) = (\ln(y))^2$, $\psi_3(y) = \ln(y)$, and $\psi_4(y) = y$, by comparison with Equation (17).

For a sample of observations on earnings, $y_1, y_2, ..., y_N$, maximum likeihood estimates are obtained by choosing the θ_is to maximize the log-likelihood function:

$$\ln L = \sum_{j=1}^{N} \sum_{i=1}^{M} \theta_i \psi_i(y_j) - N\eta \tag{25}$$

Standard iterative optimization routines can be used to determine the θ_is which maximize Equation (25). In maximizing Equation (25), the normalizing constant η in Equation (24) can be determined numerically using Gaussian quadrature routines.

Suppose instead that earnings data are available in the form of a frequency table. Lye and Martin (1994) introduced a least squares approach for estimating the parameters in Equation 23 when the data are grouped, motivated by the least squares estimator of the Pareto distribution suggested by Johnson and Kotz (1970, 19, p. 235), and the work of Finch (1989). The distinguishing feature of the least squares estimator proposed by Lye and Martin (1994) is that it is based on frequencies. The error terms are therefore more likely to satisfy the assumption of independence than in the approach of Johnson and Kotz, which uses cumulative frequencies. Let the number of classes of equal width be K, with midpoints y_k, $k = 1, 2, ..., K$, and define O_k as the observed frequency corresponding to the kth class interval. The expected frequency in the kth group, E_k, can be written as:

$$E_k = \phi^{-1} \exp\left[\sum_{i=1}^{M} \theta_i \psi_i(y_k) \right] \qquad (26)$$

where ϕ is the normalizing constant and values are assumed to be concentrated at the class midpoint.

The least squares estimator consists of defining a logarithmic linear regression relationship between the observed frequency O_k and the expected frequency E_k, as given by Equation (23). Letting v_k be an error term, the regression equation is:

$$\ln(O_k) = \ln(E_k) + v_k \qquad (27)$$

The ratio, O_k/E_k, is assumed to be lognormally distributed with unit mean, so that the estimates are constrained to be nonnegative. Substituting Equation (26) into Equation (27) gives:

$$\ln(O_k) = -\ln\phi + \sum_{i=1}^{M} \theta_i \psi_i(y_k) + v_k \qquad (28)$$

The parameters can be estimated using a standard ordinary least squares procedure. Since the sampling theory of the estimators has not been fully worked out, conventional formulae to compute standard errors and hence test statistics are not reported below. Instead, a goodness of fit measure based on a chi-square statistic is calculated in order to compare models.

Denoting the least squares estimators by ^, the estimate of the kth frequency is:

$$\hat{E}_k = \psi^{-1} \exp\left[\sum_{i=1}^{M} \hat{\theta}_i \psi_i(y_k) \right] \qquad (29)$$

where:

$$\psi = \frac{1}{N} \sum_{k=1}^{K} \exp\left[\sum_{i=1}^{M} \hat{\theta}_i \psi_i(y_k)\right] \tag{30}$$

In the case where the required maximum likelihood software is not available, the least squares estimator discussed above can also be used by grouping the data into a frequency table. Since there is a loss of information from grouping, some loss of efficiency relative to the maximum likelihood estimator can be expected from using the least squares estimator. However, the Monte Carlo experiments performed by Lye and Martin (1994) show that provided the sample size is large, the least squares estimator performs very well.

B.   The Conditional Distribution

In the estimation procedures discussed so far, individuals are assumed to be homogeneous. To allow for heterogeneity, assume that associated with the *j*th individual is a set of characteristics given by the vector z_j. In terms of the economic model presented above, this amounts to allowing the structural parameters to be functions of the variables in z. Examples that would help determine the earnings of individuals would be the level of education and experience.

Maximum likelihood parameter estimates of the heterogeneous earnings model when the data are ungrouped, are obtained by maximizing the log likelihood function:

$$\ln L = \sum_{j=1}^{N} \sum_{i=1}^{M} \theta_i(z_i)\psi_i(y_j) - \sum_{j=1}^{N} \eta_j \tag{31}$$

where the normalizing constant is:

$$\eta_j = \ln \int \exp\left[\sum_{i=1}^{M} \theta_i(z_j)\psi_i(y)\right] dy \tag{32}$$

The main difference between Equation (32) and Equation (24) is that the former needs to be computed for each individual in the sample, at each iteration. Thus the algorithm is computationally burdensome especially for large data sets.

The adaptation of the least squares procedure to the conditional distribution context is by no means straightforward as it requires the apropriate choice of conditioning of not only the dependent variables, but also the independent variables. These issues will be examined in future work.

IV.   APPLICATIONS

This section applies the equilibrium earnings model to both unconditional and conditional distributions of earnings and the results are compared with existing distributional specifications. The data are from the 1987 March Supplement (Annual Demographic File) of the United States Current Population Survey (CPS) which contains information on individual earnings and labor market characteristics in 1986. The total sample is 4,927 individuals. Since there is a bunching at the top end of the distribution caused by an upper limit on hours worked, 104 individuals are removed from the sample used in this paper. The earnings variable is a measure of weekly earnings obtained as the product of hours per week and wages per hour.

A.   Estimates of the Unconditional Earnings Distribution

Maximum likelihood estimates of the structural parameters for the unconditional generalized gamma earnings distribution in Equation (13) are given in Table 1, along with estimates of the standard gamma distribution where $\theta_3 = \theta_4 = 0$. In addition, the results of the generalized lognormal distribution as given by Equation (17) and the standard lognormal distribution where in Equation (17) $\theta_1 = \theta_4 = 0$, are reported. Inspection of the standard errors in the case of the generalized gamma distribution shows that the estimates of θ_1 and θ_2 are statistically significantly different from zero, although those of θ_3 and θ_4 are not. More important, however, is an overall measure of the model's performance. This is achieved by the Akaike Information Criterion (AIC) reported in Table 1. This is computed as $AIC = -\ln L + K$, where K, the number of estimated parameters, acts as a penalty for the inclusion of additional parameters. The result in Table 1 shows that the generalized gamma distribution is preferred to the gamma distribution as

Table 1
The Unconditional Earnings Distribution: MLE Estimates

Parameter	Generalized Gamma	Gamma	Generalized Lognornal	Lognormal
θ_1	2.0298	2.4365	−0.1604	
	(0.1556)	(0.0698)	(0.1929)	
θ_2	−4.9953	−6.8087	−0.7728	−1.3882
	(1.0931)	(0.1471)	(0.3183)	(0.0361)
θ_3	−0.5772		1.1212	−3.2810
	(1.0888)		(3.2648)	(0.0586)
θ_4	−0.1813		−5.7674	
	(0.4079)		(3.3140)	
ln	−39.9708	−50.3252	−39.1348	−318.9790
AIC	43.9709	52.3235	43.1348	320.9790

Note: Asymptotic standard errors based on the inverse of the hessian are given in parentheses.

Table 2
The Unconditional Earnings Distribution: Least Squares Estimates

Parameter	Generalized Gamma	Gamma	Generalized Lognormal	Lognormal
Constant	8.7108	5.1751	−9.4945	−3.2895
θ_1	5.6220	4.2579	−0.8182	
θ_2	−14.7650	−8.2186	−5.6642	−1.9856
θ_3	3.2468		−10.1307	−3.4505
θ_4	−0.3946		6.2802	
Chi-square	45.0612	133.9298	46.4094	110.6682
Degrees of Freedom	9	11	9	11

Table 3
Comparison of Actual and Expected Frequencies: Least Squares Estimates

Group Midpoint	Actual	Generalized Gamma	Gamma	Generalized Lognormal	Lognormal
100	17	17	21	17	14
200	180	206	179	193	276
300	598	536	443	533	657
400	785	764	663	776	817
500	729	800	754	813	772
600	650	702	720	708	636
700	622	553	611	553	487
800	428	408	474	404	359
900	301	288	344	284	258
1000	162	198	237	194	183
1100	129	134	156	132	130
1200	77	90	99	89	91
1300	77	60	61	60	65
1400	44	41	37	40	46
1500	24	27	22	28	33

the *AIC* is minimized for the generalized gamma distribution. Furthermore, inspection of the *AIC* for the generalized lognormal distribution shows that this distribution also performs very well; indeed, it is difficult to distinguish between the two generalized forms.

The results using the least squares estimator are given in Table 2 for the same four types of distribution given in Table 1. The data are grouped into 21 cells with the first cell having a mid-point of $100, the second a mid-point of $200, and so on. The chi-square statistics shown in Table 2 indicate that both of the generalized distributions perform significantly better than their standard forms even when the loss of degrees of freedom is taken into account. The superiority of the generalized distributions are further highlighted in Table 3 and Figure 1, which give the actual and expected frequencies from the alternative models.

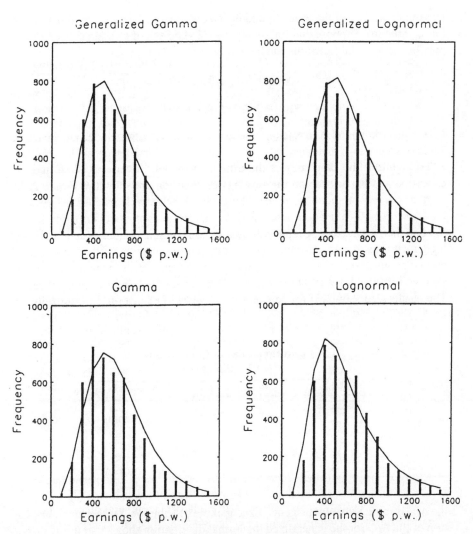

Figure 1.   Comparison of Observed and
Expected Frequencies: Least Squares Estimates

B.   ESTIMATES OF THE CONDITIONAL EARNINGS DISTRIBUTION

In order to illustrate the way in which further heterogeneity may be introduced, suppose that the demand for labor is affected by the labor market experience, t, and education of individuals, h, measured in terms of years of schooling. The constant term, δ, in Equation (4) can be specified as a function of these variables. This can be seen to imply that the terms θ_1 and θ_2 in equation (13) are, in turn, functions of those variables. Suppose that, following the standard use of a quadratic experience profile, the relevant functions can be written as:

$$\theta_1 = \delta_0 + \delta_1 h_n + \delta_2 t_n + \delta_3 t_n^2$$
$$\theta_2 = \gamma_0 + \gamma_1 h_n + \gamma_2 t_n + \gamma_3 t_n^2$$

Maximum likelihood estimates of the conditional earnings model are given in Table 4.

To highlight the properties of the estimated model, the effects of changes in education and experience on the earnings distribution are shown in Figure 2. In both cases the predictions of the model agree with well established results. Increases in both education and experience shift the earnings distribution to the right so that, on average, people with higher education and more experience have higher earnings levels. Furthermore, the dispersion increases with experience. In particular, an increase in education from 12 to 20 years, leads to an increase in the average earnings level from \$397 to \$1023 assuming that experience is 10 years. The results also show that for people with 12 years of education, a person with 25

Table 4
The Conditional Earnings Distribution:
MEL Estimates

Variable	Parameter	Generalized Gamma
Constant	δ_0	1.6021
		(0.4669)
h	δ_1	−0.0019
		(0.0329)
t	δ_2	0.0846
		(0.0442)
t^2	δ_3	−0.0016
		(0.0006)
Constant	γ_0	−18.3953
		(1.4232)
h	γ_0	0.8770
		(0.0727)
t	γ_0	0.2878
		(0.0996)
t^2	γ_0	−0.0040
		(0.0015)
	θ_3	−3.0728
		(1.6999)
	θ_4	0.0570
		(0.4717)
	$\ln L = 775.5155$	$AIC = 795.5155$

Note: Absolute standard errors based on the inverse of the hessian are given
in parentheses.

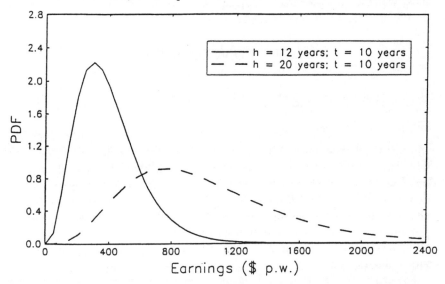

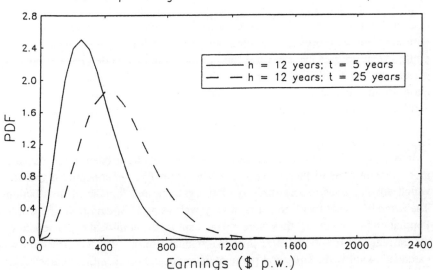

Figure 2.   Effects of Education and Experience on
Earnings Distribution: MLE Estimates

years experience earns on average $514 which is more than the amount of $327 which would be earned on average by a person with only 5 years of experience.

These figures compare with overall sample means of $504 for weekly earnings, 13 years of education, and 19 years experience.

V.   CONCLUSIONS

The main purpose of this paper has been to explore the integration of a simple economic model of labor supply and demand with a stochastic process which causes shocks to the structural form of the model. For each individual, the number of hours of labor supplied was treated as the reciprocal supply associated with the demand for goods, or real income, while the demand for labor was a function of the real wage rate. Equilibrium earnings, the product of the wage rate and the number of hours worked, were derived as the root or roots of a cubic equation. An error correction process was then used to derive the stationary distribution associated with the model. This was found to be a generalized gamma distribution. An alternative specification of the structural form of the model produced a generalized lognormal distribution.

The generalized distributions have the advantage of nesting other special cases, such as the standard gamma or lognormal, which have been used in the statistical analysis of income distribution, depending on particular assumptions about the structural form. A special feature of these generalized distributions, in contrast with their standard forms, is that they can display multimodality corresponding to multiple equilibria in the structural form of the economic model. Furthermore, the parameters can be allowed to vary over time, so that the model has the potential to allow for macroeconomic changes to alter the form of the personal distribution of earnings. In some contexts the earnings distribution may be truncated and this can be handled for the generalized exponential family following the methods of Lye and Martin (1994).

It was possible to exploit estimation methods that have been developed for a more general class of models known as the generalized exponential distribution which encompasses generalizations of the gamma and lognormal distributions. These models were found to perform very well using U.S. data from the Current Population Survey in that they were able to capture the empirical characteristics of the earnings distribution better than the standard forms. The specification was extended to allow the structural parameters to depend on specified characteristics such as the experience and education of individuals. This provided a mechanism for understanding the effects of changes in both education and experience on the shape of the conditional earnings distribution.

ACKNOWLEDGMENTS: We wish to thank Peter Lambert for detailed comments on an earlier version of this paper.

REFERENCES

Aitchison, J., and Brown, J. A. C. 1957. *The Lognormal Distribution.* Cambridge: Cambridge University Press.

Brown, J. A. C. 1976. "The Mathematical and Statistical Theory of Income Distribution." Pp. 72-97 in A. B. Atkinson (Ed.), *The Personal Distribution of Income.* London: George Allen and Unwin.

Champernowne, D. G. 1953. "A Model of Income Distribution," *Economic Journal*, 63: 316-351.

Cobb, L., Koppstein, P. and Chen, N.H. 1983. "Estimation and Moment Recursion Relations for Multimodal Distributions of the Exponential Family," *Journal of the American Statistical Association*, 78: 124-130.

Cox, D.R., and Miller, H.D. 1984. *The Theory of Stochastic Processes.* London: Chapman and Hall.

Creedy, J. and Martin, V. L. 1993. "Multiple Equilibria and Hysteresis in Simple Exchange Models," *Economic Modelling*: 339-347.

_____. 1994. "A Model of the Distribution of Prices," *Oxford Bulletin of Economics and Statistics*, 56: 67-76.

Finch, P.D. 1989. "An Approximation to ML Estimation." Monash University Department of Statistics.

Johnson, N.I., and Katz, S. 1970. *Continous Univariate Distributions 1.* Boston: Houghton Mifflin

Hart, P.E. 1973. "Random Processes and Economic Size Distributions". *Mimeo* University of Reading.

Klein, L.R. 1962. "An Introduction to Econometrics." Englewood Cliffs, NJ: Prentice-Hall.

Lydall, H.F. 1979. *A Theory of Income Distribution.* Oxford: Clarendon Press.

_____. 1976. "Theories of the Distribution of Earnings." Pp. 15-46 in A.B. Atkinson (Ed.), *The Personal Distribution of Income.* London: George Allen and Unwin.

Lye, J.N. and Martin, V.L. 1993. "Robust Estimation, Non-Normalities and Generalized Exponential Distributions," *Journal of the American Statistical Association*, 88: 253-259.

_____. 1994. *Truncated Distribution Families: With Applications to Earnings, Insurance and Income*, mimeo.

Mandelbrot, V. 1960. "The Pareto-Levy Law and the Distribution of Income," *International Economic Review*, 1: 79-106.

Marron, J.S. and Schmitz, H.P. 1992. "Simultaneous Estimation of Several Income Distributions," *Econometric Theory*, 8: 476-488.

Mincer, J. 1970. "Distribution and Labour Incomes: A Survey," *Journal of Economic Literature*, 8: 1-26.

Phelps Brown, E.H. 1977. *The Inequality of Pay.* Oxford: Oxford University Press.

Robbins, L. 1930. "On the Elasticity of Demand for Income In Terms of Effort," *Economica*, 10: 123-129.

Salem, A.Z.B. and Mount, T.D. 1974. "A Convenient Descriptive Model of Income Distribution: The Gamma Density," *Econometrica*, 42: 1115-1127.

Shorrocks, A.F. 1975. "On Stochastic Models of Size Distribution," *Review of Economic Studies*, 42: 631-641.

[3]

OXFORD BULLETIN OF ECONOMICS AND STATISTICS, 56, 1 (1994)
0305-9049

A MODEL OF THE DISTRIBUTION OF PRICES[1]

John Creedy and Vance L. Martin

I. INTRODUCTION

This paper shows how the distribution of prices can be derived explicitly from an economic model. The approach generates a generalized gamma distribution which belongs to the generalized exponential family (see Cobb, Koppstein and Chen, 1983; Cobb and Zacks, 1985; and Lye and Martin, 1993a). This distribution is extremely flexible as it contains the gamma, Rayleigh, and exponential distribution as special cases, and is related to the generalized gamma distribution studied by McDonald (1984). This flexibility is important in empirical work as the use of the generalized gamma distribution provides a consistent framework for estimating and testing alternative distributional models. A feature of this approach is that distributional characteristics such as skewness and kurtosis can be explicitly related to the parameters of the economic model and thus given economic interpretations. Furthermore, it is shown that when there are multiple equilibria, the distribution of relative prices is multimodal: the (deterministic) stable equilibrium relative prices correspond to the modes of the distribution whilst the (deterministic) unstable equilibrium relative prices correspond to the antimodes of the distribution.

The paper proceeds as follows. A simple model is introduced in Section II, along with the introduction of stochastics. The distributional implications are analysed in Section III. In this section, two types of distribution are distinguished; these are the transitional and stationary distributions respectively. The transitional distributions provide information on the changing distribution of prices resulting from exogenous changes to the system when prices do not adjust instantaneously. The stationary distribution describes the long-run properties of the sequence of transitional distributions; this represents the stochastic analogue of long-run equilibrium. Conclusions and implications of the price distribution model are given in Section IV.

[1] We are grateful to the editor and a referee for helpful suggestions.

II. THE MODEL

Consider the following model where x_d and y_d denote respectively B's demand for good X (supplied by A) and A's demand for good Y (supplied by B), and p denotes the price of X relative to that of good Y. With linear demand functions:

$$x_d = a - bp \qquad (1)$$

$$y_d = c - dp^{-1} \qquad (2)$$

The structural parameters, a, b, c, d, in (1) and (2) are in general regarded as being functions of a range of relevant economic variables which can change over time. For present purposes, these functions do not need to be defined explicitly and time subscripts can be omitted for convenience. However, as discussed below, changes in any of those variables will affect one or more of the structural parameters and will therefore have implications for the equilibrium properties of the model.

The relative price, p, is the amount of good Y that must be given up in order to obtain one unit of good X. Hence B's demand for x_d units of good X implies a supply of $x_d p = y_s$ units of good Y. Appropriate substitution into the equilibrium condition, $y_s = y_d$, gives:

$$bp^3 - ap^2 + cp - d = 0 \qquad (3)$$

The equilibrium price ratio is the appropriate real root of this cubic which can have at most three solutions. Where there are three real and distinct roots, only two will be associated with stable equilibria, whilst the 'middle' root will be unstable. For further discussion of this model, see Creedy and Martin (1993). Other examples where the equilibrium properties of an exchange model can be represented by a cubic equation are by Shapley and Shubik (1977), and Venables (1984).

Stochastic Specification

Stochastics can be introduced in various ways. One approach is to assume that (3) represents the mean of a stochastic process and that deviations from the mean are regarded as arising from continuous additive stochastic shocks. The stochastic representation of the model is given by:

$$\frac{dp}{dt} = -(bp^3 - ap^2 + cp - d) + u \qquad (4)$$

where the stochastic term, u, follows a Normal distribution with zero mean. This differential equation can be interpreted as an 'error correction model' whereby the price adjusts continuously from its mean as a result of short-run stochastic shocks, u. However, the negative sign in front of the brackets means that on average the price adjusts back, that is it 'error corrects', to the original long-run equilibrium position over time. Indeed, (3) can be regarded as a special case of (4) since in the absence of random shocks, $u = 0$, prices are in equilibrium and $dp/dt = 0$.

Since p and u are continuous random variables, it is convenient to express (4) in its stochastic continuous time form. This produces what is known as an Ito process (see Kamien and Schwartz, 1981, pp. 243–244), as follows:

$$dp = -\mu(p)dt + \sigma(p)dW \tag{5}$$

where $\mu(p)$ is the (instantaneous) mean given by (3) and $\sigma^2(p)$ is the (instantaneous) variance which in general is also a function of p. The term, $dW = udt/\omega(p)$, is distributed as $N(0, dt)$, where W is a Wiener process. For a more formal discussion of such processes, see Brock and Malliaris (1982, pp. 67–88). Equation (5) is a completely general representation which encompasses a wide range of models. The simple exchange model in Section II is used to illustrate the way in which economic structure can be added.

An alternative way to introduce stochastics into the model is to assume that the terms a, b, c and d in (1) and (2) have Wiener processes. For example, Merton (1975) adopted this approach when introducing stochastics into the Solow growth model. However, the distributional characteristics have been found using simulation procedures to be similar to those analysed below.

III.   PRICE DISTRIBUTIONS

For a given set of structural parameters, the above stochastic process implies that p is a random variable with density function $f(p)$. In view of the fact that the structural parameters themselves may change, it is necessary to distinguish two types of distribution. First, if adjustment of prices towards equilibrium is instantaneous, then the stochastic process described in (5) results in a stable distribution. This can be referred to as a long-run, or stationary, distribution. Secondly, when adjustment is not instantaneous, the process can be regarded as moving through a sequence of transitional distributions.

Transitional Distributions

If adjustment to an exogenous shock is not instantaneous, the process moves through a sequence of temporary equilibria. Associated with each temporary equilibrium is the transitional density of p. The dynamics of the process are summarized by the Kolmogorov forward equation (see, for example, Cox and Miller, 1984, p. 208):

$$\frac{\partial f}{\partial t} = \frac{\partial}{\partial p}(\mu f) + \frac{1}{2}\frac{\partial^2}{\partial p^2}(\sigma^2 f) \tag{6}$$

This partial differential equation defines the transitional density at each point in time. Unfortunately, except for very simple expressions for both the mean and the variance, no analytical solution of (6) exists. The complexity of very simple processes is highlighted in Soong (1973).

The transitional densities for general specifications can only be obtained numerically. An example is shown in Figure 1 where, $\mu(p) = 49 - 44p + 12p^2 - p^3$, and $\sigma^2 = 1$. The initial distribution of p is chosen to be unimodal with a mean of 2, and a variance of unity. The transitional densities are obtained by solving the partial differential equation in (6) numerically using subroutine MOLCH from the IMSL library. Figure 1 shows that the price distribution over time becomes bimodal and displays two stable and one unstable equilibrium points. In Figure 1 the process is seen to converge to a price distribution which is constant over time. This distribution represents the stationary density which is examined next.

Stationary Distribution

The above example shows that when the system is shocked, a sequence of transitional densities evolves which converges to the stationary density. This density represents the stochastic analogue of long-run equilibrium (see Brock and Malliaris, 1982, pp. 106–108). Unlike the transitional densities, it is possible to derive analytical expressions for the stationary density using general expressions for the mean and the variance. From (6), the stationary density, $f^*(p)$, is found by setting:

$$\frac{\partial f^*(p)}{\partial t} = 0 \tag{7}$$

This converts the partial differential equation in (6) to an ordinary differential equation in the stationary density $f^*(p)$ which is independent of time. The general expression for the stationary density is derived as follows. Write the ordinary differential equation in f^*:

$$0 = \frac{d}{dp}(\mu f^*) + \frac{1}{2}\frac{d^2}{dp^2}(\sigma^2 f^*) \tag{8}$$

Expanding the second term using the product rule, (8) can be rewritten as:

$$0 = \frac{d}{dp}(\mu f^*) + \frac{1}{2}\frac{d}{dp}(f^* d\sigma^2/dp + \sigma^2 df^*/dp)$$

Integrating both sides with respect to p gives a first-order linear differential equation:

$$k = \mu f^* + \frac{1}{2}(f^* d\sigma^2/dp + \sigma^2 df^*/dp) \tag{9}$$

A MODEL OF THE DISTRIBUTION OF PRICES   71

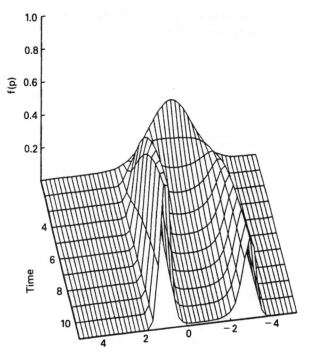

Fig. 1. Transitional price distributions

where k is a constant of integration. Solving for df^*/dp gives:

$$\frac{df^*}{dp} = \frac{2k}{\sigma^2} - \left(\frac{2\mu + d\sigma^2/dp}{\sigma^2}\right) f^*$$

(10)

Finally, the stationary density is given as the solution of this differential equation:

$$f^*(p) = \exp\left[-\int_0^p \left(\frac{2\mu(s) + d\sigma^2(s)/ds}{\sigma^2(s)}\right) ds - \eta \right]$$

(11)

where η is the normalising constant which is determined by the boundary conditions of (6) and is given by:

$$\eta = \log \int_0^\infty \left[\exp \int_0^p \left(-\frac{2\mu(s) + d\sigma^2(s)/ds}{\sigma^2(s)} \right) ds \right] dp$$

(12)

This density represents a generalized exponential distribution which has been studied by Cobb, Koppstein and Chen (1983); Cobb and Zacks (1985);

Martin (1990); Lye and Martin (1993a), and applied by Fischer and Jammer-negg (1986) to the analysis of the Phillips curve.

The number of modes and antimodes of the density is given by the number of the roots of:

$$2\mu(p) + \mathrm{d}\sigma^2(p)/\mathrm{d}p = 0 \tag{13}$$

For the case where the variance is constant, $\mathrm{d}\sigma^2(p)/\mathrm{d}p = 0$, and the modes and antimodes equal the stable and unstable equilibrium points respectively. In the general case where the variance is not constant, the modes and anti-modes are displaced from the equilibrium points by the factor $\mathrm{d}\sigma^2/\mathrm{d}p$. As demonstrated below, the variance of the process, $\sigma^2(p)$, determines the form of the stationary density.

The Generalized Gamma Distribution

Suppose that the variance is proportional to p, so that $\sigma^2(p) = \gamma p$. Making the appropriate substitution in (11) and using (3) for the mean of the process, the stationary density is:

$$f^*(p) = \exp\left[\theta_1 \log p + \theta_2 p + \theta_3 p^2 + \theta_4 p^3 - \eta\right] \tag{14}$$

for $p > 0$, with:

$$\theta_1 = 1 + 2\mathrm{d}/\gamma$$

$$\theta_2 = -2c/\gamma$$

$$\theta_3 = a/\gamma$$

$$\theta_4 = -2b/3\gamma \tag{15}$$

The normalizing constant, η, needs to be evaluated numerically since there is no closed form solution of (14). This density represents a generalized gamma distribution, an advantage of which is that it contains a variety of other well-known distributions as special cases. For example, the unimodal gamma distribution arises when $\theta_3 = \theta_4 = 0$ which implies that $a = b = 0$. For a discussion of the gamma distribution and its properties, see Johnson and Kotz (1970, pp. 197–199). In this situation the single mode of the distribution corresponds to the single equilibrium point. The generalized gamma distribution also contains the exponential distribution, when $\theta_1 = \theta_3 = \theta_4 = 0$, and the Rayleigh distribution, when $\theta_2 = \theta_4 = 0$. This distribution is also related to the generalized gamma distribution studied by McDonald (1984) and the generalized lognormal distribution discussed by Lye and Martin (1993a).

Figure 2 gives some examples of the generalized gamma distribution and the way the shape of the distribution changes as a result of changes in θ_3. The normalising constant η is evaluated numerically by using the routine INTQUAD1 in the GAUSS library. This evaluates the integral using a

A MODEL OF THE DISTRIBUTION OF PRICES   73

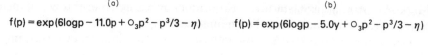

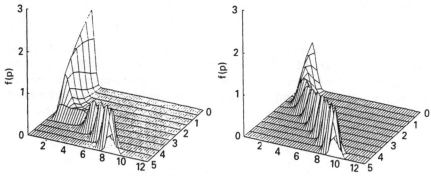

Fig. 2. Stationary price distributions: the generalized gamma distribution

Gauss-Legendre quadrature algorithm. From (15), changes in θ_3 can be interpreted as shifts in the demand for good X caused by shifts in the intercept, a. Figure 2(a) is based on the generalized gamma distribution, $f^*(p) = \exp[6\log p - 11p + \theta_3 p^2 - p^3/3 - \eta]$. For values of $0 < \theta_3 < 3$, the density is unimodal and there is a unique equilibrium price. As θ_3 increases from 0 to 2, the mode of the distribution changes very little. At $\theta_3 = 3$, the process moves into a zone of multiple equilibria where the distribution is transformed from being unimodal to being bimodal. As θ_3 increases above 3, the distribution reverts to being unimodal with the single mode corresponding to higher prices as θ_3 increases.

The effect of a change in the parameter θ_2 from -11 to -5 is illustrated in Figure 2(b). From (15) this change represents a shift in the demand for good Y caused by a shift in the intercept, c. The generalized gamma distribution is now given by $f^*(p) = \exp[6\log p - 5p + \theta_3 p^2 - p^3/3 - \eta]$. The effect of changes in θ_3 are the same as in Figure 2(a), except that there is no zone where the distribution becomes bimodal.

IV. CONCLUSIONS

The distribution of prices has been derived from a stochastic economic model. The price distribution is referred to as a generalized gamma distribution which nests a range of well-known distributions which have been used to model empirical price distributions. A property of this distribution is that it is possible to give distributional characteristics, such as skewness, kurtosis and multimodality, an economic interpretation.

The approach has implications for the interpretation of empirical price distributions derived from a frequency table constructed from a time series of prices. A potential problem with distributions constructed in this way is that they are independent of time. This represents a loss of information since the empirical distribution is a temporally aggregated distribution of a sequence of transitional densities. To highlight the limitation of this approach, consider the situation where the system is shocked, setting in motion a sequence of transitional densities. Over time, the transitional densities converge to the stationary density, provided that the adjustment speed towards the stationary distribution is faster than the time between shocks. Assuming that the sampling rate is slow enough such that realised observations represent the equilibrium solution from the stationary density, then the drawing of a single observation provides no information on the characteristics of either the transitional or stationary densities. It is possible that for particular time intervals, the distribution, transitional or stationary, is bimodal. This situation would most likely arise when the shocks are large, resulting in the price exhibiting volatility as the price shifts from one stable mode to another stable mode. Alternatively, periods of time when the distribution is unimodal would correspond to periods of tranquillity where shocks lead to gradual changes in price as it moves from one stable equilibrium to a new stable equilibrium. Combining these scenarios with temporally aggregated empirical distributions implies that, in the case of exchange rates at least, a sharp peak suggests that the exchange rate over most of the period has been stable, whereas the fatness in the tails captures the periods of volatility where the distribution is bimodal, see Lye and Martin (1993b).

The framework for modelling the distribution of prices analysed above has important implications for applied work. First, when estimating price equations, it is common practice to assume that price is a function of a set of explanatory variables plus an error term which is commonly assumed to be unimodal. By construction, the price distribution has, apart from the mean, the same characteristics as the distribution that is assumed for the error term. An implication of the above framework is that the price distribution is affected in a non-trivial way by the explanatory variables and is not just solely determined by the assumptions made about the error term. This, in general, will lead to misspecification problems resulting in biased and inconsistent parameter estimates. Problems of specification error are expected to be more severe where there are multiple equilibria, as the price distribution will be multimodal rather than unimodal. Secondly, the generalized gamma distribution is non-standard, so the usual econometric software is no longer appropriate. However, Cobb, Koppstein and Chen (1983) and Lye and Martin (1993a) show how to obtain maximum likelihood estimates of the parameters of the generalized gamma distribution.

Another application is in modelling the distribution of income. For example, the generalized gamma distribution can model the type of bimodality in the income distributions observed by Marron and Schmitz (1992). Also, the generalized gamma distribution is related to other distributions used in modelling incomes, such as those discussed by McDonald

A MODEL OF THE DISTRIBUTION OF PRICES   75

(1984), along with the familiar lognormal distributional. Generalizations of the lognormal distribution can be derived within the framework of the generalized exponential family (Lye and Martin, 1993a).

It is suggested that these results offer a potentially fruitful alternative to the conventional approach to the examination of price distributions. They allow for the explicit role of an economic model in the determination of the shape of price distributions as well as the possibility that prices may be drawn from unobserved multimodal distributions.

University of Melbourne, Victoria

Date of Receipt of Final Manuscript: May 1993

REFERENCES

Brock, W. A. and Malliaris, A. G. (1982). *Stochastic Methods in Economics and Finance.* North Holland, New York.

Cobb, L., Koppstein, P. and Chen, N. H. (1983). 'Estimation and Moment Recursion Relations for Multimodal Distributions of the Exponential Family', *Journal of the American Statistical Association*, Vol. 78, pp. 124–30.

Cobb, L. and Zacks, S. (1985). 'Applications of Catastrophe Theory for Statistical Modelling in the Biosciences', *Journal of the American Statistical Association*, Vol. 80, pp. 793–802.

Cox, D. R. and Miller, H. D. (1984). *The Theory of Stochastic Processes.* Chapman and Hall, London.

Creedy, J. and Martin, V. L. (1993). 'Multiple Equilibria and Hysteresis in Simple Exchange Models', *Economic Modelling.*

Fischer, E. O. and Jammernegg, W. (1986). 'Empirical Investigation of a Catastrophe Theory Extension of the Phillips curve', *Review of Economics and Statistics*, Vol. 68, pp. 9–17.

Johnson, N. L. and Kotz, S. (1970). *Continuous Univariate Distributions — 1.* Boston, New York.

Kamien, M. I. and Schwartz, N. L. (1981). *Dynamic Optimization: The Calculus of Variations and Optimal Control in Economics and Management.* North Holland, New York.

Lye, J. and Martin, V. L. (1993a). 'Robust Estimation, Non-Normalities and Generalized Exponential Distributions', *Journal of the American Statistical Association*, Vol. 88, pp. 253–59.

Lye, J. and Martin, V. L. (1993b). 'Non-linear Time Series Modelling and Distributional Flexibility', *Journal of Time Series Analysis.*

McDonald, J. B. (1984). 'Some Generalized Functions for the Size Distribution of Income', *Econometrica*, Vol. 52, pp. 647–63.

Marron, J. S. and Schmitz, H. P. (1992). 'Simultaneous Estimation of Several Income Distributions', *Econometric Theory*, Vol. 8, pp. 476–88.

Martin, V. L. (1990). *Properties and Applications of Distributions from the Generalized Exponential Family.* Unpublished PhD thesis, Monash.

Merton, R. (1975). 'An Asymptotic Theory of Growth Under Uncertainty', *Review of Economic Studies*, Vol. 42, pp. 375–93.

Soong, T. T. (1973). *Random Differential Equations in Science and Engineering*. Academic Press, New York.

Shapley, L. S. and Shubik, M. (1977). 'An Example of a Trading Economy with Three Competitive Equilibria', *Journal of Political Economy*, Vol. 85, pp. 873–75.

Venables, A. J. (1984). 'Multiple Equilibria in the Theory of International Trade with Monopolistically Competitive Commodities', *Journal of International Economics*, Vol. 16, pp. 103–21.

[4]

JOURNAL OF APPLIED ECONOMETRICS, VOL. 11, 669–686 (1996)

A NON-LINEAR MODEL OF THE REAL US/UK EXCHANGE RATE

JOHN CREEDY, JENNY LYE AND VANCE L. MARTIN

Department of Economics, University of Melbourne, Parkville, Victoria, 3052, Australia
E-Mail: vance_martin.economics@muwaye.unimelb. edu.au

SUMMARY

This paper provides a framework for building and estimating non-linear real exchange rate models. The approach derives the stationary distribution from a continuous time error correction model and estimates this by MLE methods. The derived distribution exhibits a wide variety of distributional shapes including multimodality. The main result is that swings in the US/UK rate over the period 1973:3 to 1990:5 can be attributed to the distribution becoming bimodal with the rate switching between equilibria. By capturing these changes in the distribution, the non-linear model yields improvements over the random walk, the speculative efficiency model, and Hamilton's stochastic segmented trends model.

1. INTRODUCTION

Most models of the exchange rate are linear, although evidence suggests that linear models are not consistent with the data (see Meese and Rogoff, 1983; Meese and Rose, 1991; Diebold and Nason, 1990). The underlying assumption of non-linear models is that while the set of market fundamental variables commonly used in empirical exchange rate models is appropriate, the relationship between the exchange rate and market fundamentals is not linear. The approach adopted is to identify the source of the non-linearity through a range of non-linear empirical techniques. Recent examples include the random coefficient model of Schinasi and Swamy (1989); the use of non-parametric estimation procedures by Meese and Rose (1991) and Chinn (1991); the stochastic segmented trends model of Engel and Hamilton (1990); and the adoption of an ARCH specification of the variance by Diebold (1988) and Domowitz and Hakkio (1985). The first three examples correspond to specifying non-linear models of the mean, while the last corresponds to a non-linear model of the variance.

This paper presents an alternative non-linear model of the exchange rate. The main differences from existing non-linear approaches are that the specification is parametric, and that the third and fourth moments are considered in addition to the mean and the variance. The approach is based on the work of Creedy and Martin (1993, 1994) which consists of building a non-linear model by solving for the real exchange rate distribution from a flexible continuous-time error correction model. The derived distribution belongs to the generalized exponential class which has been studied by Cobb, Koppstein and Chen (1983) and Lye and Martin (1993; 1994). A property of this distribution is that it encompasses the normal distribution as well as being able to capture skewness, kurtosis and even multimodality. The last property is found to be important when applying the framework to the real US/UK exchange rate over the period 1973 to 1990, since the

CCC 0883–7252/96/060669–18
© 1996 by John Wiley & Sons, Ltd.

Received 21 October 1993
Revised 14 February 1996

large swings observed in the real exchange rate correspond to periods when the distribution is bimodal.

In Section 2 a non-linear model of the real exchange rate is derived. Estimation and prediction conventions are discussed in Section 3. The framework is applied in Section 4 to the US/UK real exchange rate using monthly data for the period 1973:3 to 1990:5. These are the same data as used by Baillie and Pecchenino (1991). For comparative purposes, the forecasting properties of the non-linear model are compared with the predictions based on linear specifications which include alternative random walk specifications and speculative efficiency, and the non-linear exchange rate model of Engel and Hamilton (1990) which is based on a stochastic segmented trends model. Section 5 provides the main conclusions.

2. A NON-LINEAR MODEL OF THE REAL EXCHANGE RATE

A non-linear model of the exchange rate should be sufficiently flexible, but must have sufficient restrictions placed on it so as to limit the number of choices from a very large set of non-linear functional forms. Consider the general reduced-form relationship between the real exchange rate s, and a set of market fundamental variables contained in the vector x:

$$\mu(s, x) = 0 \tag{1}$$

In the empirical application below, this relationship occurs at each point in time. However, it is convenient in the derivation of the model to suppress the time subscript for the moment.

Simple economic models of exchange suggest that it is appropriate to include higher-order terms in s at least up to order three; see the class of models examined in Creedy and Martin (1993). If equation (1) is characterized by a cubic in s, it can display either at least one root which corresponds to a single equilibrium or, at most, three roots which occur when there are multiple equilibria. A parameterization to capture these properties is obtained, following Creedy and Martin (1994), by writing equation (1) as:

$$\mu(s, x) = a_0(x) + a_1(x)s + a_2(x)s^2 + a_3(x)s^3 \tag{2}$$

where $a_j(x)$ represent general functions of the market fundamental variables x.

2.1. The Error Correction Representation

The above specification is deterministic, but stochastics can be added to the model using the following error correction model (see Phillips, 1991):

$$ds = -\mu(s, x)\, dt + \sigma(s, x)\, dW \tag{3}$$

where $\mu(s, x)$ represents the (instantaneous) mean which is given by equation (2), $\sigma^2(s, x)$ is the (instantaneous) variance which in general is a function of s and the market fundamental variables in x, and W is a Wiener process with the property that dW is distributed as $N(0, dt)$. The stochastics of the model are captured by the term dW which represents the continuous time analogue of the normal distribution.

Equation (3) is an Ito process which shows that the real exchange rate adjusts continuously from its mean as a result of stochastic shocks, dW (see Kamien and Schwartz, 1981). The negative sign means that a positive shock, that is, $dW > 0$, leads to an increase in the real exchange rate but that over time the real exchange rate, on average, error corrects to the original equilibrium position.

2.2. Distributional Dynamics

Associated with equation (3) is the density function of s, denoted by $f(s)$. Consider a shock to the system and assume that adjustment to equilibrium is not instantaneous, so that over time the process moves through a sequence of temporary equilibria. Associated with each temporary equilibrium is the transitional distribution of s. The dynamics of the process are summarized by the Kolmogorov forward equation (see Cox and Miller, 1984, p. 208):

$$\frac{\partial f}{\partial t} = \frac{\partial}{\partial s}(\mu f) + \frac{1}{2}\frac{\partial^2}{\partial s^2}(\sigma^2 f) \tag{4}$$

This partial differential equation defines the transitional distribution of the real exchange rate at each point in time. For a given setting of the market fundamentals x, the sequence of real exchange rate transitional distributions converges to a stationary distribution. If the market fundamentals remain constant the observed real exchange rates represent realizations of drawings from the same stationary distribution. When the market fundamentals do change over time, associated with each market fundamental setting at a particular point in time is a new sequence of transitional distributions which converges to a new stationary distribution. If prices are flexible, the speed of convergence to the stationary distribution is fast. For a chosen sampling frame, the observed real exchange rate at a particular point in time represents a drawing from the stationary distribution at that point in time.

Except for very simple expressions for both the mean and the variance, no analytical solution of equation (4) exists. However, the stationary distribution can be derived representing the stochastic analogue of long-run equilibrium. Unlike the transitional distribution, it is possible to derive analytical expressions for the stationary distribution for general expressions of the mean and the variance (see Cobb, Koppstein, and Chen, 1983; Malliaris and Brock, 1982; Martin, 1990). The stationary density, f^*, is:

$$f^*(s) = \exp\left[-\int_0^s\left(\frac{2\mu(w) + d\sigma^2(w)/dw}{\sigma^2(w)}\right)dw - \eta^*\right] \tag{5}$$

where η^* is the normalizing constant which is determined by the boundary conditions of equation (4).

In specifying the variance of the real exchange rate, it is often assumed that exchange rate volatility increases with the level of the real exchange rate (Malliaris and Brock, 1982). Thus, an appropriate specification for $\sigma^2(s)$ is:

$$\sigma^2(s) = \gamma s \tag{6}$$

In most of the empirical work of exchange rates, the logarithm of the exchange rate is modelled. Defining e as the logarithm of the real exchange rate:

$$e = \log(s) \tag{7}$$

Combining equations (5) to (7), and defining

$$u = [e - \Lambda(x)]/v \tag{8}$$

where $\Lambda(x)$ and v are, respectively, the mean and the standard deviation of e, it is shown in the Appendix that:

$$f(u) = \exp[\Theta_1(x)u + \Theta_2(x)u^2/2 - u^4/4 - \eta] \qquad -\infty < u < \infty \tag{9}$$

where the normalizing constant η is given by:

$$\eta = \log \int_{-\infty}^{\infty} \exp\left[\Theta_1(x)u + \Theta_2(x)u^2/2 - u^4/4\right]du \qquad (10)$$

and the $\Theta_1(x)$ and $\Theta_2(x)$ are general functions of the market fundamental variables. The distribution given by equation (9) represents a generalized normal distribution. It can be interpreted as the error distribution from a model of the real exchange rate (see Cobb, Koppstein and Chen, 1983). By constraining this distribution to have zero mean, from equation (8) this implies that $\Lambda(x)$ is the mean of the distribution of the logarithm of the real exchange rate e. This generalization of the normal distribution contrasts with the standard class of linear models where it is common to assume that u is $N(0, 1)$, implying that the distribution of e is $N(\Lambda(x), v^2)$.

The distributional functions, $\Theta_1(x)$ and $\Theta_2(x)$, provide information which can be used in formulating the conditional expectation of e. This means that the market fundamentals can feed into the real exchange rate through two channels: a linear channel through $\Lambda(x)$ and a non-linear channel through $\Theta_1(x)$ and $\Theta_2(x)$. It is the latter channel which provides the additional information for improving conditional forecasts of the real exchange rate and highlights the main difference between the non-linear and linear real exchange rate models discussed above. Further specification of $\Theta_1(x)$ and $\Theta_2(x)$ are given in Section 4.

2.3. Properties of the Model

The generalized normal distribution given by equation (9) exhibits great flexibility in modelling skewed, kurtic and bimodal distributions. It is these properties which gives the non-linear model's potential gains for explanatory and forecasting power over both the linear model as well as other non-linear models, including non-parametric and semi-non-parametric formulations.

A simple procedure for identifying bimodality is given by inspecting the sign of Cardan's discriminant:

$$\delta = [\Theta_1(x)/2]^2 - [\Theta_2(x)/3]^3 \qquad (11)$$

Unimodality occurs when $\delta > 0$, while bimodality occurs when $\delta < 0$. Furthermore, a necessary condition for bimodality is that $\Theta_2(x) > 0$. The parameters of the canonical normal distribution in equation (8) have the interpretations that with unimodality $\Theta_1(x)$ is a measure of skewness and $\Theta_2(x)$ is a measure of kurtosis, while with bimodality, $\Theta_1(x)$ is a measure of the relative heights of the two modes and $\Theta_1(x)$ is a measure of the separateness of the two modes (see also Cobb, Koppstein and Chen, 1983).

The modes of the distribution correspond to the stable equilibria, and the antimode corresponds to the unstable equilibria, a region of relatively low probability (see Creedy and Martin, 1994). When there are multiple equilibria, shocks to the market fundamentals can result in discrete 'jumps' in the real exchange rate that are not necessarily reversible, giving rise to hysteresis.

The model highlights in an explicit way the role of higher-order moments. In particular, the distribution in equation (9) can model both skewness (third moment) and kurtosis (fourth moment). Where the reduced form in equation (1) is derived from an explicit structural model, these higher-order moments can be given an economic interpretation (see Creedy and Martin, 1994). This contrasts with previous approaches in modelling empirical exchange rate distributions which have largely concentrated on statistical approaches in modelling leptokurtosis (see, for example, Friedman and Vandersteel, 1982).

3. ESTIMATION AND PREDICTION CONVENTIONS

3.1. Maximum Likelihood Estimation

Cobb, Koppstein and Chen (1983) and Lye and Martin (1993) have shown how the parameters of distributions within the generalized exponential class can be estimated by maximum likelihood procedures. Given data on $\{e_t, x_t\}$, $t = 1, 2, ..., T$, the log likelihood is:

$$\log L = \sum_t \log f(u_t)$$

$$= \sum_t [\Theta_1(x_t) u_t + \Theta_2(x_t) u_t^2/2 - u_t^4/4] - \sum_t \eta_t \qquad (12)$$

where as in equation (8) $u_t = [e_t - \Lambda(x_t)]/v$.

Iterative procedures are required to maximize the log-likelihood function in equation (12). The Newton–Raphson algorithm in conjunction with the Berndt–Hall–Hall–Hausman algorithm are adopted here. The program MAXLIK in GAUSS is used to perform the calculations based on numerical derivatives. At each iteration, the GAUSS numerical integration program INTQUAD1 is used to compute the normalizing constant and the derivatives.

3.2. Prediction Conventions

In most models of the exchange rate, the distribution is assumed to be unimodal. The choice of the best predictor depends upon the adopted loss function, but whatever the choice of the loss function, the set of predictors is small. If the distribution is both unimodal and symmetric, this set is reduced even further: a typical choice is the mean of the distribution.

Difficulties arise when the distribution is multimodal. Some potential new conventions are:

Global: Choose the global maximum at each point in time.
Delay: Do not leave a mode until that mode disappears.
Nearest: Choose the mode or antimode closest to the data.

The global convention is based on the assumption that the process always moves (jumps) to a region of higher probability. With the delay convention, it is assumed that a process never leaves a stable region until that region becomes unstable (see Cobb, Koppstein and Chen, 1983). The nearest convention consists of choosing the mode, stable or unstable, which is closest to the data. This convention allows for the possibility that the process can settle at unstable equilibria as well as stable equilibria.

4. EMPIRICAL APPLICATION

4.1. Model Specification

This section applies the above model of the distribution of the real exchange rate to the real US/UK bilateral exchange rate. The data are those used by Baillie and Pecchenino (1991). The main market fundamental variables of the real exchange rate are based on the flexible price monetarist real exchange rate model and are the domestic and foreign real money supply, domestic and foreign real income, and domestic and foreign interest rates. The assumption of flexible prices is consistent with the underlying theory of the model developed above whereby the observed real exchange rate at time t represents a realization of a drawing from the stationary distribution at time t. The set of market fundamentals could be expanded to include other variables, while alternative definitions of the set of variables already included in the set of market fundamentals could be adopted. However, to keep the empirical analysis as comparable as possible with the Baillie and Pecchenino (1991) empirical study, these alternative variables are not considered.

The standard linear exchange rate model is embedded into the non-linear model by expressing $\Lambda(x)$ in equation (8) as a linear function of the exogenous variables, while assuming that v is constant. More elaborate versions of this model could be considered by allowing for some heterogeneity by assuming that v is a function of either market fundamentals or follows an ARCH process, and therefore is time varying. This generalization of the linear model is not pursued in the empirical analysis, but will be investigated at a later stage.

An important feature of the non-linear model is that the first four moments of the distribution of the real exchange rate are time varying. This contrasts with the standard linear model where only the first moment is time varying, or, at most, the second moment is time varying if some heterogeneity is included into the specification by making the variance time varying. To capture changes in the characteristics of the real exchange rate distribution over time, and hence to allow for non-linear relationships between the market fundamentals and the real exchange rate, $\Theta_1(x)$ and $\Theta_2(x)$ in equation (9) are also expressed as functions of the market fundamental variables. The model is given by:

$$\Lambda_t = \lambda_1 m_t^{US} + \lambda_2 m_t^{UK} + \lambda_3 y_t^{US} + \lambda_4 y_t^{UK} + \lambda_5 r_t^{US} + \lambda_6 r_t^{UK}$$

$$v_t = v$$

$$\Theta_{1,t} = \theta_{1,1} m_t^{US} + \theta_{1,2} m_t^{UK} + \theta_{1,3} y_t^{US} + \theta_{1,4} y_t^{UK} + \theta_{1,5} r_t^{US} + \theta_{1,6} r_t^{UK}$$

$$\Theta_{2,t} = \theta_{2,1} m_t^{US} + \theta_{2,2} m_t^{UK} + \theta_{2,3} y_t^{US} + \theta_{2,4} y_t^{UK} + \theta_{2,5} r_t^{US} + \theta_{2,6} r_t^{UK}$$

$$u_t = (e_t - \Lambda_t)/v \tag{13}$$

where m_t is the logarithm of the real money stock, y_t is the logarithm of real income, r_t is the nominal interest rate, and e_t is the logarithm of the real exchange rate.

The sample period consists of 207 monthly observations starting in March 1973, when the US floated its exchange rate, and ending in May 1990. The real exchange rate is computed from the nominal exchange rate, which is the end-of-month closing bid price on the New York foreign exchange market, and the CPI in the two countries. The stock of money is M1 for the US and M0 for the UK. The real income variables are the industrial production indexes of the US and the UK. The US interest rate is the Federal Funds rate, while for the UK it is London Interbank Offer. All data are adjusted for seasonality by regressing each series on a constant and three seasonal dummy variables and using the residuals as the seasonally adjusted data. Finally, to avoid numerical overflows when computing the integrals in equation (10) numerically, all data are standardized to have unit variance.

4.2. The Results

Maximum likelihood parameter estimates of the non-linear model are given in Table I and diagnostics are given in Table II. For comparison, ordinary least squares estimates of the linear real exchange rate model are also given. The non-linear model performs very well when compared with the linear model. In the case of the non-linear model, the signs of the parameter estimates of the function which determines the mean of the distribution, $\Lambda(x)$, are consistent with the basic monetarist theory of real exchange rates. This contrasts with the linear model where half of the parameter estimates have the wrong sign. There is a big improvement in goodness of fit with $\bar{R}^2$ increasing from 0·282 for the linear model to 0·736 for the non-linear

Table I. Estimates of the real exchange rate model, 1973:3 to 1990:5[a]

Variable	Parameter	Linear	Non-linear
m^{US}	λ_1	−0·066	0·081
		(0·485)	(0·503)
m^{UK}	λ_2	0·178	−1·489
		(1·349)	(7·628)
y^{US}	λ_3	−0·150	−1·679
		(0·563)	(7·005)
y^{UK}	λ_4	0·470	0·216
		(2·293)	(1·202)
r^{US}	λ_5	0·411	0·525
		(3·991)	(4·919)
r^{UK}	λ_6	0·168	−0·245
		(2·282)	(3·011)
m^{US}	$\theta_{1,1}$		−0·595
			(0·694)
m_{UK}	$\theta_{1,2}$		4·683
			(4·208)
y^{US}	$\theta_{1,3}$		5·145
			(3·683)
y^{UK}	$\theta_{1,4}$		−0·021
			(0·020)
r^{US}	$\theta_{1,5}$		−0·005
			(0·014)
r^{UK}	$\theta_{1,6}$		0·451
			(1·190)
m^{US}	$\theta_{2,1}$		−4·349
			(7·279)
m^{UK}	$\theta_{2,2}$		0·959
			(2·052)
y^{US}	$\theta_{2,3}$		5·502
			(5·477)
y^{UK}	$\theta_{2,4}$		−0·176
			(0·281)
r^{US}	$\theta_{2,5}$		−1·925
			(5·309)
r^{UK}	$\theta_{2,6}$		0·128
			(0·599)
	σ	0·847	1·034
			(22·299)

[a] Absolute values of *t*-statistics given in parentheses.

one. Both the AIC and SIC show that the non-linear model is superior to the linear model, while the Keenan test shows that the non-linear model captures all of the non-linearities in the real exchange rate. For a discussion of the properties of the Keenan test, see Lee, White and Granger (1993).

The improvement in explanatory power of the non-linear model over the linear model is highlighted in Figure 1, which compares the predictions of the two models with the actual (logarithm of the) real exchange rate. There are two periods worth highlighting: 1980–81 when the real exchange rate peaked, and 1985 when it hit a trough. In both cases, the linear model fails to capture the large swings in the real exchange rate.

J. CREEDY, J. LYE AND V. L. MARTIN

Table II. Diagnostics of the real exchange rate
model, 1973:3 to 1990:5

Test	Linear	Non-linear
$\bar{R}^2$	0·282	0·736
RSS	144·280	49·807
log L	−256·360	−132·265
AIC	524·721	300·531
SIC	544·717	360·520
K	6·915	0·430

$\bar{R}^2$ is the adjusted coefficient of determination
based on the global convention.
RSS is the residual sum of squares.
AIC is the Akaike information criterion computed
as $-2 \log L + 2q$, where q is the number of
estimated parameters excluding σ.
SIC is the Schwarz information criterion computed
as $-2 \log L + q \log T$, where q is the number
of estimated parameters excluding σ.
K   is the Keenan test for non-linearities: the
critical values are 3·84(5%, linear); and 3·84
(5%, non-linear).

4.3. Forecasting

In an important paper, Meese and Rogoff (1983) found that the simple random walk
specification performed better than many linear models of exchange rates. This work was
extended by Meese and Rose (1991), who found that the random walk model also performed
better than a number of non-linear models. In contrast Engel and Hamilton (1990) found that a
non-linear model based on stochastic segmented trends yielded superior forecasting power to the
random walk. To test the forecasting properties of the non-linear exchange rate model developed
in the present paper, its forecasting capabilities are compared with these existing methodologies.

One way to highlight the relationship between the non-linear model developed here with that
of the random walk model is to express the error correction model given by equation (3) in
terms of the logarithm of the exchange rate, $e = \log(s)$, and assume that $\mu(e, x) = \alpha_0$, and
$\sigma^2(e, x) = \beta_0$, are constant:

$$de = -\alpha_0 \, dt + \beta_0 \, dW$$

It is possible to derive a closed-form expression for the transitional density defined by equation
(4). Using the results of Cox and Miller (1984, p. 209), the transitional density is

$$f(e_t) = \frac{1}{(2\pi\beta_0 t)} \exp\left[-\frac{(e_t - \alpha_0 t)^2}{2\beta_0 t}\right] \tag{15}$$

This is simply a normal distribution of the level of the (logarithm of) the exchange rate with
mean $\alpha_0 t$, and variance $\beta_0 t$. These moments are also the moments of a random walk with drift.

Equation (15) suggests that one way to compare the random walk specification with the
non-linear model is to compute the RMSE obtained from the predictions of a model based on
regressing the exchange rate on a constant and a time trend. This result is represented in
Table III by RW (level) = 0·995, which is larger than the one-step-ahead RMSE of the non-linear
model based on the level of the exchange rate given by NL (level) = 0·491.

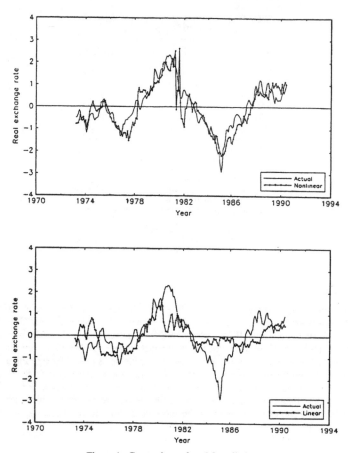

Figure 1. Comparison of model predictions

An alternative linear model of the level of the exchange rate is based on the (logarithm of the) forward exchange rate at time $t-1$ for delivery at time t, f_{t-1}. Under the assumption of speculative efficiency, $\alpha = 0$ and $\beta = 1$ in the following regression equation (see Baillie and McMahon, 1990, for a review)

$$s_t = \alpha + \beta f_{t-1} + v_t \qquad (16)$$

where v_t is a disturbance term. This suggests that a one-step-ahead prediction of the exchange rate is given by f_{t-1}. Using one-month forward exchange rate data between the US and the UK, the RMSE of this forward rate, assuming speculative efficiency, is given by SE(level) = 0·254 in Table III. As this RMSE is smaller than that obtained using the nonlinear model given by NL(level) in Table 3, this suggests that the information set used in formulating forecasts of the

678   J. CREEDY, J. LYE AND V. L. MARTIN

Table III. Forecasting comparison of models,
RMSE

Model[a]	RMSE
RW(level)	0·995
NL (level)	0·491
SE(level)	0·254
RW(sr)	0·193
NL$_1$(sr)	0·190
NL$_2$(sr)	0·183
EH(sr)	0·194

RW(level):	the random walk based on equation (15).
NL(level):	the non-linear model based on equation (13).
SE(level):	the speculative efficiency model using equation (16) with $\alpha = 0$, $\beta = 1$.
RW(sr):	the random walk based on (17) with $\phi_i = 0 \ \forall i$.
NL$_1$(sr):	the ECM in equation (17) with $\phi_4 = 0$.
NL$_2$(sr):	the ECM in equation (17) unrestricted.
EH(sr):	Engel and Hamilton model.

spot rate in forward markets is larger than the set of variables used to estimate the non-linear long-run model.

The forecasts of the non-linear model presented in Table III, discussed so far, are based on the stationary distribution and can thus be interpreted as long-run forecasts. However, it is more appropriate to generate the forecasts from the error correction representation as given by equation (3) and hence focus attention on the change in the exchange rate, that is, short-run forecasts. This has the further advantage that the forecasts of the non-linear model become commensurate with forecasts obtained using the non-linear stochastic segmented trends model which is also based on the change in the exchange rate. Having derived forecasts of the change in the exchange rate, forecasts of the level of the exchange rates can be obtained by progressively summing the forecasts of the changes.

In building an error correction model for the non-linear model several alternative specifications are possible. The approach adopted here is to estimate the following ECM:

$$e_t - e_{t-1} = \phi_1 \Theta_{1,t-1} + \phi_2 \Theta_{2,t-1} u_{t-1} + \phi_3 u_{t-1}^3 + \phi_4 (\Lambda_t - \Lambda_{t-1}) + w_t \qquad (17)$$

where $\Theta_{1,t}$, $\Theta_{2,t}$, Λ_t and u_t are defined in equation (13). The motivation behind equation (17) is that it represents a discretization of the continuous time ECM expression used to derive the stationary distribution for e_t. The first three variables in equation (17) correspond to the terms used to identify the modes of the distribution in equation (9) and thereby correspond to μ, in an error correction model of e_t in the form given by equation (3). The fourth term, $\Lambda_t - \Lambda_{t-1}$, is used to capture any short-term dynamics which have not been captured by the error correction term. While further short-run dynamics could be envisaged, the variable $\Lambda_t - \Lambda_{t-1}$ is sufficient for the purposes of this paper to highlight the forecasting properties of the non-linear model. Another approach is to estimate the continuous time version of the ECM by using the indirect estimation method of Gourieroux, Monfort and Renault (1993). This was not tried, but will be investigated in future work.

The short-run RMSE of estimating the non-linear ECM model in equation (17) with $\phi_4 = 0$ is given by NL$_1$(sr) = 0·190 in Table III. This is marginally smaller than that obtained for the random walk representation, $RW(sr) = 0.193$, which is simply the standard deviation of $e_t - e_{t-1}$. Not constraining ϕ_4 to be zero in equation (17) yields a RMSE of $NL_2(sr) = 0.183$, which constitutes just over a 5% reduction in the RMSE compared with that obtained for the random walk representation.

As a final comparison, the forecasting performance of a two-state stochastic segmented trends model adopted by Engel and Hamilton (1990) is examined. This comparison is of special interest for the present paper because the stochastic segmented trends model, as with the non-linear model developed here, is based on the assumption that the distribution governing the exchange rate is also bimodal. The one-step-ahead predictions are based on Engel and Hamilton (1990, equation (14), p.699). The RMSE is given by $EH(sr) = 0.194$, in Table III, which is marginally larger than the RMSE using the random walk, which is in turn larger than that obtained using the non-linear model.

4.4. Interpretation

The large movements in the real exchange rate during the periods 1980 and 1985 can be interpreted as resulting from multiple equilibria; see Lye and Martin (1994) who found similar distributional characteristics for the rate of growth of the nominal US/A exchange rate. This is seen from Figure 2, which shows that Cardan's discriminant, as given by equation (11), becomes negative for these periods. The changing distributional properties of the real exchange rate over the sample period are further highlighted in Figures 3 and 4. Figure 4 gives a sequence of distributions for the first nine months of 1985. This shows that at the start of the year the exchange rate distribution is bimodal with a dominant lower mode at around -2. In the next month, the upper mode increases, suggesting an increase in the probability of the real exchange rate rising. However, for the months of March to September, this upper mode gradually disappears. It is also interesting to note that the within-sample predictions of the linear model in 1985, as given in Figure 1, are closer to the antimode of the distribution. As this corresponds to a region of relatively low probability, it helps to highlight further the problems of explaining real exchange rate movements with a linear model.

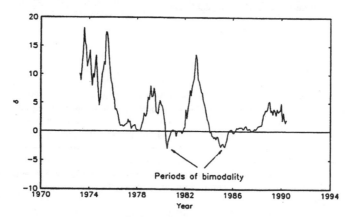

Figure 2. Properties of δ

1973:3 to 1977:12   1978:1 to 1981:12

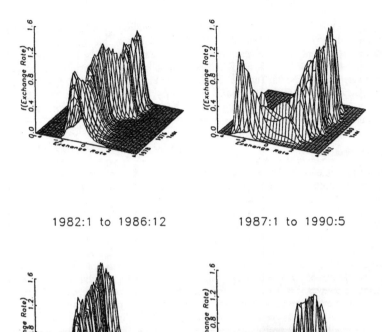

1982:1 to 1986:12   1987:1 to 1990:5

Figure 3. US/UK exchange rate distributions: 1973:3 to 1990:5

An alternative explanation of the occurrence of discrete jumps around the years 1980 and 1985 is that they were the result of structural changes. For example, there was a change in the Federal Reserve Board operating system around 1980. This property highlights further the flexibility of the modelling framework adopted in this paper. The usual approach to modelling structural change is by augmenting the model with dummy variables. This is a mechanical approach as the timing of the change is determined exogenously. In contrast, the real exchange rate model developed above enables the timing of the structural change to be endogenized.

The occurrence of bimodality has important implications for conducting policy and highlights some of the potential problems that monetary authorities may have in correctly choosing their policy settings. For example, given that the change in the way the Federal Reserve Board conducted its monetary policy in 1980 occurred during a period when the real exchange rate was

A NON-LINEAR MODEL OF THE REAL US/UK EXCHANGE RATE   681

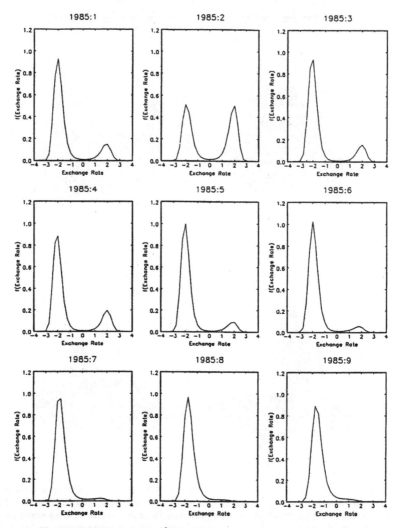

Figure 4. Snapshots of the US/UK exchange rate distribution: 1985:1 to 1985:9

in a period of bimodality, small changes in monetary settings could have been enough to generate large changes in the real exchange rate. This contrasts with other periods where the real exchange rate was operating in a unimodal zone, whereby the effect on the real exchange rate from the same change in monetary policy would be expected to be less.

Further properties of the real exchange rate distribution are highlighted in Figures 5 and 6, which show how $\Theta_{1,t}$ and $\Theta_{2,t}$ behave over time. For the periods of unimodality (bimodality),

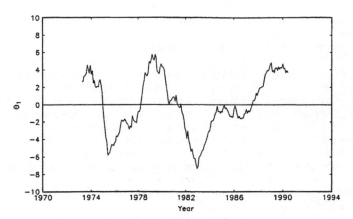

Figure 5. Properties of Θ_1

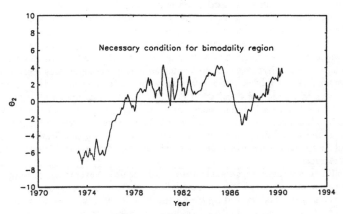

Figure 6. Properties of Θ_2

that is, when $\delta > 0$ ($\delta < 0$) in Figure 2, $\Theta_{1,t}$ identifies the skewness (relative heights of the modes) of the distribution. For example, in the period 1980–81 (1985), when the real exchange rate distribution is bimodal, the positive (negative) value of $\Theta_{1,t}$ shows that the upper (lower) mode has the highest peak. It is also interesting to note that for the last part of the sample period, $\Theta_{2,t}$ has become positive. This is the necessary condition for bimodality and suggests that the real exchange rate is moving into another period of bimodality.

5. CONCLUSIONS

This paper has provided a framework for building and estimating non-linear models of the real exchange rate. The approach is based on deriving the stationary density as the solution of a continuous-time error correction model. An important feature of this density is that it nests the standard normal distribution, as well as generating a range of distributional characteristics such as skewness, kurtosis, and bimodality.

The framework was used to estimate a non-linear model of the real US/UK exchange rate for the period 1973 to 1990 using monthly data. The non-linear model was compared with a linear model and found to be superior in terms of goodness of fit and explaining the non-linearities in the data. The non-linear model was also found to be superior to the random walk representation and the stochastic segmented trends model of Engel and Hamilton, yielding over a 5% reduction in RMSE. The reason for this superiority was that the non-linear model was able to identify periods when the distribution became bimodal. These periods corresponded to large swings in the real exchange which were caused by structural changes not explained by the linear model. The identification of structural changes in the real exchange rate provides an explanation of the slow adjustment of the exchange rate to purchasing power parity (see, for example, the approach adopted by Pesaran and Shin, 1994). The non-linear model was also able to explain why the linear model performed badly: during periods of bimodality it generated predictors corresponding to the antimode of the distribution.

Two important areas of further research stem from this paper. First, there are some obvious connections between the model developed above and the cointegration framework of Engle and Granger (1987). If the stationary distribution is interpreted as a long-run distribution then this represents the distributional form of cointegration (see Creedy, Lye and Martin, 1994). Furthermore, given the emphasis on solving non-linear models, this implies that the model derived here constitutes an appropriate framework for estimating and testing non-linear cointegrating models. This connection with cointegration gives rise to another important point: a failure to reject the null hypothesis of no cointegration does not necessarily mean a rejection of the long-run economic model, but a rejection of the functional form. For example, in the empirical work of Baillie and Pecchenino (1991) where the assumption of purchasing power parity was rejected, this could be interpreted as a rejection of the linear model used in testing for cointegration rather than a rejection of the economic fundamentals driving the long-run model. Furthermore, the model developed here could be viewed as a generalization of the work of Baillie and Pecchenino as it extends the linear cointegration framework of these authors to non-linear cointegration.

A second area of research suggested is that it would be useful to compare the properties of the exchange rate model developed here with other flexible procedures based on non-parametric and semi-parametric methods discussed by Meese and Rose (1991) (also see Chinn, 1991). Given the limited success that Meese and Rose found with the non-parametric and semi-non-parametric models, it is hypothesized that the non-linear approach adopted in this paper can give rise to potential gains from an explanatory and forecasting perspective. These potential gains arise from explicit formulation of higher-order moments of the distribution, which contrasts with other approaches where either higher-order moments are treated implicitly or attention is focused only on the mean of the distribution. Potential gains also arise from the ability of the model to exhibit multimodality, which contrasts with non-parametric approaches where the distribution is unimodal. This property is particularly useful in explaining large swings in the exchange rate as well as persistent deviations.

APPENDIX: THE DISTRIBUTION OF THE LOGARITHM OF THE REAL EXCHANGE RATE

This appendix derives the generalized normal distribution of equation (9) The derivation proceeds in three parts.

J. CREEDY, J. LYE AND V. L. MARTIN

Part 1   Derivation of the distribution of the real exchange rate, *s*

Substitute equations (2) and (6) in (5) and solve to get:

$$f_G^* = \exp[\pi_1(x)\log(s) + \pi_2(x)s + \pi_3(x)s^2 + \pi_4(x)s^3 - \eta^G] \qquad 0 < s < \infty \qquad \text{(A1)}$$

where η^G is the normalizing constant, and

$$\pi_1 = -(2a_0(x) + \gamma)/\gamma$$
$$\pi_2 = -2a_1(x)/\gamma$$
$$\pi_3 = -a_2(x)/\gamma$$
$$\pi_4 = -2a_3(x)/3\gamma$$

This distribution is known as a generalized gamma distribution as it contains as a special case the standard gamma distribution ($\pi_3 = \pi_4 = 0$).

Part 2   Derivation of the distribution of $e = \log(s)$

Given that the real exchange rate, *s*, is distributed as equation (A1), the distribution of $e = \log(s)$ is obtained by using the transformation technique to write the distribution in equation (A1) in terms of *e*. Expanding the exponential terms in Taylor series expansions up to order four around the parity level of $e = 0$, that is, $s = 1$, and rearranging the terms gives

$$f_N^* = \exp[\delta_1(x)e + \delta_2(x)e^2 + \delta_3(x)e^3 + \delta_4(x)e^4 - \eta^N] \qquad -\infty < e < \infty \qquad \text{(A2)}$$

where η^N is the normalizing constant, and

$$\delta_1 = 1 + \pi_1(x) + \pi_2(x) + 2\pi_3(x) + 3\pi_4(x)$$
$$\delta_2 = [\pi_2(x) + 4\pi_3(x) + 9\pi_4(x)]/2$$
$$\delta_3 = [\pi_2(x) + 8\pi_3(x) + 27\pi_4(x)]/6$$
$$\delta_4 = [\pi_2(x) + 16\pi_3(x) + 54\pi_4(x)]/24$$

This distribution represents a generalized normal distribution as it contains as a special case the standard normal distribution ($\delta_3 = \delta_4 = 0$).

Part 3   Derivation of the distribution of *u*

Defining the error term as $u = [e - \Lambda(x)]/v$, and using the transformation technique, the distribution of *u* is given as in equation (9)

$$f(u) = \exp[\Theta_1(x)u + \Theta_2(x)u^2/2 - u^4/4 - \eta] \qquad -\infty < u < \infty \qquad \text{(A3)}$$

where $\Theta_1(x)$ and $\Theta_2(x)$ are derived from

$$\delta_1 = \Lambda(x)^3/v^4 - 2\Lambda(x)\Theta_2(x)/v^2 + \Theta_1(x)/v$$
$$\delta_2 = -3\Lambda(x)^2/2v^4 + \Theta_2(x)/v^2$$
$$\delta_3 = \Lambda(x)/v^4$$
$$\delta_4 = -1/4v^4$$

with the remaining terms included in the normalizing constant, η.

ACKNOWLEDGEMENTS

We would like to thank the editor, three referees and seminar participants at Southern Methodist University, Latrobe University, and University of Technology of Sydney, for constructive comments. All computer programs are written in GAUSS, Version 2.2, which are available from Martin upon request.

REFERENCES

Adler, M. and B. Lehmann (1983), 'Deviations from purchasing power parity in the long run', *Journal of Finance*, **38**, 1471–1487.

Backus, D. (1984), 'Empirical models of the exchange rate: separating the wheat from the chaff', *Canadian Journal of Economics*, **XV11**, 824–846.

Baillie, R. T. and P. C. McMahon (1990), *The Foreign Exchange Market: Theory and Econometric Evidence*, Cambridge University Press, Cambridge.

Baillie, R. T. and R. A. Pecchenino (1991), 'The search for equilibrium relationships in international finance: the case of the monetary model', *Journal of International Money and Finance*, **10**, 582–593.

Baldwin, R. and R. Lyons (1989), 'Exchange rate hysteresis: the real effects of large vs small policy misalignments', NBER Working Paper, No.2828.

Chinn, M.D. (1991), 'Some linear and non-linear thoughts on exchange rates', *Journal of International Money and Finance*, **10**, 214–230.

Cobb, L., P. Koppstein, and N. H. Chen (1983), 'Estimation and moment recursion relations for multimodal distributions of the exponential family', *Journal of the American Statistical Association*, **78**, 124–130.

Cox, D. R. and H. D. Miller (1984), *The Theory of Stochastic Processes*, Chapman and Hall, London.

Creedy, J. and V. L. Martin (1993), 'Multiple equilibria and hysteresis in simple exchange models', *Economic Modelling*, 339–347.

Creedy, J. and V. L. Martin (1994), 'A model of the distribution of prices', *Oxford Bulletin of Economics and Statistics*, **56**, 67–76.

Creedy, J., J. Lye and V. L. Martin (1994), 'Non-linearities and the long-run exchange rate distribution, in J. Creedy and V. L. Martin (eds), *Chaos and Non-Linear Models in Economics*, Edward Elgar, Aldershot.

Diebold, F. X. (1988), *Empirical Modelling of Exchange Rate Dynamics*, Springer-Verlag, Berlin.

Diebold, F. X. and J. M. Nason (1990), 'Nonparametric exchange rate prediction', *Journal of International Economics*, **28**, 315–332.

Domowitz, I. and C. S. Hakkio (1985), 'Conditional variance and the risk premium in the foreign exchange market', *Journal of International Economics*, **19**, 47–66.

Dornbusch, R. (1976), 'Expectations and exchange rate dynamics', *Journal of Political Economy*, **84**, 1161–1176.

Engel, C. and J. D. Hamilton (1990), 'Long swings in the dollar: are they in the data and do markets know it?' *American Economic Review*, September, 689–713.

Engle, R. F. and C. W. J. Granger (1987), 'Co-integration and error correction: representation, estimation and testing', *Econometrica*, **55**, 251–276.

Fischer, E. O. and W. Jammernegg (1986), 'Empirical investigation of a catastrophe theory extension of the Phillips curve', *Review of Economics and Statistics*, **68**, 9–17.

Friedman, D. and S. Vandersteel (1982), 'Short-run fluctuations in foreign exchange rates: evidence from the data 1973–79', *Journal of International Economics*, **13**, 171–186.

Gourieroux, C., A. Monfort and E. Renault (1993), 'Indirect inference', *Journal of Applied Econometrics*, **8**, S85–S118.

Kamien, M. I. and N. L. Schwartz (1981), *Dynamic Optimization: The Calculus of Variations and Optimal Control in Economics and Management*, North-Holland, Amsterdam.

Koedijk, K. G. and P. Schotman (1990), 'How to beat the random walk: an empirical model of real exchange rates', *Journal of International Economics*, **29**, 311–332.

Lee, T., H. White and C. W. J. Granger (1993), 'Testing for neglected non-linearity in time series models: a comparison of neural network methods and alternative tests', *Journal of Econometrics*, **56**, 269–290.

Lye, J. and V. L. Martin (1993), 'Robust estimation, non-normalities and general exponential distributions', *Journal of the American Statistical Association*, **88**, 253–259.

Lye, J. and V. L. Martin (1994), 'Non-linear time series modelling and distributional flexibility', *Journal of Time Series Analysis*, **15**, 65–84.

Malliaris, A. G and W. A. Brock (1982), *Stochastic Methods in Economics and Finance*, North-Holland, Amsterdam.

Martin, V. L. (1990), *Properties and Applications of Distributions from the Generalized Exponential Family*, unpublished PhD thesis, Monash University.

Martin, V. L. (1992), 'Threshold time series models as multimodal distribution jump processes', *Journal of Time Series Analysis*, **13**, 79–94.

Meese, R. A. and K. Rogoff (1983), 'Empirical exchange rate models of the seventies: do they fit out of sample?' *Journal of International Economics*, **14**, 3–24.

Meese, R. A. and A. K. Rose (1991), 'An empirical assessment of non-linearities in models of exchange rate determination', *Review of Economic Studies*, **58**, 603–619.

Pesaran, M. H. and Y. Shin (1994), 'Cointegration and speed of convergence to equilibrium', mimeo.

Phillips, P. C. B. (1991), 'Error correction and long-run equilibrium in continuous time', *Econometrica*, **59**, 967–980.

Rotemberg, J. J. (1987), 'The new Keynesian microfoundations', in S. Pischer (ed.), *NBER Macroeconomics Annual 1987*, New York.

Schinasi G. and P. A. V. B. Swamy (1989), 'The out-of-sample forecasting performance of exchange rate models when coefficients are allowed to change', *Journal of International Money and Finance*, **8**, 375–390.

New Zealand Economic Papers, 32(1), 1998, 19-39

Estimating the Exponential Family Using Grouped Data: An Application to the New Zealand Income Distribution [1]

Alexander Bakker and John Creedy [*]

The exponential family of distributions offers considerable scope for the analysis of income distributions because of its ability to 'nest' many densities and the possibility of deriving special cases explicitly from labour demand and supply models. This paper presents several estimation methods based on the use of grouped data. These methods are motivated by the fact that many income distribution data are available in grouped form. The methods are applied to New Zealand income distribution data for males and females in a number of age groups. The generalised gamma distribution is found to provide the best fit to the distributions of most age groups. Three of the four parameters of the generalized gamma distribution are expressed as functions of age and conditional generalised gamma distributions are estimated using maximum likelihood, modified for grouped data. The estimated model captured the major empirical features of the changing distribution of income with age.

1. Introduction

The generalised exponential family of distributions has been used most successfully to examine a range of time series data; see, for example, Martin (1990) and Lye and Martin (1994a,b).[2] However, this very flexible family is able to contain, as special cases, a wide range of distributions that have been used to examine income distributions.[3] A substantial further advantage is that the

---

[*] *Department of Economics, The University of Melbourne, Parkville, Victoria 3052, Australia*

[1] We are grateful to the New Zealand Inland Revenue Department for making the data available and two referees for helpful comments on earlier versions.

[2] For a treatment of this family at an introductory level, see Creedy and Martin (1998).

[3] For an indication of the range of functional forms which have been used, see Bordley *et al.* (1996) and Dagum (1996).

20

distributions can be generated explicitly from labour market demand and supply models containing deterministic and stochastic components; see Creedy *et al.* (1996). Many data sources present income distributions in grouped form, so a method of estimation of the exponential family using grouped data is required. Such a method can be useful even in cases where unit record data are available, since there may be computational advantages from grouping the data.

This paper has two main aims. First, it presents several estimation methods for the exponential family which use grouped data. Secondly, the methods are applied to data on the taxable incomes of New Zealand males and females in order to examine the changing distribution of income with age. The exponential family is described in Section 2. Estimation using grouped data is examined in Section 3, and the empirical results are presented in Section 4. Conclusions are given in Section 5.

2. The Exponential Family

The exponential family of density functions, $f(y)$, is defined for the random variable y as:

$$f(y) = \exp\left[\sum_{j=1}^{J} \theta_j R_j(y,\theta) - \eta\right] \quad y \in D, \tag{1}$$

where $R_j(.)$ denotes the jth functional form, J is the number of additive terms in the density, θ is the parameter vector of dimension equal to or greater than J and is the normalising constant given by:

$$\eta = \ln \int_D \exp\left[\sum_{j=1}^{J} \theta_j R_j(y,\theta) - \eta\right] dy, \tag{2}$$

thus ensuring $\int_D f(y)dy = 1$.

Most distributions, given some rearrangement, can be expressed as special cases of the exponential family defined in (1). Consider, for example, the following generalised beta distribution defined by Bordley *et al.* (1996, p.91):

$$GB(y;a,b,c,p,q) = \frac{|a| y^{ap-1} (1-(1-c\left(\frac{y}{b}\right)^a)^{q-1}}{b^{ap} B(p,q)(1+c\left(\frac{y}{b}\right)^a)^{p+q}} \quad (b,p,q) > 0, \tag{3}$$

where $0 < y^a < b^a / (1-c)$ and zero otherwise. Assuming $c = 1$, thus defining the density over the $0 < y < \infty$ interval, and rearranging yields a density of the form:

21

$$f(y)=\exp\left[(ap-1)\ln y-(p+q)\ln\left(1+\left(\frac{y}{b}\right)^{a}\right)-\eta\right],\qquad(4)$$

where $\eta = 1nb^{ap} B(p,q) - \ln |a|$. Alternatively, (4) can be expressed in (1) notation as:

$$f(y)=\exp\left[\theta_1 \ln y+\theta_2 \ln(1+\theta_3 y^{\theta_4})-\eta\right],\qquad(5)$$

where $\theta_1 = ap - 1$, $\theta_2 = -p - q$, $\theta_3 = b^{-a}$ and $\theta_4 = a$.

The following analysis concentrates on the class of generalised exponential distributions that can be expressed in the form:

$$f(y)=\exp\left[\sum_{j=1}^{J}\theta_1 \psi_j(y)-\eta\right],\qquad(6)$$

where the parameter vector θ is of dimension J. In this case, the term $R_j(y, \theta)$ in (1) has been replaced with the simpler term $\psi_j(y)$. Since the income distribution data considered in Section 4 are non-negative, only the following non-negative forms of (6) are considered: these are the generalised gamma, gamma, generalised lognormal and lognormal. The functional forms for the distributions are given in Table 1. The generalised gamma distribution contains the gamma, exponential, Weibull and power distributions as special cases. Unlike the standard gamma distribution, proposed by Salem and Mount (1974) to describe income distributions, and the standard lognormal distribution, the generalised counterparts can model bimodal behaviour. Economic models giving rise to these forms are discussed in Creedy *et al.* (1996).

Table 1: Alternative Distributions from the Exponential Family

eneralised gamma	$f(y) = \exp[\theta_1 \ln y + \theta_2 y + \theta_3 y^2 + \theta_4 y^3 - \eta]$
gamma	$f(y) = \exp[\theta_1 \ln y + \theta_2 y - \eta]$
generalised lognormal	$f(y) = \exp[\theta_1 y + \theta_2 \ln y + \theta_3 (\ln y)^2 + \theta_4(\ln y)^3 - \eta]$
lognormal	$f(y) = \exp[\theta_1 \ln y + \theta_2 (\ln y)^2 - \eta]$

3. Estimation Using Grouped Data

This section introduces the econometric theory used to estimate exponential family densities, defined in Subsection 2, with data in frequency form. Two contexts may be distinguished. In *unconditional modelling*, the θ_j terms in (6) are constant. In *conditional modelling*, the *j*th distributional term in (6) is defined with respect to

22

the ith individual, $\theta_{j,i}$. That is, the jth distributional term is expressed as a function of relevant exogenous variables, $z_{j,i}$, such that:

$$\theta_{j,i} = v_j (\mathbf{z}_{j,i}) \tag{7}$$

where the jth function $v_j (.)$ may be nonlinear. The use of conditional modelling is particularly powerful, as this allows the *form* of the distribution to change as the exogenous variables change. For example, the distribution can change from being unimodal to being multimodal as an exogenous variable changes. This form of analysis is applied in Section 4, where age is used as a conditioning variable.

Subsection 3.1 outlines the generalised least squares frequency estimator (GLSFE) which is used to obtain unconditional distribution parameter estimates. Although the estimator represents a convenient method for unconditional modelling, it is not possible to extend the estimator to conditional modelling. Therefore Subsection 3.2 introduces unconditional frequency-based maximum likelihood (UFML) estimation for the case where data are grouped. Given that the probabilities associated with particular class-intervals must sum to unity, the framework is based on the multinomial distribution. Subsection 3.3 extends the framework to conditional frequency-based maximum likelihood (CFML) estimation with grouped data.

3.1 Unconditional Distribution Estimates: The GLSFE
Income data are often given in grouped (frequency) format, so that standard maximum likelihood methods of estimation for exponential family distributions, as described in Lye and Martin (1994b), cannot be used. Even where unit record data are available, the computational difficulties associated with the calculation of the normalising constant for each individual in a large sample can be reduced by grouping. The least squares frequency estimator (LSFE) was introduced by Martin (1990) to obtain parameter estimates of unconditional exponential family densities of the form (6) using grouped data. Efficiency improvements to the estimator, by Bakker (1997), demonstrated that to use equation (6) in a frequency context it is necessary to divide the density's domain into K class intervals, such that the probability associated with the kth class interval is:

$$p_k = \int_{a_k}^{a_k + W_k} \exp\left[\sum_{j=1}^{J} \theta_j \psi_j(y) - \eta \right] dy, \tag{8}$$

where a_k denotes the lower bound of the kth class interval of width W_k. For a sample of size N, the natural logarithm of the expected frequency in the kth class interval is $\ln E_k = \ln (N p_k)$.

The LSFE was formally derived by Bakker (1997) from two approximations of $\ln E_k$. The first approximation arises from computing the integral in equation (8) numerically. This expression can be written as:

$$\ln E_k = \ln A_k + \varepsilon_{1,k},\tag{9}$$

where $\varepsilon_{1,k}$ is the numerical integration, or 'quadrature', error. The term A_k represents a rectangular area approximation of the integral in equation (8) and is calculated as:

$$A_k = NW_k f(m_k),\tag{10}$$

where $m_k = a_k + 0.5 W_k$ is the midpoint of the kth class.

The second approximation of $\ln E_k$ represents an empirical approximation and is written:

$$\ln E_k = \ln O_k + \varepsilon_{2,k},\tag{11}$$

where O_k is the empirical frequency observed for the kth class interval and $\varepsilon_{2,k}$ is the empirical sampling error of the kth class interval[4].

Combining equations (9) and (11) yields the expression:

$$\ln O_k = \ln A_k + \varepsilon_{1,k} - \varepsilon_{2,k}.\tag{12}$$

Substituting equation (10) into equation (12) gives:

$$\ln O_k = \ln(NW_k) + \ln f(m_k) + \varepsilon_{1,k} - \varepsilon_{2,k}.\tag{13}$$

Finally, substituting equation (6) into equation (13) gives:

$$\ln O_k = \ln(NW_k) + \ln\left\{\exp\left[\sum_{j=1}^{J}\theta_j\psi_j(m_k) - \eta\right]\right\} + \varepsilon_{1,k} - \varepsilon_{2,k},\tag{14}$$

which can be written more simply as:

$$\ln\left(\frac{O_k}{NW_k}\right) = -\eta + \sum_{j=1}^{J}\theta_j\psi_j(m_k) + \varepsilon_{1,k} - \varepsilon_{2,k}.\tag{15}$$

---

[4] It is assumed that the sample size is sufficiently large such that
$$\int_{-\infty}^{\min y} f(y)\,dy + \int_{\max y}^{\infty} f(y)\,dy \simeq 0.$$

24

Equation (15) can be rearranged into the matrix linear regression form:

$$\ln\left(\frac{O_k}{NW_k}\right)=\Psi\theta+\varepsilon,\qquad(16)$$

where Ψ is a nonstochastic matrix composed by horizontally concatenating a unit vector with the column vectors $\psi_j\ (m_k)\ \forall\ j$, θ is augmented to included the constant term and $\varepsilon = \varepsilon_{1,k} - \varepsilon_{2,k}$. Ordinary least squares parameter estimates of θ, in equation (16), are those of the LSFE. There is no need to apply numerical integration to calculate η (see equation (2), as it is estimated as the negative of the constant term.

The LSFE, given by ordinary least squares estimates of equation (16), is inefficient. Efficient estimation of θ requires application of the covariance matrix Ω in the generalised least squares (GLS) framework, where:

$$\Omega \simeq \frac{1}{N}\begin{bmatrix}(O_1^{-1} N-1) & 1 & \cdots & 1\\ 1 & (O_2^{-1} N-1) & & \vdots\\ \vdots & & \ddots & 1\\ 1 & & \cdots & 1 & (O_k^{-1} N-1)\end{bmatrix}\qquad(17)$$

This covariance matrix is obtained using a first-order Taylor series expansion of the variance of the error term in (16); see Bakker (1997). Given that Ω is a known, symmetric, positive definite matrix it is possible to express the GLS estimator as:

$$\theta^* =(\Psi'\Omega^{-1}\Psi)^{-1}\Psi'\Omega^{-1}\ln\left(\frac{O_k}{NW_k}\right),\qquad(18)$$

where:

$$\text{var}\,(\theta^*)=(\Psi'\Omega^{-1}\Psi)^{-1}.\qquad(19)$$

The parameter estimates, θ *, are defined as belonging to the generalised least squares frequency estimator (GLSFE).

3.2 Unconditional Frequency-based Maximum Likelihood: UFML
Consider the following continuous unconditional distribution of N individuals:

$$f(y) =N\exp\left[\sum_{j=1}^{J}\theta_j\psi_j(y)-\eta\right].\qquad(20)$$

Maximum likelihood estimation of (20) with grouped data is performed by maximizing the multinomial likelihood function:

$$L(\theta) = N! \prod_{k=1}^{K} \frac{(p_k)^{O_k}}{O_k!}, \tag{21}$$

where O_k denotes the number of observations in the kth class and p_k denotes the probability associated with the kth class. As in (8), where the width of the kth class is W_k the formal definition of p_k is:

$$p_k = \int_{d_k}^{a_k+W_k} \exp\left[\sum_{j=1}^{J} \theta_j \psi_j(y) - \eta\right] dy, \tag{22}$$

where a_k denotes the lower bound of the kth class interval. Therefore, the log-likelihood function associated with (21) is derived as:

$$\ln L(\theta) = \ln\Gamma(N+1) + \sum_{k=1}^{K}\left[O_k \ln p_k - \ln\Gamma(O_k+1)\right] \tag{23}$$

$$= C_1 + \sum_{k=1}^{K} O_k \ln p_k.$$

where $C_1 = \ln\Gamma(N+1) - \sum_{k=1}^{K} \ln\Gamma(O_k+1)$ is independent of θ. Parameter estimates obtained by maximizing $\ln L$ in equation (23) are referred to below as unconditional frequency-based maximum likelihood (UFML) estimates.

Consider the special case where the p_k integral in (22) is approximated by a single rectangle of width W_k and height $f(m_k)$, where m_k denotes the kth class midpoint, to give

$$\ln L(\theta) = C_1 + \sum_{k=1}^{K} O_k \ln\left(W_k \exp\left[\sum_{j=1}^{J} \theta_j \psi_j(m_k) - \eta\right]\right)$$

$$= C_2 + \sum_{k=1}^{K} O_k\left[\sum_{j=1}^{J} \theta_j \psi_j(m_k) - \eta\right], \tag{24}$$

where $C_2 = C_1 + \sum_{k=1}^{K} O_k \ln W_k$. Parameter estimates obtained by maximizing $\ln L$ in equation (24) are referred to as approximate unconditional frequency-based maximum likelihood (AUFML) estimates.

In contrast to AUFML, Subsection 3.1 outlined the GLSFE for unconditional grouped data which is also constructed using a multinomial framework and equivalent integration approximation. A difference between the estimators is that

26

the covariance matrix given by equation (17) is constructed using a first-order Taylor series expansion of the variance of the error term in (16). Unreported Monte Carlo simulation experiments demonstrated only marginal differences between the small sample properties of the GLSFE and AUFML estimators.

3.3 Conditional Frequency-based Maximum Likelihood: CFML

The results in Subsection 3.2 can be extended to conditional analysis by considering the joint distribution of y and the conditioning variable matrix, $\mathbf{z}$, as:

$$f(y,\mathbf{z}) = f(y|\mathbf{z}) f(\mathbf{z}).$$

It is convenient to consider the conditioning variable matrix $\mathbf{z}$ to be sorted such that identical rows in $\mathbf{z}$ are contiguous and indexed as the qth conditional classification. Therefore, the probability associated with the kth class and qth conditional classification is given as:

$$P_{q,k} = \int_q \int_{a_k}^{a_k+W_k} f(y|\mathbf{z}_q) f(z_q)\, dydz. \qquad (25)$$

Assuming conditional variables are also grouped, the marginal probabilities in (25) can be replaced with empirical probabilities to give the probability associated with the kth class and qth conditional classification as:

$$P_{q,k} = \int_{a_k}^{a_k+W_k} f\left(y \middle| z_q\right) \frac{O_q}{N}\, dy. \qquad (26)$$

where O_q is the total number of observations associated with the qth conditional classification. Given that:

$$\sum_{q=1}^{Q}\sum_{k=1}^{K} P_{q,k=1}$$

$$\sum_{q=1}^{Q}\sum_{k=1}^{K} O_{q,k=N},$$

where $O_{q,k}$ is the empirical frequency observed for the qth conditional classification and kth class interval, the multinomial framework is appropriate. Therefore, combining (26) and (20) yields:

$$P_{q,k} = \frac{O_q}{N} \int_{a_k}^{a_k+W_k} \exp\left[\sum_{j=1}^{J} \theta_{j,q}(z_q)\psi_j(y) - \eta_q\right] dy, \qquad (27)$$

where the normalising constant, η_q, is defined:

$$\eta_q = \ln \int \exp\left[\sum_{j=1}^{J} \theta_{j,q}(\mathbf{z}_q)\psi_j(y)\right] dy,$$

thus ensuring $\int f(y|\mathbf{z}_q)dy = 1$. Hence, the conditional form of likelihood function (21) is defined as:

$$L(\theta) = N! \prod_{q=1}^{Q}\prod_{k=1}^{K} \frac{(p_{q,k})^{O_{q,k}}}{O_{q,k}!}, \tag{28}$$

and the log-likelihood function associated with (28) is derived as:

$$\ln L(\theta) = \ln \Gamma(N+1) + \sum_{q=1}^{Q}\sum_{k=1}^{K}\left[O_{q,k}\ln p_{q,k} - \ln \Gamma(O_{q,k}+1)\right]$$

$$\tag{29}$$

$$= C_2 + \sum_{q=1}^{Q}\sum_{k=1}^{K} O_{q,k} \ln p_{q,k},$$

where $C_2 = \ln \Gamma(N+1) - \sum_{q=1}^{Q}\sum_{k=1}^{K} \ln \Gamma(O_{q,k}+1)$ is independent of θ and (27) defines $p_{q,k}$. Parameter estimates obtained by maximizing $\ln L$ in equation (29) are referred to below as conditional frequency-based maximum likelihood (CFML) estimates.

Consider the special case where the $p_{q,k}$ integral in (29) is approximated by a single rectangle of width W_k and height $f(m_k)$, where M_k denotes the kth class midpoint, to give:

$$\ln L(\theta) = C_2 + \sum_{q=1}^{Q}\sum_{k=1}^{K}\left[O_{q,k}\ln\left(W_k \frac{O_q}{N}\exp\left[\sum_{j=1}^{J}\theta_{j,q}(\mathbf{z}_q)\psi_j(m_k)-\eta_q\right]\right)\right]$$

$$\tag{30}$$

$$= C_3 + \sum_{q=1}^{Q}\sum_{k=1}^{K}\left[O_{q,k}\sum_{j=1}^{J}\theta_{j,q}(\mathbf{z}_q)\psi_j(m_k)-\eta_q\right],$$

where $C_3 = C_2 + \sum_{q=1}^{Q}\sum_{k=1}^{K} O_{q,k} W_k | N$ is independent of θ. Maximum likelihood estimation using (30) is computationally less burdensome than (29). Parameter estimates obtained by maximizing ln L in equation (30) are referred to below as approximate conditional frequency-based maximum likelihood (ACFML) estimates.

4. Application to New Zealand Data

This section applies the above methods of estimating unconditional and conditional distributions to New Zealand data. Details of the data sets are provided in Subsection 4.1. Subsection 4.2 examines the goodness-of-fit of densities listed in Table 1 when applied to unconditional distributions of particular age groups. Subsection 4.3 reports conditional modelling estimates where the distributional parameters are expressed as functions of age.

4.1 New Zealand Income Distribution Data

The New Zealand income distribution data were derived from a random sample of 2 per cent of IR3 and IR5 income tax returns filed for 1991. IR5 returns are filed by taxpayers whose income predominantly has tax withheld; that is, income from wages and salaries, taxable welfare benefits, NZ superannuation, interest and dividends. Individuals who have income from other sources, or who have been paying provisional tax, file an IR3. Taxable income is used for IR5 taxpayers, incorporating wage/salary income, interest, dividends, and other income less tax agent fees for return preparation. For IR3 the "income after expenses" definition is used, incorporating current losses, but not losses brought forward from prior years. This includes income from wages and salaries, interest, dividends, overseas, trusts, self employment, partnerships, shareholder salaries, and rents. Private superannuation income is not included since this is not taxable in New Zealand.

Wages and salaries include all income from which PAYE was withheld at source. This includes welfare benefits, NZ superannuation, withholding payments (e.g. from shearing, domestic employment), redundancy payments, lump sum retiring allowances and taxable ACC payments. Welfare beneficiaries and NZ superannuitants cannot be separately identified, and their income is lumped together with any wage or salary income they may have received from other jobs during the year. The sample used here consists of those regarded as obtaining their income mainly from wages and salaries; that is, their taxable income was between 67 and 133 per cent of salary income.

Individuals with income below \$20,000 and who have tax withheld at source, are not in receipt of income-related transfer payments or student loans, are not required to file. Such individuals may nevertheless choose to file, usually to receive a tax refund. Hence, people in the sample with incomes below \$20,000 are not representative of the full tax-paying population with incomes below \$20,000.

Age is calculated in years as at 31 March 1991. Gender was determined using a "title" variable (Mr, Mrs, Brig, Rev etc.). Where title was missing, sex was imputed assuming 50% males. Where title was Dr, 79% males were assumed.

Where title was numeric, the assumption was 92% males (this situation seems to be restricted to army serial numbers).

For confidentiality reasons, the data are only available in grouped form. Tables 2 and 3 show the available data for males and females respectively[5]. The 19 income midpoints, m_k, for males and females are given in the first column of each table. The first ten class intervals have a width of 5000, the next five class intervals have a width of 10000 and the last four class intervals have a width of 20000, thus defining the vector W_k. The ten conditional age group classifications, a_q, are shown in the first row of the tables.

Table 2. 1991 New Zealand Grouped Data: Males

$m_k \backslash a_q$	22	27	32	37	42	47	52	57	62	67
2500	·16	17	9	5	3	6	4	2	1	3
7500	117	43	46	39	27	33	36	44	117	147
12500	105	61	55	43	26	25	23	22	141	160
17500	113	79	61	50	40	27	19	29	38	26
22500	198	148	132	99	95	72	58	67	30	12
27500	164	218	207	151	126	107	87	67	31	9
32500	91	183	193	156	131	116	80	75	41	3
37500	46	131	165	152	133	123	84	56	23	4
42500	22	88	137	144	129	97	67	35	30	8
47500	10	45	92	116	103	74	56	39	11	4
55000	3	23	97	108	101	92	64	35	15	1
65000	2	15	30	38	44	56	33	21	9	0
75000	2	4	9	20	25	15	21	12	5	0
85000	1	1	7	10	10	9	6	3	3	0
95000	0	0	4	10	5	8	2	0	1	1
110000	0	1	0	6	4	8	3	3	2	0
130000	0	1	0	1	3	5	5	0	1	0
150000	0	0	3	0	2	0	0	0	0	0
170000	0	0	0	3	2	1	1	1	0	0

Notes: m_k denotes the annual income midpoint of the kth class interval and a_q denotes the age midpoint of the qth conditional distribution

4.2 Unconditional Distribution Estimates

One method of determining the most appropriate statistical distribution for conditional analysis is to examine how well the density fits various unconditional empirical distributions. Therefore, this subsection compares the fit of alternative distributions from the exponential family to 1991 New Zealand unconditional

---

[5] Data for the class intervals (y ≤ 0), (180000 < y ≤ 200000) and (y > 200000\right) were not used here. For the male sample of 8307 observations this removed 42 individuals and for the female sample of 7399 individuals this removed 167 individuals.

30

income distributions classified by age group and sex. The criterion used is the chi-square statistic:

$$\chi^2 = \sum_k \frac{(f_{o,k} - f_{e,k})^2}{f_{e,k}}, \tag{31}$$

where k indexes class intervals, $f_{o,k}$ is the unconditional empirical distribution's observed frequency in the kth class and $f_{e,k}$ is the expected frequency for the kth class. Given the large number of unconditional distributions to be estimated, 88 in total[6], the GLSFE as described in Subsection 3.1 is adopted for its computational speed and the relative simplicity of the computer programming necessary for its implementation. Expected frequencies are calculated as:

$$f_{e,k} = NW_k \exp(\Psi\theta^*),$$

where θ^* are obtained from the GLSFE given by equation (18) and Ψ is defined with reference to equation (16).

Table 3. 1991 New Zealand Grouped Data: Females

$m_k \backslash a_q$	22	27	32	37	42	47	52	57	62	67
2500	55	95	105	70	41	16	17	10	6	1
7500	162	111	143	118	94	65	55	105	164	137
12500	125	131	141	136	143	78	62	89	211	258
17500	144	112	142	140	128	90	68	35	31	14
22500	235	157	90	108	134	132	73	46	26	7
27500	168	188	98	109	129	110	81	26	15	3
32500	64	141	94	80	112	100	72	34	13	3
37500	18	57	55	51	54	47	42	12	13	1
42500	6	29	28	26	37	26	20	5	7	0
47500	1	11	12	11	18	15	11	5	2	0
55000	1	15	17	12	7	8	11	3	5	0
65000	0	3	4	2	2	5	3	0	2	0
75000	0	1	2	0	1	3	0	0	0	0
85000	0	1	1	2	0	0	0	0	0	0
95000	0	0	1	0	0	0	0	0	0	0
110000	0	0	0	1	0	1	0	0	0	0
130000	0	0	0	0	0	0	0	0	0	0
150000	0	0	0	1	0	0	0	0	0	0
170000	0	0	0	0	1	0	0	0	0	0

Notes: m_k denotes the annual income midpoint of the kth class interval and a_q denotes the age midpoint of the qth conditional distribution

[6] This is because 4 distributions are fitted to 10 age distributions for males and females, along with distributions for all ages combined.

Table 4. χ^2 Statistics of Unconditional Income Distributions

Age	Generalised Gamma	Gamma	Generalised Lognormal	Lognormal
Male				
22	**72.54**	111.94	106.22	243.68
27	**44.82**	223.37	128.38	509.08
32	**50.23**	217.06	138.32	411.87
37	**66.86**	226.04	138.91	373.31
42	**46.07**	156.74	93.37	344.60
47	**44.99**	111.48	87.48	272.30
52	**65.34**	96.00	88.98	171.44
57	**53.14**	79.07	72.50	94.18
62	113.63	197.34	**58.55**	94.01
67	**45.56**	408.67	62.96	124.98
Aggregate	**493.71**	828.40	849.83	1593.50
Female				
22	99.82	226.18	**53.67**	404.48
27	**49.16**	218.34	83.39	447.93
32	**22.22**	48.58	28.24	136.92
37	**18.87**	73.87	32.64	122.65
42	**15.79**	183.71	61.21	178.51
47	**25.59**	65.03	53.62	162.76
52	12.77	39.86	**7.97**	92.59
57	21.69	54.52	**19.73**	33.57
62	**68.82**	207.93	71.37	103.73
67	52.50	124.05	**21.56**	103.80
Aggregate	**227.86**	858.68	826.33	1080.28

Notes: χ^2 statistics are calculated using equation (31) and bold type denotes the minimum χ^2 statistic for a particular age group.

Table 4 reports the 88 χ^2 values, for the four unconditional densities given in Table 1 applied to each age group and all ages combined for males and females. The minimum χ^2 value for each age group is shown in bold. The generalised gamma density provides superior results in nine of the ten cases for males and six of the ten cases for females. In addition, the generalised gamma distribution dominates alternatives for males and females aggregated over all age groups.

A graphical example of the fit provided by alternative forms is provided in Figure 1 which compares the empirical income distribution for males aged 42 to expected GLSFE frequencies of the densities described in Table 1.[7] This shows

---

[7] For graphical purposes the frequencies are represented in a common \$5000 interval basis, as described in Yule and Kendall (1940, p.89).

32

that both the standard gamma and lognormal forms provide a poor fit the the mode and place too much weight in the tails. The generalised gamma can be seen to model the mode and the tails slightly closer than the generalised lognormal. Hence, the following conditional analysis is restricted to the generalised gamma distribution.

Figure 1: Empirical and Expected GLSFE Frequencies: Males Aged 42

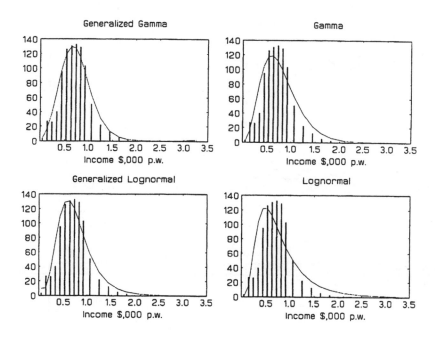

4.3 Conditional Model Specification

This subsection extends the unconditional generalised gamma distribution by allowing the distributional parameters, $\theta_{j,q}$, to be functions of age, a_q. Adopting the notation of equation (7) gives:

$$\theta_{j,q} = \upsilon_j (a_q) . \tag{32}$$

Selecting the functional forms, $\upsilon_j (.)$, is a non-trivial task. One approach is to express each θ_j as a polynomial function of age, and successively eliminate statistically insignificant terms. However, given the considerable present data limitations, this approach was not followed.[8]

---

[8] Alternatively, different structural models of the type examined in Creedy *et al.* (1996) could be produced, but this approach was not adopted given the emphasis on examining the functional form.

The method adopted involves examining the unconditional distributions in order to determine the most appropriate conditional specification. The GLSFE estimates of the unconditional generalised gamma distributions for each age group $(\hat{\theta}_{1,q}, \hat{\theta}_{2,q}, \hat{\theta}_{3,q}, \hat{\theta}_{4,q})$ are plotted against a_q in Figure 2 for males and females. The figure provides insight into the appropriate form of $v_j(.)$ in equation (32).

Figure 2: Unconditional Distribution Parameters

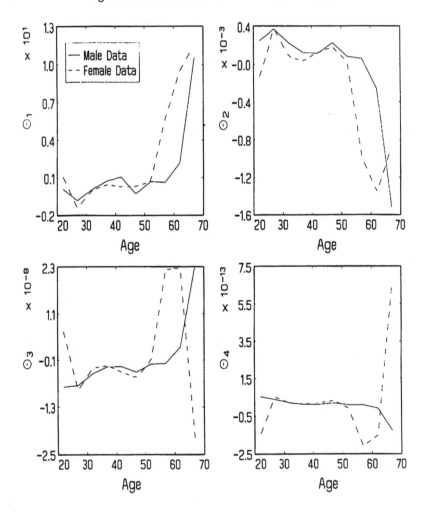

Figure 2 exhibits an approximate quadratic relationship $(\hat{\theta}_{1,q}, \hat{\theta}_{2,q})$ and a_q for males. Results are less apparent for females and hence a more flexible cubic

34

relationship was adopted between $(\hat{\theta}_{1,q}, \hat{\theta}_{2,q})$ and a_q. The relationship between $\hat{\theta}_{3,q}$ and a_q is less clear, with significant departures between males and females in the older age groups. However, estimation results favoured inclusion of a second-order term only. Given the small scale of the θ_4 term, for both males and females, a negative constant value was imposed during estimation, thus ensuring that the density does not become explosive as $y \to \infty$. Therefore, the following conditional distribution was adopted to model the 1991 New Zealand income distribution:

$$f(y) = \exp\left[\theta_{1,q} \ln y + \theta_{2,q} y + \theta_{3,q} y^2 + \theta_{4,q} y^3 - \eta_q\right], \qquad (33)$$

Table 5. Generalised Gamma Conditional Distribution Estimates: CFML

MALE

$\hat{\theta}_{1,q}$ = 0.2587 + 0.1209 a_q - 1.5363 a_q^2
(0.4847)   (0.0261)   (0.3030)

$\hat{\theta}_{2,q}$ = -15.2367 + 0.6349 a_q - 8.1909 a_q^2
(1.0116)   (0.0557)   (0.7096)

$\hat{\theta}_{3,q}$ = -2.0907 + 0.7015 a_q^2
(0.2463)   (0.0589)

$\hat{\theta}_{4,q}$ = -0.0001

FEMALE

$\hat{\theta}_{1,q}$ = 6.2015 - 0.4156 a_q + 8.1231 a_q^2 - 0.0340 a_q^3
(1.3250)   (0.1025)   (2.5433)   (0.0201)

$\hat{\theta}_{2,q}$ = 3.2300 - 0.3336 a_q + 20.6361 a_q^2 - 0.3316 a_q^3
(4.2560)   (0.3276)   (8.2017)   (0.0663)

$\hat{\theta}_{3,q}$ = -7.7018 + 2.2620 a_q^2
(0.4822)   (0.1136)

$\hat{\theta}_{4,q}$ = -0.0001

Notes: Standard errors are given in parentheses.

where the specification for males is given as:

$$\theta_{1,q} = \gamma_1 + \gamma_2 a_q + \gamma_3 a_q^2 \tag{34}$$

$$\theta_{2,q} = \gamma_4 + \gamma_5 a_q + \gamma_6 a_q^2 \tag{35}$$

$$\theta_{3q} = \gamma_7 + \gamma_8 a_q^2 \tag{36}$$

$$\theta_{4q} = -0.0001, \tag{37}$$

where the specification for females is given as:

$$\theta_{1,q} = \gamma_1 + \gamma_2 a_q + \gamma_3 a_q^2 + \gamma_4 a_q^3 \tag{38}$$

$$\theta_{2,q} = \gamma_5 + \gamma_6 a_q + \gamma_7 a_q^2 + \gamma_8 a_q^3 \tag{39}$$

$$\theta_{3q} = \gamma_9 + \gamma_{10} a_q^2 \tag{40}$$

$$\theta_{4q} = -0.0001, \tag{41}$$

During estimation m_k were divided by (1000 x 52), thus converting income into a thousand dollar per week measure, and (a_q^2, a_q^3) values were divided by 1000. This scaling improved the convergence behaviour of the GAUSS maximum likelihood algorithms.

CFML, as described by the log-likelihood function (29) in Subsection 3.2, was used to obtain parameter estimates of γ and associated standard errors for 1991 male and female data as presented in Tables 2 and 3. Estimation results are reported in Table 5. Except for the male estimate of $\hat{\gamma}_1$ and the female estimates of $(\hat{\gamma}_4, \hat{\gamma}_5, \hat{\gamma}_6)$, all parameter estimates in Table 5 are statistically significant. However, the properties of standard errors for CFML are unknown, so caution with interpretation is recommended.

Parameter estimates in Table 5 were used to construct the probability density surfaces for males and females shown in Figures 3 and 4. These figures demonstrate that the fitted densities capture the features of their corresponding empirical distributions, namely, high peaks at young and elderly age groups, with a relatively higher peak observed for the elderly and more dispersed distributions corresponding to middle-aged people. The fitted density surface for females appears relatively more skewed than that of males, again consistent with empirical observation. Figure 5 compares mean and median values calculated using estimates from Table 5 with empirical means from the grouped data presented in Tables 2 and 3. Figure 5 demonstrates that the mean income of females is substantially lower than that of males, for a given age group. Moreover, the mean values calculated from the conditional income density of males more closely correspond to the empirical counterpart than for females.

Figure 3: Estimated Density Surface: Males 1991

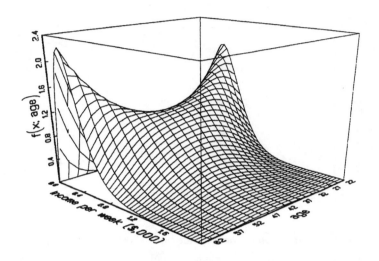

Figure 4: Estimated Density Surface: Females 1991

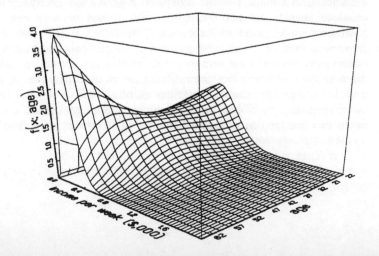

Figure 5: Estimated Conditional Density means and Grouped Data Means

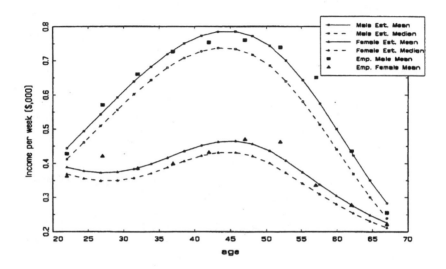

5. Conclusions

The exponential family of distributions offers considerable scope for the analysis of income distributions because of its ability to 'nest' many well-known densities and the possibility of deriving special cases explicitly from labour demand and supply models. This paper has presented several estimation methods based on the use of grouped data. These methods were motivated by the fact that many income distribution data are available in grouped form, combined with the fact that they offer computational advantages even when unit record data are available.

The methods were applied to New Zealand income distribution data for males and females in a number of age groups. The generalised gamma distribution was found to provide the best fit to the distributions of most age groups. The generalised least squares frequency-based estimator (GLSFE) was shown to be a convenient method of estimating these unconditional distributions. Following further examination of the unconditional distributions in each age group, three of the four parameters of the generalised gamma distribution were expressed as functions of age. Conditional generalised gamma distributions were then estimated using maximum likelihood, modified for grouped data (CFML). The estimated model captured the major empirical features of the changing distribution of income with age.

It is suggested that the flexibility of the model offers much potential for further income distribution modelling. For example, it would be of interest to apply the model to particular occupations. Furthermore, the approach could be adapted to examine the changing aggregate income distribution over time, thereby allowing the influence of macroeconomic variables on the income distribution to be estimated. Such an approach would allow the *form* of the distribution to change over time.

References

Bakker, A. (1997), "Estimation of Generalised Distributions", Chapter 5 in J. Creedy and V.L. Martin (eds.) *Nonlinear Economic Models: Cross-sectional, Time Series and Neural Network Applications*, Edward Elgar, pp.91-110.

Bordley, R., McDonald, J.B. and Mantrala, A. (1996), "Something New, Something Old: Parametric Models for the Size Distribution of Income", *Journal of Income Distribution*, 6, 91-103.

Cobb, L., Koppstein, P. and Chen, N.H. (1983), "Estimation and Moment Recursion Relations for Multimodal Distributions of the Exponential Family", *Journal of the American Statistical Association*, 78, 124-130.

Cox, D.R. and Miller, H.D. (1984), *The Theory of Stochastic Processes*, London: Chapman and Hall.

Creedy, J., Lye, J. and Martin, V.L. (1996), "A Labour Market Equilibrium Model of The Personal Distribution of Earnings", *Journal of Income Distribution*, 6, 127-144.

Creedy, J. and Martin, V.L. (1998), "Nonlinear Modelling Using the Generalized Exponential Family of Distributions", forthcoming in *Bulletin of Economic Research*.

Dagum, C. (1996), "A Systematic Approach to the Generation of Income Distribution Models", *Journal of Income Distribution*, 6, 105-126.

Kamien, M.I. and Schwartz, N.L. (1991), *Dynamic Optimization: The Calculus of Variations and Optimal Control in Economics and Management*, Amsterdam: North-Holland.

Lye, J. and Martin, V.L. (1994a), "Towards a Theory of Non-Linear Models", in J. Creedy and V.L. Martin (eds.) *Chaos and Non-Linear Models in Economics*, Aldershoot: Edward Elgar, pp.70-86.

Lye, J. and Martin, V.L. (1994b), "Robust Estimation with the Generalized Exponential Family", in J. Creedy and V.L. Martin (eds.) *Chaos and Non-Linear Models in Economics*, Aldershoot: Edward Elgar, pp.151-165.

Martin, V.L. (1990), "Properties and Applications of Distributions from the Generalized Exponential Family", Ph.D. Thesis, Monash University.

Salem, A.Z.B. and Mount, T.D. (1974), "A Convenient Descriptive Model of Income Distribution: the Gamma Density", *Econometrica*, 42, 1115-1127.

Yule, G.U. and Kendall, M.G. (1940), *An Introduction to the Theory of Statistics*, London: Charles Griffin.

PART II

MACRO-VARIABLES AND INCOME DISTRIBUTION

JOURNAL OF
INCOME
DISTRIBUTION

NORTH-HOLLAND   Journal of Income Distribution 9 (2000) 183–197

Macroeconomic variables and income distribution Conditional modelling with the generalised exponential

Alex Bakker, John Creedy*

Department of Economics, University of Melbourne, Parville, Victoria 3052, Melbourne Australia

Accepted 1 September 1999

Abstract

This paper presents a method of examining the effects of macroeconomic variables on the personal distribution of income over time. The approach involves modelling the complete distribution of income in each year using a flexible functional form from the generalised exponential family of distributions. The parameters of the distribution are specified as functions of the macroeconomic variables. It is shown how comparative static analyses, involving the modes and Atkinson inequality measures, can be performed. The method is applied to male New Zealand income distribution data for the period 1985–1994. The rate of unemployment is found to be the primary influence on the form of the distribution. Higher unemployment is found to decrease the modal income and increase the Atkinson inequality measure. © 2001 Elsevier Science Inc. All rights reserved.

JEL classification: C51; D31; D63

Keywords: Income inequality; Conditional modelling; Unemployment; Generalised exponential

1. Introduction

The aim of this paper is to explore a method of examining the effects of macroeconomic variables on the personal distribution of income over time. A variety of approaches has been used to examine this issue. In view of the complexity of the relationship between macroeconomic variables and the personal distribution, involving a "mapping" from just a few variables to a very large number of incomes. it is not surprising that statistical approaches

---

* Corresponding author.
E-mail address: j.creedy@ecomfac.unimelb.edu.au (J. Creedy).

0926-6437/00/$ – see front matter © 2001 Elsevier Science Inc. All rights reserved.
PII: S0926-6437(00)00006-8

have typically been adopted. For example, large-scale macroeconomic models have not been extended to include the personal distribution. However, Bud and Whiteman (1978) and Nolan (1987, 1989) used a simulation approach based on household expenditure data, using assumptions about the incidence of an increase in aggregate unemployment (in terms of higher durations and entrants to unemployment).

The statistical approaches can be roughly divided into three broad groups, where in the first two cases, summary measures of the distribution are related to the macro-economic variables. One broad approach has been to use a measure of inequality as dependent variable. For example, Schultz (1969) examined the Gini coefficient over time, while Beach (1977) examined a range of inequality measures, including the Gini and Atkinson measures. Using several measures of inequality and allowing for the impact of monetary and fiscal policy variables, Haslag and Slottje (1994) considered the question of causality.

A second approach has been to carry out several regressions, using as dependent variables the income shares of specified percentiles of the distribution (see, for example, Blejer & Guerrero, 1990; Blinder & Esaki, 1978; Flückiger & Zarin-Nejadan, 1994; Nolan, 1989; Silber & Ziberfarb, 1994). This has been extended by Bishop, Formby and Sakano (1994), who examined Lorenz ordinates, thereby allowing the application of results concerning Lorenz dominance. They also examined the behaviour of quintile conditional mean incomes (the quintile share multiplied by average income). Bishop et al. (1994) suggested that the use of percentile shares means that some shares must, because of the adding up requirement, move in opposite directions, making interpretation awkward.

Instead of using one or more summary measures, a third approach, pioneered by Metcalf (1972), uses summary statistics to fit a functional form to describe the distribution in each year. He used a displaced lognormal distribution. The approach suggested in this paper can be considered as an extension of that used by Metcalf (1972). Here, the complete distribution of income in each year is estimated using individual data from a time series of cross-sectional surveys. The parameters of the distribution are specified as functions of the macroeconomic variables and the relevant functional forms are all estimated simultaneously using conditional distribution modelling.

The question of the choice of functional form to describe the income distribution arises, where it is desirable to allow the shape of the distribution to change substantially over time. For example, the distribution may change from being unimodal to being bimodal, so the functional form must be flexible. There are obviously varying views about the appropriate functional form. This paper uses the generalised exponential family of distributions. Conditional distribution modelling with the generalised exponential family has been explored in a variety of other contexts. For a general introduction to the use of the generalised family, and a variety of applications, see Creedy and Martin (1994, 1997). This family is highly flexible and has been found to provide a good approximation to a number of empirical income distributions. An advantage of this specification is that the distribution is sufficiently flexible to be able to handle changes from single to multi-modality, and vice versa, over time. It has been used to describe income distributions in Creedy, Lye, and Martin (1996), where the form of the distribution was generated from a labour demand and supply model of the labour market, with the addition of a stochastic process. This allows for the possibility in future work of developing a more detailed structural model of the changing distribution over time.

The distributional framework of analysis is described in Section 2, along with the estimation method. Section 3 shows how summary measures of the distribution, particularly the modes and the Atkinson (1970) measure of inequality, change as a result of a change in a macroeconomic variable. An empirical application, using New Zealand male income data for the period 1985–1994, is given in Section 4. Brief conclusions are stated in Section 5.

2. The distributional framework

This section describes how macroeconomic variables can be incorporated into a conditional income distribution specification. The exponential family of distributions is outlined in Section 2.1. Section 2.2 outlines how this family of distributions can be utilised for conditional modelling, and Section 2.3 briefly describes the method of estimation used.

2.1. The exponential family

The unconditional generalised exponential family of distributions, denoted as $f(x)$, is defined for the random variable x (where $x \in D$) as:

$$f(x) = \exp\left[\sum_{j=1}^{J} \theta_j \psi_j(x) - \eta\right] \tag{1}$$

where J is the number of additive terms in the exponential function, $\psi_j(.)$ denotes the functional form of the jth additive term, and θ_j represents the associated parameter. The term η is the normalising constant, which ensures that $\int_D f(x)dx = 1$. It is given as:

$$\eta = \ln \int_D \exp\left[\sum_{j=1}^{J} \theta_j \psi_j(s)\right] ds \tag{2}$$

For a general discussion of this family of distributions, see Cobb, Koppstein, and Chen (1983) and Lye and Martin (1994a, 1994b). Many density functions used in statistics and economics can be written in the form given in Eq. (1). The simplest case occurs when $J=1$ and $\psi_1(x)=x$, for which Eq. (1) gives the standard exponential distribution. Adding a quadratic term, so that $J=2$, $\psi_1(x)=x$, and $\psi_2(x)=x^2$, gives the normal distribution. Further examples of standard and generalised forms of well-known distributions consistent with Eq. (1) are presented in Table 1. The generalised distributions are more flexible than the standard forms and a valuable property is that they are capable of demonstrating multimodality.

Restrictions on some of the θ's must be imposed in order to ensure boundedness. A necessary condition for boundedness of (1) over infinite and semiinfinite domains is that the coefficient associated with the $\psi_j(.)$ that dominates tail regions is negative. For example, boundedness of the generalised exponential distribution requires $\theta_J < 0$. A further restriction is

Table 1
Examples of generalized exponential family distributions

Generalised gamma	$\exp[\theta_1\ln x + \theta_2 x + \theta_3 x^2 + \theta_4 x^3 - \eta]$
Gamma	$\exp[\theta_1\ln x + \theta_2 x - \eta]$
Generalised lognormal	$\exp[\theta_1 x + \theta_2\ln x + \theta_3(\ln x)^2 + \theta_4(\ln x)^3 - \eta]$
Lognormal	$\exp[\theta_1\ln x + \theta_2(\ln x)^2 - \eta]$
Normal	$\exp[\theta_1 x + \theta_2 x^2 - \eta]$
Generalised exponential	$\exp[\sum_{j=1}^{J}\theta_j x^j/j - \eta]$
Beta	$\exp[\theta_1\ln x + \theta_2\ln(1-x) - \eta]$
Generalised beta	$\exp[\theta_1\ln x + \theta_2\ln(1-x) + \theta_3 x + \theta_4 x^2 - \eta]$

required for boundedness of distributions defined over a semiinfinite domain where a pole has the potential to occur at the finite boundary. For example, boundedness of the generalised gamma distribution in Table 1 requires $\theta_4 < 0$ and $\theta_1 > -1$.

2.2. Conditional modelling: time-varying distributions

The present context is one in which the random variable x is generated from the distribution in Eq. (1), but the shape of the distribution changes over time. The distribution changes because the coefficients, θ_j (and hence, η), change over time. The approach suggested here is to model the changes in the distributional coefficients, $\theta_{j,t}$, as functions of exogenous macroeconomic variables, which at time t are placed in the vector z_t. For example, z_t many include the unemployment ratio and the growth rate. In general, conditional distribution modelling involves the distributional coefficients, $\theta_{j,t}$, being defined as [Eq. (3)]:

$$\theta_{j,t} = g_j(z_t, \beta_j) \tag{3}$$

where β_j denotes the parameter vector associated with $\theta_{j,t}$. The function $g_j(.)$ indicates that the functional form used to model the jth parameter may vary with j, if required. For highly flexible distributions, such as the generalised gamma distribution shown in Table 1, this type of conditional modelling allows for transitions to take place between unimodal and bimodal specifications over time. In a time series context, this feature can be exploited to model the large "jumps" experienced in stock markets and foreign exchange markets in terms of sudden transitions between unimodal and bimodal price distributions.

2.3. Maximum likelihood estimation

Suppose that a time series of cross-sections is available where individual data are provided, and $x_{t,j}$ refers to the income of the ith individual in the tth period. N_t refers to the total number of individuals in the tth period, and T refers to the total number of time periods. Following Lye and Martin (1994b), the log-likelihood function for the exponential family (Eq. (1)) is written as:

$$\ln L = \sum_{t=1}^{T}\sum_{i=1}^{N_t}\sum_{j=1}^{J}\theta_{j,t}\psi_j(x_{t,i}) - \sum_{t=1}^{T}N_t\eta_t \tag{4}$$

where a modification of Eq. (2) yields Eq. (5):

$$\eta_t = \ln \int_D \exp\left[\sum_{j=1}^{J} \theta_{j,t}\psi_j(s)\right] ds \tag{5}$$

For example, the log-likelihood function associated with the generalised gamma distribution in Table 1 is derived from Eq. (4) as shown in Eq. (6):

$$\ln L = \sum_{t=1}^{T}\sum_{i=1}^{N_t}(\theta_{1,t}\ln x_{t,i} + \theta_{2,t}x_{t,i} + \theta_{3,t}x_{t,i}^2 + \theta_{4,t}x_{t,i}^3) - \sum_{t=1}^{T} N_t\eta_t \tag{6}$$

where the normalising constant at time t is defined as:

$$\eta_t = \ln \int_0^\infty \exp[\theta_{1,t}\ln s + \theta_{2,t}s + \theta_{3,t}s^2 + \theta_{4,t}s^3]ds \tag{7}$$

Unfortunately, the integral in Eq. (7) does not have a closed-form solution, which means that numerical techniques must be applied (see Bakker, 1995 for an investigation of alternative approaches to numerical integration in this context). Alternatively, grouped income distribution data may be available in each year, in which case, the methods suggested by Bakker (1997) and used by Bakker and Creedy (1997) can be employed.

3. Comparative static analysis

Changes in the distributional parameters, the θ's, give rise to changes in the characteristics of the distribution, in particular, the measures of location and dispersion. The way in which particular macroeconomic variables influence the parameters is determined by the form of the functions, $\theta_{j,t} = g_j(z_t,\beta_j)$. However, the implications of changes in macroeconomic variables for summary measures of the distribution of income over time, such as inequality measures, are not transparent. This is because of the fact that, except in special cases such as the standard normal and lognormal distributions, the summary measures of interest are more or less complex functions of the θ's.

The analysis of changes in the distributional characteristics as a result of a change in one of the exogenous variables contained in z is referred to here as comparative static analysis. This section shows how comparative statics can be carried out in terms of two important characteristics of the distribution. Section 3.1 examines how changes in macroeconomic variables affect modal locations of the estimated distribution. Section 3.2 examines how the parameter estimates can be used to calculate comparative static changes in the Atkinson measures of inequality.

3.1. Modal incomes

The effects on the mode of changes in a structural variable, say z_t (where this represents a variable from z_t and the subscript has been dropped for convenience) can be obtained in an

188   *A. Bakker, J. Creedy / Journal of Income Distribution 9 (2000) 183–197*

analytical form for distributions from the generalised exponential family shown in Eq. (1). Consider the simple monotonic transformation of Eq. (1) given by the function:

$$Q(x_t) = \sum_{j=1}^{J} \theta_{j,t} \psi_j(x_t) \tag{8}$$

The turning points, or modes, of the density, $Q(x_t)$, correspond to the roots of $dQ(x_t)/dx_t = 0$ and, in view of the monotonicity of the transformation, these must correspond also to the turning points of $f(x_t)$. Hence, the modes are the roots of:

$$\frac{dQ(x_t)}{dx_t} = \sum_{j=1}^{J} \theta_{j,t} \frac{d\psi_j(x_t)}{dx_t} - 0 \tag{9}$$

As an example, consider the special case of the generalised gamma distribution, shown in Table 1, for which Eq. (8) yields Eq. (10):

$$Q(x_t) = \theta_{1,t} \ln x_t - \theta_{2,t} x_t + \theta_{3,t} x_t^2 + \theta_{4,t} x_t^3 \tag{10}$$

Application of Eq. (9) gives the modal incomes in the tth period, M_t, as the roots of the cubic:

$$P(M_t) = \theta_{1,t} + \theta_{2,t} M_t - 2\theta_{3,t} M_t^2 + 3\theta_{4,t} M_t^3 = 0 \tag{11}$$

where $P(M_t)$ is used to define the cubic. If Eq. (11) contains three real and distinct roots, there are three turning points in the generalised gamma distribution, of which the middle one is the antimode.

For comparative statics, it is required to obtain an expression for changes in the modes resulting from a change in z_t. Applying the implicit function theorem to Eq. (11) yields Eq. (12):

$$\frac{dM_t}{dz_t} = -\frac{\partial P/\partial z_t}{\partial P/\partial M_t} \tag{12}$$

which can be written as:

$$\frac{dM_t}{dz_t} = -\frac{\frac{\partial \theta_{1,t}}{\partial z_t} + M_t \frac{\partial \theta_{2,t}}{\partial z_t} + 2M_t^2 \frac{\partial \theta_{3,t}}{\partial z_t} + 3M_t^3 \frac{\partial \theta_{4,t}}{\partial z_t}}{\theta_{2,t} + 4\theta_{3,t} M_t + 9\theta_{4,t} M_t^2} \tag{13}$$

This is the most general form, in view of the fact that no restrictions have so far been placed on the function $\theta_{j,t} = g_j(z_t, \beta_j)$. A convenient case arises where all of the $\theta_{j,t}$ distributional terms are expressed as linear functions of exogenous variables such that Eq. (14) holds:

$$\theta_{j,t} = z_t \beta_j \tag{14}$$

where the number of parameters in the β_j vectors corresponds to the number of exogenous variables. In this case, and if z_t is the rth variable in z_t, Eq. (13) can be rewritten as:

$$\frac{dM_t}{dz_{r,t}} = -\frac{\beta_{2,r} + 2M_t^2 \beta_{3,r} + 3M_t^3 \beta_{4,r}}{\theta_{2,t} + 4\theta_{3,t} M_t + 9\theta_{4,t} M_t^2} \tag{15}$$

This clearly illustrates the point, made above, that the changes in the modes are far from transparent.

3.2. Atkinson measure of inequality

This subsection explores the use of conditional distribution modelling, using the generalised exponential family of distributions, in measuring the effect on an inequality measure of changes in macroeconomic variables. Special attention is given to the widely used Atkinson (1970) measure of inequality, I_t, in period t. This is based on the additive social welfare function 5 $W_t = \int_0^\infty \frac{1}{1-\varepsilon} x_t^{1-\varepsilon} f(x_t) dx_t$, where $\varepsilon \neq 1$, and ε is the degree of relative inequality aversion. Let $\bar{x}_t$ denote the arithmetic mean income in the tth period, so that $x_t = \int_0^\infty x_t f(x_t) dx_t$. The Atkinson measure is defined as:

$$I_t = 1 - \frac{x_{e,t}}{\bar{x}_t} \tag{16}$$

where $x_{e,t}$ denotes the equally distributed equivalent level of income in the tth period, defined as that value of income, which, if equally distributed, gives rise to the same social welfare as the actual income distribution. Hence,

$$x_{e,t} = \left[\int_0^\infty x_t^{1-\varepsilon} f(x_t) dx_t \right]^{\frac{1}{1-\varepsilon}} \tag{17}$$

If $\varepsilon = 0$, it follows from Eq. (17) that $\bar{x}_{e,t} = x_t$ and $I_t = 0$. If $\varepsilon = 1$, Eq. (17) simplifies to $x_{e,t} = \exp \left[\int_0^\infty \ln x_t f(x_t) dx_t \right]$. In view of the fact that the choice of ε reflects a value judgement, it is usual to report results for a range of values of ε. In the case of the standard lognormal distribution, it is possible to obtain a closed-form solution to Eq. (17) by making use of the moment generating function of the standard normal distribution. However, for the generalised forms, the evaluation of the Atkinson measure requires the use of numerical integration.

The effect of changes in an exogenous variable, z_t, on the Atkinson measure of inequality may be analysed from the following partial derivative of Eq. (16):

$$\frac{\partial I_t}{\partial z_t} = \frac{1}{x_t} \left[(1 - I_t) \frac{\partial x_t}{\partial z_t} - \frac{\partial x_{e,t}}{\partial z_t} \right] \tag{18}$$

The partial derivative, $\partial x_{e,t} / \partial z_t$ in Eq. (18) can be derived from Eq. (17) as follows:

$$\frac{\partial x_{e,t}}{\partial z_t} = \frac{1}{1-\varepsilon} \left[\int_0^\infty x_t^{1-\varepsilon} f(x_t) dx_t \right]^{\frac{1}{1-\varepsilon}} \left[\frac{\theta}{\partial z_t} \int_0^\infty x_t^{1-\varepsilon} f(x_t) dx_t \right] \tag{19}$$

$$= \frac{x_{e,t}^\varepsilon}{1-\varepsilon} \int_0^\infty x_t^{1-\varepsilon} \left\{ \frac{\partial}{\partial x_t} f(x_t) \right\} dx_t$$

Given the generalised exponential family definition in Eq. (1), it is possible to rewrite Eq. (19) as:

$$\frac{\partial x_{e,t}}{\partial z_t} = \frac{x_{e,t}^\varepsilon}{1-\varepsilon} \int_0^\infty \left(\sum_j \psi_j \frac{\partial \theta_{j,t}}{\partial z_t} - \frac{\partial \eta_t}{\partial z_t} \right) x_t^{1-\varepsilon} f(x_t) dx_t \tag{20}$$

In addition, it can be shown from the expression for the normalising constant given in Eq. (2) that Eq. (21) holds:

$$\frac{\partial \eta_t}{\partial z_t} = \int_0^\infty \left(\sum_j \psi_j \frac{\partial \theta_{j,t}}{\partial z_t} \right) f(x_t) dx_t \tag{21}$$

The expression for $\partial \bar{x}_t / \partial z_t$ is obtained from Eq. (20) as a special case when $\varepsilon = 0$. Therefore, Eq. (18) can be rewritten as:

$$\frac{\partial I_t}{\partial z_t} = \frac{1}{\bar{x}_t} \left[(1 - I_t) \int_0^\infty h(x_t) x_t f(x_t) dx_t - \frac{x_{e,t}^\varepsilon}{1 - \varepsilon} \int_0^\infty h(x_t) x_t^{1-\varepsilon} f(x_t) dx_t \right] \tag{22}$$

where $h(x_t)$ is defined as (Eq. (23)):

$$h_{x_t} = \sum_j \psi_j \frac{\partial \theta_{j,t}}{\partial z_t} - \frac{\partial \eta_t}{\partial z_t} \tag{23}$$

Hence, the change in the Atkinson inequality measure resulting from a change in an exogenous variable requires the numerical evaluation of the two integrals shown in Eq. (22). Even the determination of the direction of change in the inequality measure, which involves signing the partial derivative, $\partial x_{e,t} / \partial z_t$ (and the corresponding case where $\varepsilon = 0$), represents a nontrivial task.

4. The New Zealand male income distribution: 1985–1994

This section explores the application of the conditional modelling framework presented above, and presents the empirical results of applying the model to income distribution data for males in New Zealand over the 10-year period 1985–1994. The data are described in Section 4.1. Conditional generalised gamma distribution estimates are given in Section 4.3.

4.1. The income distribution data

The income distribution data used consist of a specially compiled data set based on the individual observations on males, from the New Zealand Household Expenditure Surveys (HES) for each year over the period 1985–1994. The data set was assembled in the New Zealand Treasury. (As mentioned above, it would alternatively be possible to use a time series of grouped frequency distributions if individual data are not available.) The relevant calendar year is used to refer to the HES data, although they actually cover the period from April 1 to March 30 the following year. The measure of income is of income before tax, but including transfer payments. The use of individuals, rather than households, as the unit of analysis provides a closer focus on labour market influences that may be expected to be associated with macroeconomic changes, and avoids the complexities associated with multiple-earner units.

The samples include those whose income was predominantly obtained from wages and salaries, in order to exclude the self-employed. This avoids the difficulties of measuring self-employment incomes (and the negative values that are often reported) and also provides a closer emphasis on labour market aspects. Furthermore, the largest 1% of observations were

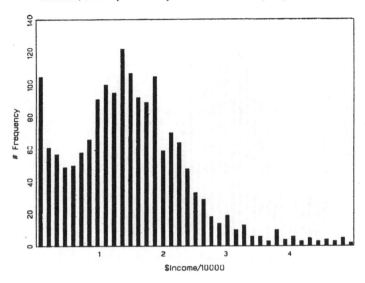

Fig. 1. 1985 Income distribution: New Zealand males (1984 prices).

removed in each year to negate the influence of outliers on parameters; this is often required in fitting distributions to individual data since a small number of extreme incomes can distort the estimates. The number of observations in the male data set for $t = 1985$ to $t = 1994$ is given by the vector [Eq. (24)]:

$$N_t = [2384, 2307, 2907, 2161, 2071, 1704, 1627, 2548, 1719, 1706] \qquad (24)$$

This yields a total sample of 20 916 observations.

The income data were converted to 1984 real values by using the consumer price index. That is, the nominal annual income of the ith individual for the tth period, $x_{i,t}$, was expressed in real terms by dividing by $\prod_{q=1}^{t}(1+\rho_q)$, where ρ denotes inflation. This, in turn, is calculated from the consumer price index, CPI, as $\rho_q = (CPI_q - CPI_{q-1})/CPI_{q-1}$.

In order to illustrate the general form of the distributions of annual income, the 1985 and 1994 distributions are represented in Figs. 1 and 2 as histograms with 40 class intervals. A noticeable feature of these distributions is that they demonstrate that the density used to model the empirical forms must be capable of exhibiting bimodality. Standard unimodal forms such as the gamma and lognormal distributions cannot possibly capture the complete distribution. The bimodality in the distributions clearly arises as a consequence of the inclusion of means-tested transfer payments in the measure of income.

4.2. Macroeconomic variables

The following analysis concentrates on the role of the unemployment ratio, u_t, and the growth rate of real GDP, y_t. These may be said to capture variables associated with the trade

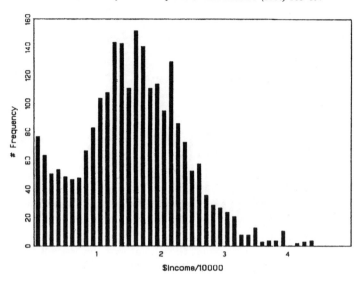

Fig. 2. 1994 Income distribution: New Zealand males (1984 prices).

cycle. The range of variables that can be used is also restricted by the 10-year period over which incomes are available. The use of real incomes and real GDP growth was found to be superior to the use of the inflation rate as a separate macroeconomic variable. Experiments demonstrated that the inclusion of inflation as a separate explanatory variable resulted in the inability to invert the estimated Hessian, which appears to be due to the strong negative correlation between inflation and unemployment. A more important independent role for inflation concerns a possible differential impact on different income groups, associated with variations in expenditure patterns with income, but this raises quite different issues from those examined here. A more complete analysis would perhaps wish, in addition, to compile indices to represent fiscal and monetary policy variables. Furthermore, it would be of interest to explore the use of demographic variables (representing, for example, the age structure) to model variations in the θ's.

The macroeconomic data are listed in Table 2. These data were kindly made available from *Statistics New Zealand* (*Te Tari Tatau*). The *Statistics New Zealand* home page is ⟨http://www.stats.govt.nz⟩. All variables are annualised for the year ending in March for consistency. *Statistics New Zealand* commenced official unemployment data in late 1986, hence, 1987 is the first unemployment rate observation. Prior to this date the number of Labour Department registered unemployed were the only available data. Superscript b in Table 2 identifies the two observations taken from the DX database for Windows ((OECD New Zealand), code: Y.NZL.UNR), used to complete the time series. Gross domestic product data, in 1991/1992 prices, are taken from the New Zealand official yearbook (1997), Table 17.2, column 7.

Table 2
Exogenous variable data

Year	Annual percent ΔCPI	Annual percent ΔGDP[a]	Unemployment rate
1985	13.41	4.9335	3.525[b]
1986	12.96	0.7711	3.994[b]
1987	18.29	2.1022	4.0
1988	8.98	0.4365	4.3
1989	4.02	− 0.4305	6.2
1990	7.02	0.6973	7.1
1991	4.53	− 0.4471	8.4
1992	0.80	− 1.2172	10.6
1993	0.96	1.1546	10.1
1994	1.30	6.2086	9.3

[a] Expressed in 1991/1992 prices.

[b] Due to a break in series, 1985/1986 values were obtained from the DX database for Windows.

As can be seen from Table 2, the New Zealand economy experienced substantial variation in the growth rate over the 10-year period. Growth was very low during the late 1980s and early 1990s and was actually negative in several of those years. The unemployment ratio increased steadily over the period, from a low of about 3.5% in 1985 to a high of 10.6% in 1992, after which it fell slightly.

The variation in the Atkinson Inequality measure over the period, for an inequality aversion coefficient of 0.5, is shown in Fig. 3 by the dashed line. Measured

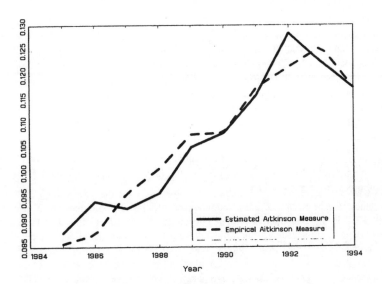

Fig. 3. Atkinson inequality measures: 1985–1994 ($\Sigma = 0.5$).

inequality increased quite steadily over the period, until a peak in 1993, after which it fell slightly. These data therefore initially suggest that the increase in inequality over the period was perhaps dominated by the increase in the unemployment rate, though the reduction in inequality at the end of the period was perhaps also influenced by the rising growth rate. It must be remembered that changes in the distribution also arise as a result of microeconomic changes taking place over the period, which are not modelled here.

4.3. Conditional distribution analysis

The first stage of the empirical analysis involved estimating the alternative forms of the generalised exponential distribution shown in Table 1, using unconditional modelling applied to each year. Comparisons of the goodness of fit were made using log-likelihood values. These showed that the generalised gamma distribution consistently provided the best fit to the New Zealand data, although the generalised lognormal also performed well. Hence, this section concentrates on the use of the generalised gamma distribution to model the changing form of the male New Zealand income distribution in the conditional modelling framework. The preliminary unconditional estimates demonstrated that the coefficient associated with x^3 is statistically insignificant, and so this is excluded in the following analysis. Hence, the distribution is defined for the tth period as:

$$h(x_t) = \exp[\theta_{1,t}\ln x_t + \theta_{2,t}x_t - \theta_{3,t}x_t^2 - \eta_t]. \tag{25}$$

The unconditional estimates of the parameters, $\theta_{1,t}$, $\theta_{2,t}$, and $\theta_{3,t}$ were plotted against the macroeconomic variables y_t and u_t, which denote respectively the annual percentage change in gross domestic product and the unemployment ratio, expressed in percentage form. These plots suggested the use of linear specifications for the functions, $\theta_{j,t} = g_j(z_t, \beta_j)$. Hence, changes in the distribution were modelled using the following:

$$\theta_{1,t} = \beta_{1,1} + \beta_{1,2}y_t + \beta_{1,3}u_t \tag{26}$$

$$\theta_{2,t} = \beta_{2,1} + \beta_{2,2}y_t + \beta_{2,3}u_t \tag{27}$$

$$\theta_{3,t} = -|\beta_{3,1} + \beta_{3,2}y_t - \beta_{3,3}u_t| \tag{28}$$

The $\theta_{3,t}$ parameter must be restricted to be negative in order to ensure boundedness of Eq. (25).

Maximum likelihood estimates of specification (Eqs. (25)–(28)), obtained following the procedure described Section 2, are:

$$\theta_{1,t} = \underset{(0.0800)}{-0.2522} - \underset{(0.0162)}{0.0130y_t} + \underset{(0.0083)}{0.0091u_t} \tag{29}$$

$$\theta_{2,t} = \underset{(0.2197)}{2.4793} + \underset{(0.0462)}{0.0525y_t} - \underset{(0.0236)}{0.1469u_t} \tag{30}$$

$$\theta_{3,t} = -\left|\underset{(0.0445)}{-0.7435} - \underset{(0.0092)}{0.0099y_t} + \underset{(0.0049)}{0.0345u_t}\right| \tag{31}$$

where estimated standard errors from the inverse of the computed Hessian appear in parentheses.[1] The constant terms $\beta_{1,1}$, $\beta_{2,1}$, and $\beta_{3,1}$ are significantly different from zero, as are the coefficients on the unemployment rate in the equations for $\theta_{2,t}$ and $\theta_{3,t}$, that is, the coefficients $\beta_{2,3}$, and $\beta_{3,3}$. However, the coefficients on the growth rate are insignificant. These results therefore indicate that unemployment has been the primary macroeconomic variable responsible for structural shifts in the real income distribution over the period.

Fig. 3 (solid line) also shows the Atkinson inequality measure for each year (for inequality aversion of 0.5), calculated from the fitted distributions, using Eq. (16) and numerical integration of Eq. (17). It can be seen that, despite the use of only two macroeconomic variables (and a density function containing only three parameters to describe bimodal distributions), the fitted Atkinson measures generally follow the empirical values closely. In only two periods, 1986–1987 and 1992–1993, the fitted Atkinson measures decline while the sample values increase. In general, it could perhaps be argued on the basis of these results that the main changes in inequality over the 10-year period were driven by macroeconomic changes, in particular, the unemployment rate, rather than microeconomic factors.

4.4. Comparative statics

It has been seen above that comparative static results are rather cumbersome to obtain in the present framework because of the need to use numerical integration at several stages. This subsection is therefore restricted to a brief illustration of the effects of changes in unemployment, since these have been found to have the strongest influence. Results are reported for the 1994 estimated density, the last year for which the income data are available.

Firstly, consider the application of Eq. (11), which gives the modal incomes in the 1994 period, M_{94}, as the roots of the quadratic [Eq. (32)]:

$$P(M_{94}) = \theta_{1,94} + \theta_{2,94}M_{94} + 2\theta_{3,94}M_{94}^2 = 0 \tag{32}$$

Eqs. (29)–(31) yield $\theta_{1,94} = -0.2485$, $\theta_{2,94} = 1.4385$, and $\theta_{3,94} = -0.4843$. Substitution of these values into the standard expression for the roots of a quadratic equation give the two values, 0.1996 and 1.2854. The smallest root corresponds to the antimode, and the largest corresponds to the mode. Appropriate substitution into Eq. (15) gives values of dM_{94}/du_{94} for the antimode and mode of 0.0218 and -0.27926, respectively. Therefore, an increase in unemployment has the effect of reducing the mode of the distribution and increasing the antimode slightly.

Consider next the Atkinson inequality measure. Appropriate substitution gives, for the estimated distribution in 1994, an arithmetic mean of $\bar{x}_{94} = 1.4631$ and an equally distributed equivalent income, $x_{e,94}$, of 1.2937 for an inequality aversion of 0.5, so that $I_{94} = 0.1158$. It can be found that $(\partial\bar{x}_{94}/\partial u_{94}) = -0.2051$ and $(\partial x_{e,94}/\partial u_{94}) = -0.1999$. The reduction in both the arithmetic mean and the equally distributed equivalent income as a result of an increase in unemployment gives rise to an increase in the Atkinson measure, whereby $(\partial I_{94}/$

---

[1] The computer programs were written in GAUSS, and are described in more detail in the references given above.

$\partial u_{94}) = 0.0127$. Hence, as expected from the above results, an increase in unemployment produces an increase in inequality. It can also be shown that the effect on inequality increases as the degree of aversion to inequality increases.

5. Conclusions

This paper has presented a method of examining the effects of macroeconomic variables on the personal distribution of income over time. The approach suggested here involves modelling the complete distribution of income in each year using a flexible functional form from the generalised exponential family of distributions. The parameters of the distribution were specified as functions of the macroeconomic variables. The paper showed how comparative static analyses, involving the modes and Atkinson inequality measures, can be performed. The method was applied to male New Zealand income distribution data for the period 1985–1994 where the rate of unemployment was found to be the primary influence on the form of the distribution. The expected results of higher unemployment decreasing the modal income and increasing the Atkinson inequality measure were verified.

The empirical exercise reported here must be considered as exploratory, but the results are sufficiently encouraging to suggest that the approach has considerable potential. It would be useful in future research to explore a longer period using a wider range of macroeconomic variables.

Acknowledgments

This research was supported by a University of Melbourne Faculty of Economics and Commerce Research Grant. We should like to thank Statistics New Zealand for permission to use the HES data, and Helen Zarifeh for extracting the data from the basic files. We have also benefited from the constructive comments of two referees.

References

Atkinson, A. B. (1970). On the measurement of inequality. *Journal of Economic Theory, 2,* 244–263.

Bakker, A. (1995). The generalised exponential distribution: some numerical issues of estimation. The University of Melbourne Department of Economics Research Paper, No. 460.

Bakker, A. (1997). Estimation of generalised distributionsm. In: J. Creedy, & V. L. Martin (Eds.), *Nonlinear economic models: cross-sectional, time series and neural network applications* (pp. 91–110). Aldershot: Edward Elgar.

Bakker, A., & Creedy, J. (1997). Age and the distribution of earnings. In: J. Creedy, & V. L. Martin (Eds.), *Nonlinear economic models: cross-sectional, time series and neural network applications* (pp. 111–128). Aldershot: Edward Elgar.

Beach, C. (1977). Cyclical sensitivity of aggregate income inequality. *Review of Economics and Statistics, 59,* 56–66.

Bishop, J. A., Formby, J. P., & Sakano, R. (1994). Evaluating changes in the distribution of income in the United States. *Journal of Income Distribution, 4,* 79–105.

Blinder, A. S., & Esaki, H. Y. (1978). Macroeconomic activity and income distribution in the postwar United States. *Review of Economics and Statistics, 60*, 604–607.

Blejer, M. I. and Gueriero, I. (1990). The impact of macroeconomic policies on income distribution: an empirical study of the Philippines. *Review of Economics and Statistics, 72, 414–23.*

Bud, E. C., & Whiteman, T. C. (1978). Macroeconomic fluctuations and the size distribution of income and earnings in the US. In: Z. Griliches, N. Krelle, H-J. Krupp & O. Kyn (eds.) *Income Distribution and Economic Inequality.* New York: Campus–Verlag.

Cobb, L., Koppstein, P., & Chen, N. H. (1983). Estimation and moment recursion relations for multimodal distributions of the exponential family. *Journal of the American Statistical Association, 78*, 124–130.

Creedy, J., Lye, J., & Martin, V. L. (1996). A labour market equilibrium model of the personal distribution of earnings. *Journal of Income Distribution, 6*, 127–144.

Creedy, J., & Martin, V. L. (1994). *Chaos and non-linear models in economics — theory and applications.* Aldershot: Edward Elgar.

Creedy, J., & Martin, V. L. (1997). *Non-linear economic models: cross-sectional, time series and neural network applications.* Aldershot: Edward Elgar.

Flückiger, Y., & Zarin-Nejadan, M. (1994). The effect of macroeconomic variables on the distribution of income: the case of Switzerland. *Journal of Income Distribution, 4*, 25–39.

Haslag, J. H., & Slottje, D. (1994). Cyclical fluctuations, macroeconomic policy, and the size distribution of income: some preliminary evidence. *Journal of Income Distribution, 4*, 3–23.

Lye, J. N. & Martin, V. L. (1994a). Nonlinear time series modelling and distributional flexebility. *Journal of Time Series Analysis, 15*, 65–84.

Lye, J. N., & Martin, V. L. (1994b). Robust estimation with the generalised exponential family. In: J. Creedy, & V. L. Martin (Eds.), *Chaos and non-linear models in economics* (pp. 151–165). Aldershot: Edward Elgar.

Metcalf, C. E. (1972). *An econometric model of the income distribution.* Chicago: Markham.

New Zealand official yearbook. Wellington: Statistics New Zealand.

Nolan, B. (1987). *Income distribution and the macroeconomy.* Cambridge: Cambridge Univ. Press.

Nolan, B. (1989). Macroeconomic conditions and the size distribution of income: evidence from the UK. In: P. Kregel, & J. Kregel (Eds.), *Macroeconomic problems and policies of income distribution* (pp. 115–137). Aldershot: Edward Elgar.

Schultz, T. P. (1969). Secular trends and cyclical behaviour of income distributionin the US 1944–1965. In: L. Soltow (Ed.), *Six papers on the size distribution of wealth and income* (pp. 75–100). New York: NBER.

Silber, J., & Ziberfarb, B. Z. (1994). The effect of anticipated and unanticipated inflation on income distribution: the Israeli case. *Journal of Income Distribution, 4*, 41–49.

[7]

New Zealand Economic Papers, 33(2), 1999, 59-80   *59*

Macroeconomic Variables and Income Inequality in New Zealand: An Exploration Using Conditional Mixture Distributions

Alex Bakker and John Creedy[*]

This paper explores a method of examining the effects of macroeconomic variables on the personal distribution of income over time. The approach involves modelling the complete distribution of income in each year using a conditional mixture distribution. The parameters of the distribution are specified as functions of the macroeconomic variables. The paper shows how comparative static analysis, involving the Atkinson inequality measure, can be performed. The method is applied to male New Zealand income distribution data for wage and salary earners over the period 1985 to 1994. It appears that cyclical variations in unemployment and GDP contributed substantially to the observed increase in inequality over the period 1987 to 1991 and the reduction in inequality during the years 1993 and 1994.

1. Introduction

The aim of this paper is to explore an approach for analysing the effects of macroeconomic variables on the personal distribution of income over time. There is a well-established literature on this subject, complementing those studies which focus on microeconomic influences on income distribution. For example, macroeconomic changes may frustrate microeconomic policies designed to influence the income distribution, so it is useful to be able to separate their effects. Given the complexity of the relationship between macroeconomic variables and the personal distribution, involving a 'mapping' from just a few variables to a very large number of incomes, it is perhaps not surprising that statistical approaches have been taken. For example, large-scale macroeconomic models have not been extended to include the personal distribution, although Bud and Whiteman (1978) and Nolan (1987, 1989) used a simulation model based on household expenditure data, using assumptions about the incidence of an increase in aggregate unemployment, in terms of higher unemployment duration and entrants to unemployment.

---

[*] This research was supported by a University of Melbourne Faculty of Economics and Commerce Research Grant. We are grateful to the editor and three referees for valuable comments on an earlier draft. We should also like to thank Statistics New Zealand for permission to use the Household Expenditure Survey data, and Helen Zarifeh for extracting the data from the basic files.

60

The majority of studies have used an approach in which summary measures of the income distribution are related to the macroeconomic variables using regression analysis. Several variables have been used as the dependent variable. One broad strategy has been to use a measure of inequality. For example, Schultz (1969) examined the Gini coefficient over time, while Beach (1977) examined a range of inequality measures, including the Gini and Atkinson measures. A second method involves carrying out several regressions, using the income shares of a specified percentile of the distribution as dependent variable; see, for example, Blinder and Esaki (1978), Nolan (1989), Blejer and Guerrero (1990), Silber and Zilderfarb (1994) and Flückiger and Zarin-Nejadan (1994). This procedure has been extended by Bishop *et al.* (1994), who examined Lorenz ordinates, thereby allowing the application of results concerning Lorenz dominance.[1] Using several measures of inequality, Haslag and Slottje (1994) considered the question of causality.[2]

Instead of using one or more summary measures of the income distribution in each year, this paper explores a method based on modelling the complete distribution of income in each year using a flexible functional form. In spirit, this approach is closest to that of Metcalf (1972), who used summary statistics to fit a functional form to describe the distribution in each year, using a displaced lognormal distribution. However, the present paper uses income data on a large sample of individuals for each year. Furthermore, the parameters of the distribution which determine its shape, and thus changes in the shape over time, are specified as functions of the macroeconomic variables, at the initial estimation stage.[3] That is, the macroeconomic variables determine the form of the conditional income distribution in each period. It is thereby possible to provide a comparative static analysis of changes in a measure of income inequality that result from given changes in the macroeconomy.

Empirical income distributions are often complicated by the existence of a second mode, found in the lower range of incomes. This means that it is often difficult to obtain a good fit to the complete range of the distribution.[4] The present paper explores the use of a mixture of two distributions. The use of two familiar distributions makes it possible to obtain expressions for standard inequality measures of the complete distribution, even though the form of the latter can be quite complex.

The distributional framework of analysis is described in section 2. Empirical estimates, using New Zealand male income data for wage and salary earners over

[1] They also examined the behaviour of quintile conditional mean incomes (the quintile share multiplied by average income). Bishop *et al.* (1994) suggested that the use of percentile shares means that some shares must (because of the adding up requirement) move in opposite directions, making interpretation awkward.
[2] They also allowed for the impact of monetary and fiscal policy variables.
[3] This contrasts with an approach in which unconditional estimates of the parameters are obtained for each year independently, and then time series regressions of the parameters are carried out using the macroeconomic variables.
[4] On the use of the generalised exponential family of distributions, and references to the large literature on functional forms used for income distribution, see Creedy *et al.* (1997).

the period 1985-1994, are given in section 3, which explores the use of lognormal-exponential mixtures. Gamma-exponential mixtures are examined in Appendix B. Changes in the Atkinson (1970) measure of inequality which result from changes in macroeconomic variables are examined in section 4. Concluding remarks are made in section 5.

2. The Distributional Framework

This section describes the use of mixture distributions and the way in which macroeconomic variables can be incorporated into the conditional income distribution specification. Mixture distributions are examined in subsection 2.1. Subsection 2.2 outlines the conditional modelling approach and subsection 2.3 briefly describes the estimation procedure.

2.1 Mixture Modelling

A mixture distribution, $M(x)$, is defined on the random variable, x, as a linear combination of two independent distributions. $f_1(x)$ and $f_2(x)$, such that:

$$M(x) = \tau f_1(x) + (1-\tau)f_2(x) \tag{1}$$

where τ defines the proportion of density mass associated with the first distribution. The use of a mixture distribution, in contrast to the search for a much more complex functional form of a single distribution that can handle the observed bimodality, has several advantages. Firstly, relatively simple distributions can be combined intuitively in order to match particular features of an empirical distribution. For example, one distribution (such as the exponential distribution can be selected in order to capture the lower mode while also assisting in fattening the tail of upper incomes. The other distribution (such as the gamma or lognormal distribution) may be primarily selected to model the middle component of the income distribution, including the dominant mode.[5]

A second advantage of using a mixture distribution is that relatively straightforward analytical results can be derived for summary measures, despite the overall complexity of the form of the mixture, where well-established analytical results exist for the constituent distributions. For example, the mean and variance associated with (1) are:

$$E[M(x)] = \tau E[f_1(x)] + (1-\tau) E[f_2(x)] \tag{2}$$

$$V[M(x)] = \tau V[f_1(x)] + (1-\tau) V[f_2(x)] \tag{3}$$

---

[5] It is not appropriate to view the mixture in terms of, say, the employed and unemployed.

which can be evaluated using the means and variances of the constituent distributions. Section 4 uses this property when examining the Atkinson measure of inequality. A third advantage is that estimation of a mixture distribution is relatively straightforward.

2.2 Conditional Mixture Modelling

The present context is one in which the random variable x_t is generated from a mixture distribution of the general form in (1) but the shape of the distribution changes over time, t. The distribution changes because the coefficients change over time. The approach suggested here is to model the changes in the distributional coefficients, $\theta_{j,t}$, as functions of exogenous macroeconomic variables which at time t are placed in the vector z_t. For example, z_t may include the unemployment rate and the growth rate. In general, the distributional coefficients are defined as:

$$\theta_{j,t} = g_j(z_t) \tag{4}$$

where z_t represents the relevant information set for modelling the tth period, and $g_j(.)$ indicates that the functional form used to model the jth parameter may be different for different parameters. Certain parameters, which influence special features of the distribution, may be influenced by particular macroeconomic variables in substantially different ways compared with other parameters.

2.3 Conditional Mixture Estimation

The above modelling procedure is applied below to a time series of cross-sectional micro-data sets. Suppose that $x_{t,i}$ refers to the ith individual in the tth period, N_t refers to the total number of individuals in the tth period, and T refers to the total number of time periods available. The log-likelihood function for the mixture distribution (1) is written as:

$$\ln L = \sum_{t=1}^{T} \sum_{i=1}^{N_t} \{ \tau \ln f_1(x_{t,i}) + (1-\tau) \ln f_2(x_{t,i}) \} \tag{5}$$

This can be maximised using standard software for maximum likelihood estimation.

3   Application to 1985-1994 NZ Male Incomes

This section presents the empirical results of estimating a mixture distribution model using income distribution data for New Zealand male wage and salary earners. The data are described in subsection 3.1. Conditional mixture distribution estimates are given in subsection 3.2.

3.1   The Data

The data were obtained from the individual observations on males, from the New Zealand Household Expenditure Surveys (HES) for each year over the period 1985 to 1994.[6] The relevant calendar year is used to refer to the HES data, although they actually cover the period from 1 April to 30 March the following year. The use of individuals, rather than households, as the unit of analysis provides a closer focus on labour market influences that may be expected to be associated with macroeconomic changes, and avoids the complexities associated with multiple-earner units. The income data are expressed in 1984 real values by using the consumer price index data listed in Appendix A. [7] The samples include those whose income was predominantly obtained from wages and salaries, in order to exclude the self-employed.[8] Furthermore, the largest one per cent of observations were removed in each year to negate the influence of outliers on parameters; this is often required in fitting distributions to individual data since a small number of extreme incomes can distort the estimates. The number of observations in the male data set for $t = 1985$ to $t = 1994$ is given by the vector:

$$N_t = [2384, 2307, 2907, 2161, 2071, 1704, 1627, 2548, 1719, 1706]. \qquad (6)$$

This yields a total sample of 20916 observations.

In order to illustrate the general form of the distributions of annual income, the 1985 and 1994 distributions are represented in Figures 1 and 2 as histograms with 40 class intervals. A noticeable feature of these distributions is that they demonstrate that the density used to model the empirical forms must be capable of exhibiting bimodality. Standard unimodal forms such as the gamma and lognormal distributions cannot capture the complete distribution, but may be useful in combination with a second distribution.

---

[6] It would of course be possible to use a time series of grouped frequency distributions if individual data are not available.

[7] That is, the nominal annual income of the ith individual for the tth period, $x_{i,t}$ is expressed in real terms by dividing by $\Pi_{q=1}^t (1+\rho_q)$, where ρ denotes inflation which is calculated from the consumer price index, CPI, as $\rho_q = (CPI_q - CPI_{q-1}) / CPI_{q-1}$.

[8] Those with relatively small amounts of self-employment income, in addition to wage and salary income, were included. This avoids the difficulties of measuring self-employment incomes (and the negative values that are often reported) and also provides a closer emphasis on labour market aspects.

Figure 1. 1985 Real Male New Zealand Income Distribution (1984 prices)

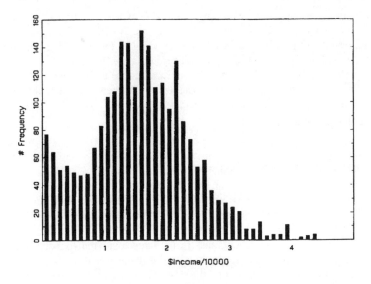

Figure 2. 1994 Real Male New Zealand Income Distribution (1984 prices)

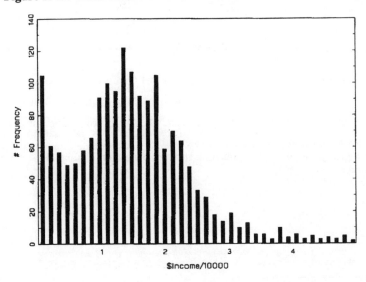

The following analysis concentrates on the role of the unemployment rate, U_t, and the growth rate of real GDP, $\dot{Y}_t$. These may be said to capture variables associated with the trade cycle. The range of variables that can be used is also restricted by the ten-year period over which incomes are available. The use of real incomes and real GDP growth was found to be superior to the use of the inflation rate as a separate macroeconomic variable.[9] These data are listed in Appendix A. A more complete analysis would perhaps wish, in addition, to compile indices to represent fiscal and monetary policy variables. Furthermore, demographic variables (representing, for example, the age structure) may be used to model variations in the θ s and perhaps also τ.

3.2   Lognormal-Exponential Mixture

After some experimentation, it was found that the best results were obtained using a mixture distribution based on the linear combination of a lognormal distribution and an exponential distribution. The use of a gamma-exponential mixture is discussed in Appendix B. If $f_1(x_t)$ and $f_2(x_t)$ represent the lognormal and exponential respectively, the functional forms are:

$$f_1(x_t) \; = \; \frac{1}{x_t \theta_2 (2\pi)^{0.5}} \; \exp\left[\frac{-(\ln x_t - \theta_1)^2}{2\theta_2^2}\right] \tag{7}$$

$$f_2(x_t) \; = \; \theta_3^{-1} \exp\left[-\theta_3^{-1} x_t\right] \tag{8}$$

The conditional form of the mixture distribution was obtained by expressing each of the three parameters, θ_1, θ_2 and θ_3 as linear functions of $\dot{Y}_t$ and U_t. It would also be possible to allow the mixture parameter, τ_t, to vary over time but in the present context no significant variation was found.

The conditional lognormal-exponential mixture maximum likelihood estimates are obtained as:

---

[9]   A more important independent role for inflation concerns a possible differential impact on different income groups, associated with variations in expenditure patterns with income. This raises quite different issues from those examined here.

66

$$\hat{\theta}_{1,t} = 0.5488 + 0.0047 \ \dot{Y}_t - 0.0088 \ U_t \tag{9}$$
$$\phantom{\hat{\theta}_{1,t} = } (0.0110) \quad (0.0018) \quad\quad (0.0015)$$

$$\hat{\theta}_{2,t} = 0.3529 - 0.0043 \ \dot{Y}_t + 0.0085 \ U_t \tag{10}$$
$$\phantom{\hat{\theta}_{2,t} = } (0.0083) \quad (0.0013) \quad\quad (0.0011)$$

$$\hat{\theta}_{3,t} = 0.9136 + 0.0021 \ \dot{Y}_t - 0.0426 \ U_t \tag{11}$$
$$\phantom{\hat{\theta}_{3,t} = } (0.0549) \quad (0.0049) \quad\quad (0.0056)$$

$$\hat{\tau} = 0.7394 \tag{12}$$
$$\phantom{\hat{\tau} = } (0.0092)$$

where $ln \ L = -24764$. This was found to provide a statistically significant improvement over the use of an unconditional mixture distribution in which the parameters were assumed to be constant over time. It is also an improvement over the use of a time-series specification in which the θs are simply assumed to be quadratic functions of t. Hence it can be inferred that the two macroeconomic variables play a significant role in influencing the shape of the male income distribution.

The estimated value of τ indicates that 74 per cent of the empirical distribution is modelled with the lognormal distribution and 26 per cent is modelled with the exponential form. The coefficients are significantly greater than zero, except for that on $\dot{Y}_t$ in $\theta_{3,t}$, which is statistically insignificant. In each case, the estimated coefficients on $\dot{Y}_t$ and U_t variables are of opposite sign. The orders of magnitude of the coefficients indicate that a one percentage point reduction in the unemployment rate will have a greater impact on the form of the conditional distribution than a one percentage point increase in the rate of GDP growth. The coefficient on U_t in the equation for $\theta_{2,t}$, which is the variance of the logarithms of income in the lognormal component of the mixture distribution, is positive, suggesting that an increase in unemployment is likely to be associated with an increase in inequality. On the other hand, an increase in $\dot{Y}_t$ has the effect of reducing $\theta_{2,t}$ and therefore is likely to reduce inequality of the mixture distribution.

The ability of the conditional mixture specification to provide a good fit to the income distributions is illustrated in Figure 3, which presents fitted and empirical distributions for the years 1985, 1988, 1991 and 1994. The exponential form is clearly playing an important role in capturing the lower mode of each distribution, as well as fattening the higher tail, while the lognormal form, as expected, contributes substantially to modelling the major mode and the bulk of the distribution.

Figure 3. Estimated versus Empirical Distribution

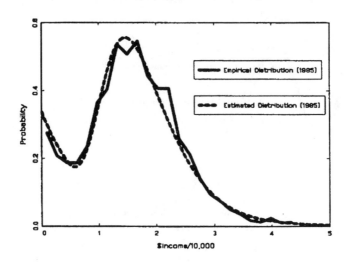

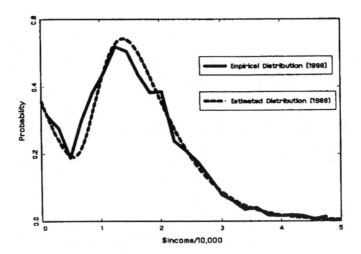

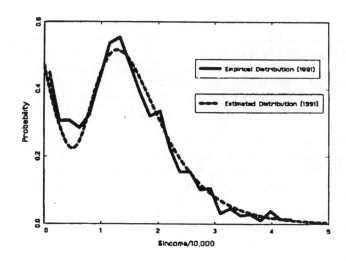

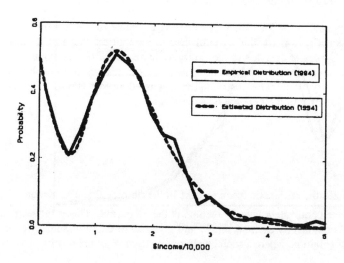

4 Inequality and Macroeconomic Changes

As mentioned in the introduction, most studies of the role of macroeconomic variables on income inequality first calculate sample values of an inequality measure for each year, and then regress these on the macroeconomic variables. Typically, only a single inequality measure is used, but in view of the fact that different measures are relatively more sensitive to changes in particular ranges of the distribution, and macroeconomic variables can have differential impacts on different parts of the distribution, it would seem useful to consider a range of inequality measures.

The present approach, by explicitly modelling each of the parameters of the distribution as conditional on macroeconomic variables, is able to capture such differential impacts. Furthermore, having obtained the form of the distribution, a range of inequality measures, reflecting alternative value judgements, can be obtained. Such measures could obviously be obtained (as sample statistics) directly from the empirical distributions, but the aim here is to be able to investigate how hypothetical changes are likely to affect inequality. Changes specifically associated with macroeconomic variables can then be separated from changes that may occur for other reasons. Most observers would wish to see a reduction in the unemployment rate and an increase in the growth rate for a variety of reasons, but it is useful to know if such changes are likely to be associated with an increase or a decrease in inequality.

4.1 The Atkinson Inequality Measure

Although a large range of inequality measures is available, the Atkinson (1970) measure of inequality is particularly useful here in view of the fact that it allows for a range of degrees of aversion to inequality to be examined by varying a single parameter. The evaluation of the Atkinson measure can also usefully exploit the convenient property of mixture distributions discussed in subsection 2.2. The Atkinson measure in period t. denoted I_t, is defined as:

$$I_t = 1 - \frac{x_{e,t}}{\overline{x}_t} \tag{13}$$

where $\overline{x}_t$ denotes the arithmetic mean income in the tth period and $x_{e,t}$ denotes the equally distributed equivalent level of income in the tth period. This is the level of income that, if obtained by each person, would give rise to the same social welfare as the actual distribution, where a social welfare function, W. of the form:

$$W = \frac{1}{1-\varepsilon} \int_o^\infty x_t^{1-\varepsilon} f(x_t)\, dx_t \tag{14}$$

is used, and $\varepsilon \neq 1$ denotes the degree of relative inequality aversion.[10] Hence, $x_{e,t}$ is defined by:

$$x_{e,t} = \left[\int_o^\infty x_t^{1-\varepsilon} f(x_t)\, dx_t \right]^{\frac{1}{1-\varepsilon}} \tag{15}$$

If $\varepsilon = 0$, it follows from (15) that $x_{e,t} = \bar{x}_t$ and $I_t = 0$.[11] Given that the choice of ε reflects a value judgement, it is usual in investigating income distributions to report results for a range of values of ε.[12]

In terms of a mixture distribution, by substituting $M(x_t)$ for $f(x_t)$, it is possible to rewrite $x_{e,t}$ from (15) as:

$$x_{e,t} = \left[\tau \int_o^\infty x_t^{1-\varepsilon} f_1(x_t)\, dx_t + (1-\tau) \int_o^\infty x_t^{1-\varepsilon} f_2(x_t)\, dx_t \right]^{\frac{1}{1-\varepsilon}} \tag{16}$$

Using the lognormal-exponential specifications for $f_1(x_t)$ and $f_2(x_t)$ given in (7) and (8), the components within the equally distributed equivalent level of income for the mixture distribution expression (16) are calculated as follows. For the exponential distribution given by (8), it can be shown that:

$$\int_o^\infty x_t^{1-\varepsilon} f_2(x_t)\, dx_t = \theta_3^{1-\varepsilon} \Gamma(2-\varepsilon) \tag{17}$$

where $\Gamma(\xi) = \int_o^\infty y^{\xi-1} e^y\, dy$ represents the gamma function.

Results for the lognormal distribution are derived as follows. Using the moment generating function of the normal distribution, it can be shown that.[13]

---

[10] For the case where $\varepsilon = 1$ then $W = \int_o^\infty x_t f(x_t)\, dx_t$

[11] If $\varepsilon = 1$, then (15) simplifies to $x_{e,t} = \exp \left[\int_o^\infty \ln x_t f(x_t)\, dx_t \right]$

[12] One way to view the size of ε is to consider judgements about the effect of taking $1 from a richer person, giving some of this to a poorer person and destroying the rest. Suppose that one person has twice the income of another. When $\varepsilon = 0$, then the judge would only approve of the transfers if $1 is given to the poorer person. But it can be shown that when ε takes the values 0.5, 1, 2 and 3 respectively, the amounts of $0.71, $0.50 and $0.13 must be given to the poorer person from the $1 taken from the richer person, in order for the resulting distributions to give the same social welfare.

$$\int_0^\infty x_t^{1-\varepsilon} f_1(x_t) dx_t = \exp\left\{(1-\varepsilon)\theta_1 + (1-\varepsilon)^2 \frac{\theta_2^2}{2}\right\} \tag{18}$$

Therefore $x_{e,t}$ is obtained by combining (17) and (18) in (16), giving:

$$x_{e,t} = \left[\tau \exp\left\{(1-\varepsilon)\theta_1 + (1-\varepsilon)^2 \frac{\theta_2^2}{2}\right\} + (1-\tau)\theta_3^{1-\varepsilon}\Gamma(2-\varepsilon)\right]^{\frac{1}{1-\varepsilon}} \tag{19}$$

The expression for $\bar{x}_t$ is obtained as a special case of $x_{e,t}$ by setting $\varepsilon = 0$ to give:

$$\bar{x}_t = \tau \exp\left\{\theta_1 + \frac{\theta_2^2}{2}\right\} + (1-\tau)\theta_3 \tag{20}$$

Substituting (19) and (20) into (13) yields the Atkinson measure:

$$I_t = 1 - \frac{\left[\tau \exp\left\{(1-\varepsilon)\theta_1 + (1-\varepsilon)^2 \frac{\theta_2^2}{2}\right\} + \theta_3^{1-\varepsilon}(1-\tau)\Gamma(2-\varepsilon)\right]^{\frac{1}{1-\varepsilon}}}{\tau \exp\left\{\theta_1 + \frac{\theta_2^2}{2}\right\} + (1-\tau)\theta_3} \tag{21}$$

This expression enables the Atkinson measure to be easily obtained for the lognormal-exponential distribution.

4.2   Empirical Results

Figure 4 compares the lognormal-exponential mixture distribution Atkinson measure (21), using parameter estimates in (9)-(12), with the Atkinson measure calculated directly as a sample statistic from empirical data, for a value of inequality aversion of $\varepsilon = 0.5$. This figure clearly indicates the observed increase in inequality in male incomes up to 1993, after which it falls.

A comparison of the estimated and empirical measures suggests that, over the period 1987 to 1991 inclusive, the increase in inequality was closely associated

---

[13]   See Aitchison and Brown (1957).

72

with the cyclical macroeconomic changes in GDP growth and the unemployment rate. Over this period there was a general increase in unemployment and a reduction in the growth rate, which reinforced each other in generating the observed increase in inequality. Furthermore, over the last two years, 1993 and 1994, the reduction in inequality appears to be associated with macroeconomic changes, that is a reduction in unemployment and an increase in growth. However, for the first two years of the sample period, 1985 and 1986 and for 1992, other factors would seem to have played an important role. In both cases these additional factors have been effective in reducing the levels of inequality below what they would otherwise have been.

Figure 4. Comparison of Estimated and Empirical Atkinson Measures
($\mathcal{E}$ = 0.5)

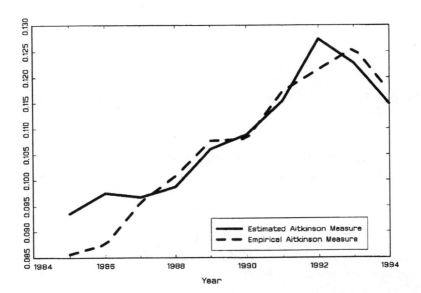

4.3   Comparative Statics

The effect of a change in an exogenous variable, on z_t the Atkinson measure of inequality (13) may be analysed from the following partial derivative:[14]

$$\frac{\partial I_t}{\partial z_t} = \frac{1}{\overline{x}_t}\left[(1-I_t)\frac{\partial \overline{x}_t}{\partial z_t} - \frac{\partial x_{e.t}}{\partial z_t}\right] \qquad (22)$$

This result effectively decomposes changes in I_t as a function of changes in $\overline{x}_t$ and $x_{e.t}$ The partial derivatives contained in (22) are derived as follows. Given (19):

$$\frac{\partial x_{e.t}}{x_{e.t}^e \partial z_t} = \left\{\frac{\partial \theta_1}{\partial z_t} + (1-\varepsilon)\theta_2\frac{\partial \theta_2}{\partial z_t}\right\}\left\{x_{e.t}^{1-\varepsilon} - \theta_3^{1-\varepsilon}(1-\tau)\Gamma(2-\varepsilon)\right\}$$

$$+ (1-\tau)\theta_3^{-\varepsilon}\frac{\partial \theta_3}{\partial z_t}\Gamma(2-\varepsilon) \qquad (23)$$

This can be simplified as follows.   First, notice that equation (19) can be rearranged to give:

$$x_{e.t}^{1-\varepsilon} - \theta_3^{1-\varepsilon}(1-\tau)\Gamma(2-\varepsilon) = \tau\exp\left[(1-\varepsilon)\theta_1 + (1-\varepsilon)^2\frac{\theta_2^2}{2}\right]$$

Hence:

$$\frac{\partial x_{e.t}}{\partial z_t} = k_\varepsilon x_{e.t} + \left(\frac{x_{e.t}}{\theta_3}\right)^\varepsilon (1-\tau)\Gamma(2-\varepsilon)\left(\frac{\partial \theta_3}{\partial z_t} - k_\varepsilon\theta_3\right) \qquad (24)$$

where:

$$k_\varepsilon = \frac{\partial \theta_1}{\partial z_t} + (1-\varepsilon)\theta_2\frac{\partial \theta_2}{\partial z_t} \qquad (25)$$

---

[14]   In terms of percentage changes and elasticities, this can be rearranged to give

$$\frac{z_t\partial I_t}{I_t\partial z_t} = -\frac{1-I_t}{I_t}\left[\frac{z_t\partial \overline{x}_t}{\overline{x}_t\partial z_t} - \frac{z_t\partial x_{e.t}}{x_{e.t}\partial z_t}\right]$$

The variable z_t is one of the variables in z_t

74

Therefore, as a special case of (24):[15]

$$\frac{\partial \bar{x}_t}{\partial z_t} = \frac{\partial x_{e.t}}{\partial z_t} \Big|_{\varepsilon=0} = k_0 \bar{x}_t + (1-\tau)\left(\frac{\partial \theta_3}{\partial z_t} - \theta_3 k_0\right) \qquad (26)$$

Table 1. An Increase in Unemployment

Variable	ε		
	0	0.5	1.5
$x_{e.94}$	1.4564	1.2891	0.6685
k_ε	-0.0053843	-0.0071098	-0.010561
$\partial x_{e.94}/\partial U$	-0.018205	-0.02315	-0.031239
$\partial I_{94}/\partial U$		0.0048313	0.015712

4.4 An Increase in Unemployment

In order to illustrate the use of this approach, consider the effect of a change in unemployment on the estimated Atkinson measure of the 1994 distribution: the earlier results indicated that unemployment has a relatively larger effect on the parameters of the mixture distribution. The partial derivatives, $\partial\theta_1/\partial U_t, \partial\theta_2/\partial U_t$ and $\partial\theta_3/\partial U_t$ are taken directly from the above estimates, giving –0.0088, 0.0085 and –0.0426 respectively. Appropriate substitution into the $\theta_{i.t}$ s gives $\theta_{1.94}$ =0.4961, $\theta_{2.94}$ =0.4051 and $\theta_{3.94}$ =0.5306.

The other values required are displayed in Table 1. for the two values of inequality aversion. The values corresponding to $\varepsilon = 0$ are for the arithmetic mean. The final row of Table 1 gives the required partial derivative, $\partial I_{94}/\partial U$ which shows, as expected, that an increase in unemployment increased the Atkinson inequality measure slightly.

---

[15] Alternatively an equivalent expression can be obtained by direct partial differentiation of (20).

5   Conclusions

This paper has presented a method of examining the effects of macroeconomic variables on the personal distribution of income over time. The approach involves modelling the complete distribution of income in each year using a conditional mixture distribution. The parameters of the distribution were specified as functions of the macroeconomic variables. The paper showed how comparative static analyses, involving the Atkinson inequality measure, can be performed. The method was applied to male New Zealand income distribution date for wage and salary earners over the period 1985 to 1994. Both increases in unemployment and reductions in the rate of GDP growth have the effect of increasing inequality.

The fact that these variables are found to affect inequality in general may not be regarded as surprising. However, the method is able to isolate the precise effect of such changes on the form of the distribution. Furthermore, it is able to determine whether there were periods during which other influences on the form of the income distribution appeared to play a more important role. For example, the results suggest that the observed increase in the Atkinson measure of inequality was closely associated with macroeconomic changes over the period 1987 to 1991. Furthermore, over the years 1993 to 1994 the reduction in inequality appears also to be associated with increases in growth and reductions in unemployment. Other factors seem to have played an important role in the years 1985, 1986 and 1992. This exploratory analysis suggests that it may be worth applying the model to more extensive data sets and countries. The use of a conditional distribution approach also offers the potential to augment the statistical approach with some economic modelling relating to particular features of the distribution.

References

Aitchison, J. and Brown, J. A. C. (1957) *The Lognormal Distribution.* Cambridge: Cambridge University Press.

Atkinson, A. B. (1970) On the Measurement of Inequality. *Journal of Economic Theory,* 2, pp. 244-263.

Creedy, J. (1996) *Fiscal Policy and Social Welfare.* Aldershot: Edward Elgar.

Creedy, J., Lye, J. and Martin, V. L. (1997) A model of income distribution. In *Nonlinear Models in Economics: Cross-Sectional, Time Series and Neural Network Applications* (ed. by J. Creedy and V. L. Martin), pp. 29-46. Aldershot: Edward Elgar.

Beach, C. (1977) Cyclical sensitivity of aggregate income inequality. *Review of Economics and Statistics,* 59, pp. 56-66.

Bishop, J. A., Formby, J. P. and Sakano, R. (1994) Evaluating changes in the distribution of income in the United States. *Journal of Income Distribution*, 4, pp. 79-105.

Blinder, A. S. and Esaki, H. Y. (1978) Macroeconomic activity and income distribution in the postwar United States. *Review of Economics and Statistics*, 60, pp. 604-607.

Flückiger, Y. and Zarin-Nejadan, M. (1994) The effect of macroeconomic variables on the distribution of income: the case of Switzerland. *Journal of Income Distribution*, 4, pp. 25039.

Haslag, J. H., Russell, W. R. and Slottje, D. (1989) *Macroeconomic Activity and Income Inequality in the United States*. Greenwich: JAI Press.

Haslag, J. H. and Slottje, D. (1994) Cyclical fluctuations, macroeconomic policy, and the size distribution of income: some preliminary evidence. *Journal of Income Distribution*, 4, pp. 3-23.

Metcalfe, C. E. (1972) *An Econometric Model of the Income Distribution*. Chicago: Markham.

New Zealand Official Yearbook 1997. Published by Statistics New Zealand (Te Tari Tatau), Wellington. New Zealand.

Nolan, B. (1987) *Income Distribution and The Macroeconomy*. Cambridge: Cambridge University Press.

Nolan, B. (1989) Macroeconomic conditions and the size distribution of income: evidence from the UK. In *Macroeconomic Problems and Policies of Income Distribution*. (ed. Davidson, P. and Kregel, J.), pp. 115-137. Aldershot: Edward Elgar.

Silber, J. and Ziberfarb, B-Z. (1994) The effect of anticipated and unanticipated inflation on income distribution: the Israeli case. *Journal of Income Distribution*, 4, pp. 41-49.

Schultz, T. P. (1969) Secular trends and cyclical behaviour of income distribution in the US 1944-1965. In *Six Papers on the Size Distribution of Wealth and Income*. (ed. Soltow, L.), pp. 75-100. New York: NBER.

Appendix A.   Macroeconomic Data

The data contained in Table 2 were kindly made available from *Statistics New Zealand (Te Tari Tatau).*[16]   All variables are annualised for the year ending in March for consistency.   *Statistics New Zealand* commenced official unemployment data in late 1986, hence 1987 is the first unemployment rate observation.   Prior to this date the number of *Labour Department* registered unemployed were the only available data.   Superscript (b) in Table 2 identifies the two observations taken from the DX database for windows (OECD New Zealand, code: Y.NZL.UNR), used to complete the time series.   Gross domestic product data, in 1991/92 prices, are taken from the *New Zealand Official Yearbook 1997,* Table 17.2, column 7.

Table 2. Exogenous Variable Data

Year	Annual % Δ CPI	Annual % $\Delta Y^{(a)}$	Unemployment Rate U
1985	13.41	4.9335	3.525 [b]
1986	12.96	0.7711	3.994 [b]
1987	18.29	2.1022	4.0
1988	8.98	0.4365	4.3
1989	4.02	-0.4305	6.2
1990	7.02	0.6973	7.1
1991	4.53	-0.4471	8.4
1992	0.80	-1.2172	10.6
1993	0.96	1.1546	10.1
1994	1.30	6.2086	9.3

(a)   Expressed in 1991/92 prices.
(b)   Due to a break in series, 1985/86 values were obtained
         from the DX database for windows

---

[16]   The Statistics New Zealand home page is http://www.stats.govt.nz.

Appendix B.   Gamma-exponential Mixture

Consider the use of the gamma and exponential distributions, given respectively by:

$$f_1\left(x_t\right) = \left(\theta_1 \; \Gamma(\theta_2) \;\right)^{-1} \left(\frac{x_t}{\theta_1}\right)^{\theta_2 - 1} \exp\left[-\theta_1^{-1} x_t\right] \tag{27}$$

$$\tag{28}$$

$$f_2\left(x_t\right) = \theta_3^{-1} \exp\left[-\theta_3^{-1} \; x_t\right] \tag{29}$$

where $\left(\theta_1, \theta_2, \theta_3\right) > 0.$[17] The mean and variance associated with (1) are:

$$E\left[M\left(x_t\right)\right] = \tau\theta_1\,\theta_2 + \left(1 - \tau\right)\theta_3 \tag{30}$$

$$V\left[M\left(x_t\right)\right] = \tau\theta_1^2\,\theta_2 + \left(1 - \tau\right)\theta_3^2 \tag{31}$$

using the convenient known expressions for the mean and variance of the gamma and exponential distributions.

The following maximum likelihood estimates are obtained for the conditional gamma-exponential mixture:

$$\begin{aligned}
\theta_{1,t} &= \quad 0.2539 \quad -\,0.0027\,Y_t \; +0.0113\,U_t \\
&\qquad (0.0115) \qquad (0.0016) \qquad\;\; (0.0015) \\[4pt]
\theta_{2,t} &= \quad 6.7878 \;\; +\,0.0632\,Y_t \;\; -\,0.2273\,U_t \\
&\qquad (0.2159) \qquad (0.0271) \qquad\;\; (0.0247) \\[4pt]
\theta_{3,t} &= \quad 0.6418 \;\; +\,0.0022\,Y_t \;\; -\,0.0348\,U_t \\
&\qquad (0.0527) \qquad (0.0044) \qquad\;\; (0.0050) \\[4pt]
\tau_t &= \quad 0.8168 \\
&\qquad (0.0075)
\end{aligned}$$

where $\ln L\; =\; -24800$. Hence, Y_t is not significant in explaining $\theta_{1,t}$ and $\theta_{3,t}$

The estimated value of τ_t indicates that 82 per cent of the empirical distribution is modelled with the gamma distribution and 18 per cent is modelled with the exponential distribution. Using a likelihood ratio test, the lognormal-exponential mixture is a significant improvement over the gamma-exponential.

---

[17] If $\theta_2 = 1$, the gamma distribution (27) collapses to an exponential distribution (29).

Appendix C.   The Atkinson Inequality Measure

Components within the equally distributed equivalent level of income expression (16) are calculated as follows. For the gamma distribution;

$$\int_0^\infty x_t^{1-\varepsilon} f_1(x_t)\, dx_t = \frac{1}{\theta_1^{\theta_2}\Gamma(\theta_2)}\int_0^\infty x_t^{\theta_2-\varepsilon}\, \exp\left[-\theta_1^{-1}x_t\right] dx_t$$

$$= \frac{\theta_1^{1-\varepsilon}\Gamma(1+\theta_2-\varepsilon)}{\Gamma(\theta_2)} \tag{32}$$

The exponential distribution is given above in (17). Hence:

$$x_{e.t} = \left[\frac{\tau\theta_1^{1-\varepsilon}\Gamma(1+\theta_2-\varepsilon)}{\Gamma(\theta_2)} + (1-\tau)\theta_3^{1-\varepsilon}\Gamma(2-\varepsilon)\right]^{\frac{1}{1-\varepsilon}} \tag{33}$$

The expression for $\bar{x}_t$ is obtained as a special case of $x_{e.t}$ when $\varepsilon = 0$ in (33) to give:

$$\bar{x}_t = \tau\theta_1\theta_2 + (1-\tau)\theta_3 \tag{34}$$

Substituting (33) and (34) into (13) yields the Atkinson measure.

PART III

INCOME REDISTRIBUTION

8

OXFORD BULLETIN OF ECONOMICS AND STATISTICS, 63, 3 (2001) 0305-9049

Close equals and calculation of the vertical, horizontal and reranking effects of taxation[†]

Justin van de Ven*, John Creedy** and Peter J. Lambert[‡]

**University of Oxford*, ** *University of Melbourne, Australia and* [‡]*University of York, UK.*

I. Introduction

This paper presents a simple spline technique that may be easily adopted by practitioners for decomposing the redistributive effect of taxation. The redistributive effect of a tax and transfer system is partially reduced by the existence of non-income differences between individuals or income units. Aronson and Lambert (1994) decomposed the redistributive effect of taxation, *L*, in terms of the Gini coefficient, into three components, which they refer to as the vertical, horizontal, and reranking effects. The vertical effect measures the progressivity of the effective tax schedule, which incorporates no horizontal or reranking effects and is derived from the actual tax schedule by allocating to each individual the average tax paid by the respective pre-tax equals. The horizontal effect relates to the unequal treatment of equals, and reranking captures the presumably unintended treatment of unequals, by the tax system.[1]

Exact equals are not often observed in survey data, and consequently Aronson *et al.* (1994) use groups of close-equals to identify the horizontal effect. It is shown that an arbitrary specification of close-equals groups can lead to misleading results. The aim of this paper is to suggest an appropriate strategy for defining the groups of close-equals used. Section II outlines the decomposition method and considers associated issues of interpretation. Section III explores the impact of different close-equals group sizes on the

---

[†]We are grateful to David Bevan for comments on earlier drafts of this paper.

[1]The treatment of Aronson and Lambert (1994) was in terms of income taxation, but the method has been applied to indirect taxes by Decoster *et al.* (1997a, b). An application of the approach suggested below to indirect taxes is in Creedy (1998) and Creedy and van de Ven (2001a) apply the decomposition in a lifetime context.

decomposition measures and defines a strategy for selection. A practical application is provided in Section IV, where the redistributive effect of the Australian tax and transfer system is analyzed. Section V concludes.

II.   The Decomposition Method

The method of decomposing the redistributive effect of taxation suggested by Aronson and Lambert (1994) is based on a decomposition of the Gini coefficient by population sub-groups that was first explored by Bhattacharya and Mahalanobis (1967).[2] The decomposition of the Gini coefficient by population sub-groups is described in sub section (i), and the redistributive effect of taxation is considered in sub section (ii).

(i)   Decomposing the Gini by population groups

For a population consisting of K groups the Gini coefficient can be divided into three components. These are the between-groups Gini, G_B, the within-groups Gini, G_W, and a residual, E. Each group, $k = 1, \ldots, K$, is comprised of N_k individuals (with $\sum_{k=1}^{K} N_k = N$) earning an average income of μ_k, where the groups are ordered so that $\mu_k \leqslant \mu_{k+1}$. The between-groups Lorenz curve, from which G_B is calculated, is derived from the income distribution that results if each individual is assigned the mean income of the respective group. Lambert and Aronson (1993) showed that within-groups inequality can be expressed as:

$$G_W = \sum_{k=1}^{K} \frac{N_k^2 \mu_k}{N^2 \mu} G_k = \sum_{k=1}^{K} a_k G_k \qquad (1)$$

where G_k is the Gini coefficient of group k taken in isolation, and $a_k = N_k^2 \mu_k / N^2 \mu$, which is the product of the population and income shares of group k.

An alternative method of obtaining G_W uses the concentration curve obtained from the observed incomes of individuals, where individuals are ranked in ascending order within their groups and groups are ranked in ascending order based upon mean income. The within-groups Gini measure is equal to the difference between the concentration index associated with the concentration curve, C_W, and G_B:

$$G_W = C_W - G_B \qquad (2)$$

The concentration index C_W can be obtained using the covariance form, following Jenkins (1988).

[2]See also Pyatt (1976), and Lambert and Aronson (1993).

Some individuals in group k may have higher incomes than individuals in group $k + 1$, while others may have lower incomes than individuals in group $k - 1$. Where this occurs, the concentration curve is not based upon the same ranking of individuals as the Lorenz curve of the entire population. Lambert and Aronson (1993) use twice the area captured between the two curves as a measure of the residual, E, which is equal to the difference between the Gini coefficient, G, of the income distribution, and the concentration index; hence $E = G - C_W$. Using this equation, and substituting for C_W from equation (2) gives:

$$G = G_B + G_W + E \tag{3}$$

(ii) Decomposing the redistributive effect of taxation

Let the subscripts x and y denote measures associated with the pre-tax and post-tax income distributions respectively. Where the population considered is divided into groups (over pre-tax equals or near-equals for example), equation (3) gives $G_y = G_{B,y} + G_{W,y} + E_y$ and $G_x = G_{B,x} + G_{W,x} + E_x$. Defining the redistributive effect of taxes in terms of the Gini coefficient:

$$L = G_x - G_y$$

$$= (G_{B,x} - G_{B,y}) - (G_{W,y} - G_{W,x}) - (E_y - E_x)$$

$$= (G_{B,x} - G_{B,y}) - \left(\sum_{k=1}^{K} a_{k,y} G_{k,y} - \sum_{k=1}^{K} a_{k,x} G_{k,x} \right) - (E_y - E_x) \tag{4}$$

When the population groups contain exact pre-tax equals, $G_{k,x} = 0$ for all k and $E_x = 0$, which implies that $G_{B,x} = G_x$. This gives the decomposition suggested by Aronson and Lambert (1994, p.285)[3]:

$$L = (G_x - G_{B,y}) - \sum_{k=1}^{K} a_{k,y} G_{k,y} - E_y$$

$$= V - H - R \tag{5}$$

The term $G_{B,y}$ is the Gini coefficient obtained when each individual's pre-tax income is adjusted by the average tax paid by their respective pre-tax equals. The reranking effect, $R = E_y$, can be shown to equal the Atkinson-Plotnick measure of reranking, R_{AP}, where:[4]

---

[3] This extends the decomposition produced by Kakwani (1984) in which $L = (\frac{g}{1-g})K - R$, where g is the aggregate tax rate and K is a measure of tax disproportionality.
[4] See Atkinson (1979) and Plotnick (1981); this is sometimes normalised by dividing by $2G_y$.

$$R_{AP} = G_y - C_y \tag{6}$$

In equation (6), C_y is the concentration index obtained when post-tax incomes are ranked by x, and G_y is the standard Gini measure which involves ranking by y. Equation (5) highlights the fact that, for any population where $H > 0$, R_{AP} understates the full inequity of the tax system.

To consider issues of interpretation associated with the measures derived from the decomposition analysis, assume that a government must form and implement taxation policy subject to imperfections, such that the net tax paid by any individual, i, is:

$$T_i(x) = T(x) + \varepsilon_{i,x} \tag{7}$$

where $T(x)$ is the government's effective tax schedule, and $\varepsilon_{i,x}$ is a random variable that identifies departures of the actual from the effective tax schedule. In this framework, three effects associated with the random element $\varepsilon_{i,x}$ can be identified that reduce the progressivity of $T_i(x)$ relative to $T(x)$. These are horizontal inequity arising due to the unequal treatment of pre-tax equals, divergence where the richer of two individuals obtains a net gain relative to the poorer when moving from the pre-tax to the post-tax distribution (a form of vertical inequity), and reranking where the rank of individuals is reversed from the pre-tax to the post-tax distribution.

Add to this framework the following two assumptions. First, assume that the government specifies taxation policy to minimise the three regressive effects identified above. Second, suppose the government's objective is achieved on average such that the distributions of expected pre-tax and post-tax incomes calculated for pre-tax equals groups exhibit no reranking or divergence. Under these conditions, any reranking or vertical inequity that arises must also be identified as horizontal inequity, and all horizontal inequity may be identified as either divergence or reranking and possibly as both. From equation (5) it can be seen that the aggregate of H and R is equal to the total regressive effect of income variation associated with departures of the actual from the effective tax schedule, $\varepsilon_{i,x}$, where the two are distinguished by the type of income variation observed.

Given the analytical framework described above, it is necessary to estimate $\varepsilon_{i,x}$ for every individual before H and R can be calculated. When survey data provide groups of pre-tax equals of sufficient size and number, the assumed framework implies that the effective tax schedule, $T(x)$, can be estimated by the arithmetic mean of the observed tax burdens for groups of pre-tax equals:

$$\hat{T}(x_k) = \frac{\sum_{i=1}^{N_k} T_i(x_k)}{N_k}$$

$$= T(x_k) + \frac{\sum_{i=1}^{N_k} \varepsilon_{i,x_k}}{N_k} \tag{8}$$

where $\hat{T}(x_k)$ is the estimate obtained for $T(x)$ at the value x_k. As the number of pre-tax equals increases, the likely error associated with the estimate of $\hat{T}(x)$ falls. This result arises because the expectation of $\bar{\varepsilon}_{x_k} = \sum_{i=1}^{N_k} \varepsilon_{i,x_k}/N_k$ is equal to the expectation of ε_{i,x_k}, which equals zero by assumption, and the variance of $\bar{\varepsilon}_{x_k}$ falls with N_k. The value of $\varepsilon_{i,x}$ can consequently be estimated by subtracting $\hat{T}(x)$ from $T_i(x)$. However, this approach is usually not practicable because the number of individuals possessing any given pre-tax income is negligible in most microdata surveys.

One solution to the sampling problem described above is to adopt a definition of pre-tax equals that is more inclusive than identifying individuals with exactly the same pre-tax incomes. For example, Aronson *et al.* (1994) suggest the use of a bandwidth that defines the maximum difference between the incomes of any two pre-tax equals. The method is desirable in that it does not impose any restriction upon the schedule of $T(x)$, and may consequently be applied in any general case, provided the assumptions that underlie the framework of the analysis are valid. However, the method implies that the use of equation (5) produces misleading results since $G_{k,x} \neq 0$ for all k, $G_{B,x} \neq G_x$ and R does not equal the Atkinson-Plotnick reranking measure when reranking occurs within groups of close-equals (or if entire groups are reranked).[5] Where groups of close-equals are used, it is therefore appropriate to use the bracketed terms in equation (4) to measure V, H, and R (with $E_x = 0$ because the groups of close-equals are identified by pre-tax income bandwidths that do not overlap).

III.   Identifying an Optimal bandwidth

Consider a sample population where the pre-tax incomes of no two individuals are the same. Estimating $T(x)$ for this population by taking the arithmetic mean of the tax burden of all true pre-tax equals (individuals with

---

[5]Consider an income band defined as 100–105, and two pre-tax income observations of 101 and 102. Let the post-tax incomes of the two individuals equal, respectively, 99 and 98. These observations would increase R_{AP}, since they involve reranking, but would affect H rather than R, since they are defined in the same pre-tax equals group.

exactly the same pre-tax income) produces a tax schedule that is identical to $T_i(x)$, which implies that the associated estimates of H and R, as they are defined in Section II(ii), equal zero. However, the estimate obtained for the effective tax schedule is likely to violate the progressivity assumptions that underlie the decomposition analysis, a measure of which is provided by the sample value of R_{AP}.

Increasing the bandwidth used to identify pre-tax equals, w, has two effects, one that improves and another that corrupts the estimate derived for the effective tax schedule. These are referred to as the averaging and appropriation effects. As w is increased, the number and disparity of individuals allocated to each close-equals group increases. Increasing the number of individuals identified in each close-equals group results in an improved estimate for the impact of the effective tax schedule. This averaging effect consequently reduces the degree to which the arithmetic mean incomes of pre-tax equals groups violate the progressivity assumptions of the effective tax schedule. However, the inclusion of increasingly disparate individuals into close-equals groups implies that increasing proportions of V and R observed in a given sample population are attributed to H.

To demonstrate this, consider a progressive tax system for which H and R both equal zero. Increasing the bandwidth from zero implies estimating the Lorenz curves of the pre-tax and post-tax income distributions by splines composed of fewer linear segments. The area between each Lorenz curve and the associated spline is identified by equation (4) as contributing toward H. Given that the Lorenz curve of pre-tax income will exhibit more curvature than that of post-tax income (due to the assumed progressivity of taxation), a larger area is captured between the pre-tax Lorenz curve and its associated spline than for the post-tax distribution. By equation (4), this implies that the values of both V and H fall, such that some of the progressivity associated with V is identified as a deduction from H. Similarly, where reranking occurs between the pre-tax and post-tax income distributions, increasing w implies that some of the regressivity associated with R is identified as a contribution to H. In the extreme case when w is set so that the entire sample population is allocated to the same close-equals group, the observed progressivity is identified as a negative horizontal effect, with V and R both equal to zero. This appropriation effect consequently corrupts the estimate derived for the effective tax schedule as w is increased.

Increasing the bandwidth, and hence the number of individuals identified in any pre-tax equals group, tends to decrease the impact of the averaging effect. Consider the effect on $\hat{T}(x_k)$ of a marginal increase in the size of pre-tax equals group k. The effects of the averaging effect can be considered independently from the appropriation effect by assuming that the additional observations contributing to increase group k's size possess the same statistical properties as all pre-existing observations in group k; hence define $E(\varepsilon_{i,x_k}) = 0$, and $var(\varepsilon_{i,x_k}) = \sigma_k^2$ for all $i \in k$. Taking the expectation and variance of equation (8):

$$E(\hat{T}(x_k)) = T(x_k) \tag{9}$$

$$var(\hat{T}(x_k)) = v = \frac{\sigma_k^2}{N_k} \tag{10}$$

Equation (9) indicates that the expectation of $\hat{T}(x_k)$ is independent of any marginal change in group k's size (N_k). However, the variance of $\hat{T}(x_k)$ is inversely related to N_k. Taking the first and second derivatives of equation (10) with respect to N_k:

$$\frac{\partial v}{\partial N_k} = \frac{-\sigma_k^2}{N_k^2} \tag{11}$$

$$\frac{\partial^2 v}{\partial N_k^2} = \frac{2\sigma_k^2}{N_k^3} \tag{12}$$

Equation (11) indicates that the appropriation effect improves the estimate obtained for $\hat{T}(x_k)$ by reducing its variance; and equation (12) reveals that the improvement associated with the averaging effect, if initially high, diminishes with increased N_k and consequently w. In addition, the range of bandwidths for which negligible averaging is achieved depends crucially upon the sample. As the number of observations in a randomly drawn sample increases, the number of individuals identified in each pre-tax equals group can be expected to rise for any given w, which reduces the benefit of increasing w.

The appropriation effect also decreases with the size of the bandwidth. Consider a population defined on a continuous pre-tax distribution specified between a minimum, x_{min}, and a maximum, x_{max}. For a given bandwidth, the number of pre-tax equals groups is given by:

$$m = \frac{(x_{max} - x_{min})}{w} \tag{13}$$

Taking the first and second derivatives of equation (13):

$$\frac{dm}{dw} = \frac{-(x_{max} - x_{min})}{w^2} = \frac{-m}{w} \tag{14}$$

$$\frac{d^2m}{dw^2} = \frac{2(x_{max} - x_{min})}{w^3} = \frac{2m}{w^2} \tag{15}$$

These equations indicate that as w is increased, the number of pre-tax equals groups decreases at a decreasing rate. Recall from the previous discussion that the decomposition method estimates the pre-tax and post-tax Lorenz curves by splines comprised of linear segments, where the number of segments is equal to the number of pre-tax groups. Hence, as w increases and m falls, the fit that can be achieved by the splines is increasingly restricted, albeit at a decreasing rate. These observations imply that, as the band-width used is raised, increasing proportions of V and R are identified as contributing to H, although the rate of appropriation falls with the bandwidth.

The combination of the averaging and appropriation effects imply the existence of a bandwidth that minimizes the error associated with the estimate of the effective tax schedule. At excessively low levels of w, insufficient averaging is undertaken and the error associated with the decomposition method is high. As w is increased, the gains in terms of increased decomposition accuracy associated with the averaging effect are likely to be initially greater than the losses caused by the appropriation effect. However, in practice, the gains derived from the averaging effect diminish relative to the losses associate with the appropriation effect as w is increased, which implies an optimal w that minimises the decomposition error.[6]

The averaging effect associated with increasing w tends to increase H and R, and consequently V, as a more accurate estimate of the effective tax schedule is obtained. However, the appropriation effect tends to decrease V and R, and have an ambiguous effect on H.[7] Hence, it is logical to set the bandwidth to maximise the estimate derived for V. An estimate for the horizontal effect can be obtained after calculating R_{AP} and L as sample statistics:

$$\tilde{H} = V_{max} - R_{AP} - L \qquad (16)$$

Let $\bar{V}$ define the measure of progressivity that would be obtained if the tax system incorporated no inequity. In practice this statistic cannot be observed due to the limited size of survey data-sets. The proposed decomposition method attempts to counter this small-sample problem by estimating horizontal inequity using groups of close-equals defined by a bandwidth w. As w is increased, it is evident that the estimate V obtained from equation (4) *must* be less than or equal to $\bar{V}$ due to the appropriation effect (as the decomposition method identifies progressivity within pre-tax equals groups as subtracting from H rather than contributing to V). Hence, $(\tilde{H} - R_{AP}) = V_{max} - L$,

---

[6]Simulation experiments also revealed that the error associated with the vertical effect at relatively high values of w is similar for all sample sizes, such that reasonably accurate measures can be obtained for relatively small sample sizes.

[7]The impact of the appropriation effect on H is ambiguous because the relative transfers from V (which makes a negative contribution to H) and R (which makes a positive contribution to H) are dependent on the sample.

derived from (16) must be less than or equal to the total inequity of the tax system, and is strictly less than total inequity if any progressivity is observed within the pre-tax equals groups used.

This result can be illustrated as follows. Consider the effect of increasing w for a population of three individuals, A, B, and C, with pre-tax incomes of 10, 15, and 20, and post-tax incomes of 10, 12, and 14 respectively. These are specified so that there is no reranking or horizontal inequity. When $w = 0$, there are three pre-tax equals groups each containing a single individual, and the value of H derived from equation (4) is zero. Since there is no over-lapping of the post-tax incomes of pre-tax equals groups, R also equals zero and observed redistribution, L, is equal to V. When w is expanded so that A and B are in the same pre-tax equals group and C is in a separate group, the value H derived from equation (4) is negative due to the redistribution observed between A and B; H is a weighted sum of the changes of within group inequality from the pre-tax to the post-tax distribution, and is negative when redistribution is observed. The associated reduction in V can be seen by noting, from equation (4), that $V = L + R + H$, where L and R are unaffected by the increase of w, and H decreases as described. When w is expanded further, such that A, B, and C are all in the same pre-tax equals group, it is evident that $H = -L$, and $V = R = 0$.

IV. A Practical Application

This section explores the properties of the decomposition method outlined in section III by analysing the redistributive effect of the Australian tax and transfer system during the 1995 to 1996 financial year.[8] The 1996 Income Distribution Survey (IDS), undertaken by the Australian Bureau of Statistics (ABS), provides demographic and income microdata for a representative cross-section of 9253 nuclear families, defined as a single adult or a couple and their dependant children. After removing 59 families from the sample because they were identified as earning negative annual incomes, the IDS data were used to obtain distributions of pre-tax and post-tax and transfer annual per capita incomes. These are analyzed below.[9]

Figure 1 displays measures of V, expressed as percentages of the net redistributive effect, L, calculated using bandwidths that range between \$50 and \$5000. As can be seen from the figure, $100V/L$ initially increases from 111.304 ($w = \$50$) up to a maximum of 112.590 ($w = \$650$), before falling

---

[8]The Australian financial year commences on the first of July.

[9]The focus here is on the practical implications of the decomposition method. Hence, no sensitivity analysis is undertaken with regard to the equivalence scale adopted. For a detailed examination of the effects of equivalence scales on measured reranking, see Creedy and van de Ven (2001b).

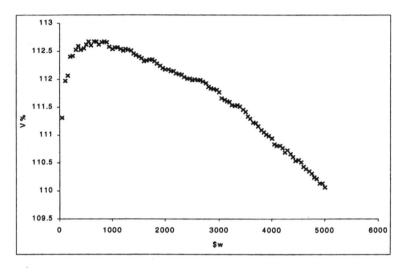

Figure 1. Vertical Redistributive Effect (percent of Net Redistributive Effect) versus Bandwidth

away at higher bandwidths; this is consistent with the discussion of section III. The slight variation observed for the curve in Figure 1 is caused by the changing close equals groups identified as *w* is altered. This variability implies that care should be taken to select the global maximum when applying the decomposition method.

The relationship between the bandwidth and the Atkinson-Plotnick measure of reranking for the average incomes of pre-tax equals groups is displayed in Figure 2. As mentioned previously, this index measures the degree to which the estimated effective tax schedule violates the progressivity assumptions that underlie the decomposition method. When the bandwidth is set to zero, it takes a value close to R_{AP} due to the few true pre-tax equals in the sample. For the sample population considered here $R_{AP} = 0.0202$, which is ten times the value shown for $w = \$50$ in the figure. This observation, together with the trend displayed in Figure 2, indicate that the estimated effective tax schedule approaches the progressivity assumptions as the bandwidth is increased, where the rate of approach is initially high and diminishes with the bandwidth. The trend exhibited in Figure 2 is consequently consistent with the averaging effect as discussed in Section III.

With regard to the impact of the appropriation effect, Figure 3 displays the extent that R_{AP}, obtained from the individual data using equation (6), exceeds the estimate of R, derived from equation (4), for a range of bandwidths. In Section III it was demonstrated that increasing the bandwidth

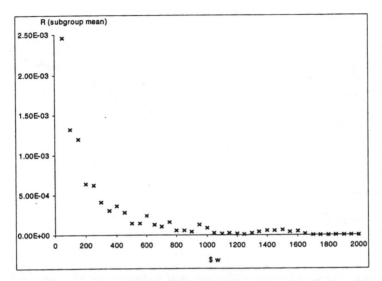

Figure 2. Atkinson-Plotnick Reranking Measure for the Mean Income Distributions of Pre-tax
Equals Groups, versus Bandwidth

causes increasing proportions of V and R observed in the sample to be
identified as contributions to H. Consequently, the larger the value of
$(R_{AP} - R)$, the larger the appropriation effect.[10] Figure 3 indicates that,
following some initial variation at the low end of the bandwidth scale
($w \leqslant \$250$), which is caused by the impact of the averaging effect, there
exists a consistent upward and concave relationship between the appropriation effect and w, which is consistent with the discussion of Section III.

Adopting the method of identifying the optimal bandwidth described in
section III and expressing the values of V, R, and H as percentages of
progressivity, $L = 0.1825$, gives:

$$V_{\max} = 112.681$$

$$R_{AP} = 11.057$$

$$\tilde{H} = 1.533$$

[10]Consider three individuals, A, B and C, with pre-tax incomes of 100, 101 and 102, and post-tax
incomes of 99, 97 and 98 respectively. When $w = 0$, $H = 0$ (there are no pre-tax equals), and $R > 0$
(compare A with B and C). When w gives a class of 100–101, $H > 0$ (compare A and B), $R > 0$
(compare A and C) but is less than when $w = 0$ (in view of A and B). When the pre-tax income
class is 100–102, $H > 0$, but $R = 0$. In all cases R_{AP} is the same since it is a sample statistic (which
may be thought of as being defined when $w = 0$), so that $R_{AP} - R$ measures the extent of the
appropriation effect.

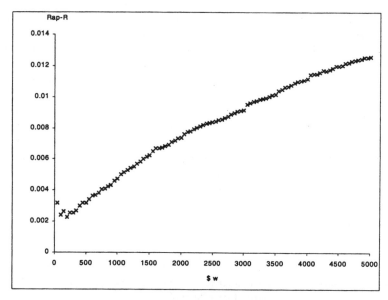

Figure 3. $(R_{AP} - R)$ versus Bandwidth.

Given that $\tilde{H}$ comprises at least $13.865 = 100(1.533/11.057)$ percent of the regressivity implied by R_{AP}, these results highlight the need to include $\tilde{H}$ when evaluating the effectiveness of a taxation system.[11] Calculations based on true equals observed in the survey population (predominantly individuals with no income), obtained an estimate for $H = 0.0027$, 1.479 percent of L. This implies that the vertical progressivity that could be calculated directly from the sample population is less than the estimate of vertical progressivity obtained by the method used to calculate $V_{\max}$. The result is a consequence of comparing every income in the sample with the respective imputed mean. Specifically, the method used to calculate $V_{\max}$ captures all deviations from the associated estimates of $T(x)$, which includes cases in which no horizontal inequity or reranking is observed in the sample population. The result is therefore consistent with the estimation objective of correcting for omissions that are presumably due to small survey populations.

Using U.K. data derived from the 1991 Family Expenditure Survey, Aronson *et al.* (1994, Table 3) report that the vertical effect is greater for a bandwidth of £5 per week than for bandwidths of either £2.50 or £10 per week. Adjusting for inflation and exchange rate differences, these bandwidths correspond to, respectively, $633.63, $316.82, and $1267.27 per annum,

[11]Creedy and van de Ven (2001b) obtain similar measures of reranking for per-capita household income distributions from Australia and the UK, 1993.

expressed in Australian dollars.[12] Figure 1 indicates that the same ordering is described by measures of the vertical effect calculated from the 1996 IDS data considered here. Although Aronson *et al.* use the £5 per week bandwidth for the majority of their applied analysis, they give no justification for the selection. The analysis undertaken here consequently helps to support the results that they report.

The results displayed here are different from those reported by Aronson *et al.* in two respects. First, Aronson *et al.* use equation (5) to calculate their horizontal and reranking effects, which results in a significantly smaller difference between the two than is reported here, because of the appropriation effect. Secondly, Aronson *et al.* report vertical effects that are 6 percent less than the vertical effect found here. This difference is in line with the intertemporal variation that Aronson *et al.* discuss, and the fact that Australian rather than UK data are considered.

V. Conclusions

This paper has examined the theoretical foundation upon which the method of decomposing the redistributive effect of taxation suggested by Aronson and Lambert (1994) is based. Particular attention was paid to the effect of varying the bandwidth that is used to identify close-equals in estimation of the effective tax schedule. This analysis produced a strategy for selecting the bandwidth used to estimate potential vertical redistribution, V, and the regressive effects, denoted by H and R, associated with a tax system.

It is suggested that the bandwidth should be adjusted to maximise the estimate obtained for V. Given that progressivity, L, and the Atkinson-Plotnick measure of reranking, R_{AP}, can be calculated as sample statistics, a lower limit of the value H can be obtained by subtraction: $\tilde{H} = V_{max} - L - R_{AP}$. The method was applied to Australian data, showing that the redistributive effect of the tax and transfer system would be about 12.5 percent higher without the effects of R and H.

Date of Receipt of Final Manuscript: May 2001.

References

Aronson, J. R. and Lambert, P. J. (1994). 'Decomposing the Gini coefficient to reveal vertical, horizontal and reranking effects of income taxation', *National Tax Journal*, Vol. 47, pp. 273–94.

[12] Wages were rescaled by an inflation factor of $(132.3/108.2) = 1.2227$ and an exchange rate of 0.5017 AUD/GBP (annual average for 1996). Wage rate data were derived from Table 6.16, *Annual Abstract of Statistics*, 1995 and 1998.

Aronson, J. R., Johnson, P. and Lambert, P. J. (1994). 'Redistributive effect and unequal income tax treatment', *Economic Journal*, Vol. 104, pp. 262–70.

Atkinson, A. B. (1979). 'Horizontal equity and the distribution of the tax burden', in Aaron H. J. and Boskins M. J. (eds) *The Economics of Taxation* Brookings Institution, Washington DC.

Bhattacharya, N. and Mahalanobis, B. (1967). 'Regional disparities in household consumption in India', *Journal of the American Statistical Association*, Vol. 62. pp. 143–61.

Creedy, J. (1998). 'Non-uniform indirect taxation, horizontal inequity and reranking', *University of Melbourne Department of Economics Research Paper*, No. 647.

Creedy, J. and van de Ven, J. (2001a). 'The redistributive effect of selected Australian taxes and transfers on annual and lifetime inequality', *Australian Economic Papers*, (forthcoming).

Creedy, J. and van de Ven, J. (2001b). 'Taxation, Reranking and Equivalence Scales', *University of Melbourne Department of Economics Research Paper*, No. 782.

Decoster, A., Schokkaert, E. and Van Camp, G. (1997a). 'Is redistribution through indirect taxes equitable?' *European Economic Review*, Vol. 41, pp. 599–608.

Decoster, A., Schokkaert, E. and Van Camp, G. (1997b). 'Horizontal neutrality and vertical redistribution with indirect taxes', *Research on Economic Inequality*, Vol. 7, pp. 219–39.

Jenkins, S. P. (1988). 'Calculating income distribution indices from micro-data', *National Tax Journal*, Vol. XLI, pp. 139–42.

Kakwani, N. C. (1984). 'Welfare rankings of income distributions', *Advances in Econometrics*, Vol. 3, pp. 191–213.

Lambert, P. J. and Aronson, J. R. (1993). 'Inequality decomposition analysis and the Gini coefficient revisited', *Economic Journal*, Vol. 103, pp. 1221–7.

Plotnick, R. (1981). 'A measure of horizontal inequity', *Review of Economics and Statistics*, Vol. 63, pp. 283–87.

Pyatt, G. (1976). 'On the interpretation and disaggregation of Gini coefficients', *Economic Journal*, Vol. 86, pp. 243–55.

[9]

DECOMPOSING REDISTRIBUTIVE EFFECTS OF TAXES AND TRANSFERS IN AUSTRALIA: ANNUAL AND LIFETIME MEASURES

JOHN CREEDY AND JUSTIN VAN DE VEN*
The University of Melbourne

This paper decomposes the redistributive effect on annual and lifetime inquality of a range of taxes and transfers in Australia, using a dynamic cohort lifetime simulation model. The redistributive effect is decomposed into vertical, horizontal and reranking effects. Horizontal inequities in the tax and transfer system are found to be negligible. The extent of reranking is greater in the lifetime than in the annual context and is affected by the equivalence scales used to adjust household incomes. If no adjustment is made to household incomes, reranking is about nine per cent of the reduction in lifetime inequality. However, if each child is counted as equivalent to one-third of an adult, reranking is found to be less than one per cent.

I. INTRODUCTION

This paper decomposes the redistributive effect on annual and lifetime incomes of a range of Australian tax and transfer programmes into vertical, horizontal and reranking effects. A dynamic cohort microsimulation model is used and decompositions are obtained using a range of equivalent adult scales and alternative time periods. The basic decomposition was first derived by Aronson and Lambert (1994) and has been applied to annual incomes in several countries. However, it has not previously been applied to lifetime income measures, where the variability of incomes over the life cycle may be expected to reduce the relative importance of vertical redistribution. In addition, the present paper applies a procedure suggested by van de Ven *et al.* (1998) to overcome the problem raised by the use in earlier studies of an arbitrary income class width within which individuals are considered to have near-equal incomes.

The intended vertical redistribution of income from relatively rich to poor households that is achieved by a tax and transfer system may be partially frustrated by horizontal inequity and reranking. Horizontal inequality relates to the 'unequal treatment of equals', where two households with the same pre-tax income have different post-tax incomes. The use of the term 'inequity' involves the presumption that it is not an intended consequence of the progressive tax structure. Reranking relates to the 'unequal treatment of unequals', where

* This research was supported by an Australian Research Council Large Grant and the Ronald Henderson Research Foundation. We should also like to thank two referees and Sheila Cameron for constructive comments on an earlier version.

households with different pre-tax incomes find their rank-order in the income distribution reversed when moving from pre-tax-and-transfer to post-tax-and-transfer incomes.

In the context of a single year, these effects can arise where non-income differences between households are treated differently by the tax and transfer system compared with the procedure used to adjust household incomes for inequality measurement.[1] The primary non-income consideration arises from differences in household composition. For example, income taxation may be applied to individuals irrespective of the number and composition of household members. Alternatively, transfer systems may impose complex rules depending on household composition and use different rules for each type of transfer payment.[2] Consequently, in measuring inequality, household incomes could be adjusted using adult equivalence scales that bear little relation to those implied by the tax and transfer system.

The use of a longer-period measure of income can introduce horizontal inequities and reranking even without non-income differences between households. These effects arise from the combination of income fluctuations from year to year with a tax and transfer system having a progressive marginal rate structure. Households with more highly fluctuating income streams pay relatively more tax because they move into higher-rate tax brackets during some of the years.[3]

The decomposition method is outlined in Section II. The microsimulation model is briefly described in Section III. The simulation results regarding annual and lifetime inequality and the extent of reranking and horizontal inequity are reported in Section IV. Section V concludes.

II. DECOMPOSING THE REDISTRIBUTIVE EFFECT

The Reynolds-Smolensky (1977) measure of the redistributive impact of a tax structure is the reduction in the Gini measure of inequality from pre-tax income, y, to post-tax income, x. If the Gini measure is denoted by G, then

$$L = G_y - G_x \qquad (1)$$

The possibility of reranking, when moving from the pre-tax to the post-tax distribution, introduces an 'unequal treatment of unequals' which is contrary to the vertical redistribution intended by the form of the tax function. The Atkinson (1979)-Plotnick (1981) measure of reranking, R, is[4]

$$R = G_x - C_x \qquad (2)$$

The concentration index, C_x, of x is similar to the associated Gini coefficient, G_x, but with the exception that it ranks by y rather than x. Consequently, an absence of reranking implies that $R = 0$.

Aronson *et al.* (1994) and Aronson and Lambert (1994) showed that the redistributive

---

[1] The extent of redistribution within a single year is likely to vary over the life cycle of a cohort because it depends on the precise form of the distribution of pre-tax-and-transfer income, which does not remain fixed from year to year.

[2] See, for example, Banks and Johnson (1994).

[3] Under a concave tax function $t(x)$, the annual average tax paid on a variable income stream x_t ($t = 1, \ldots, T$) exceeds that which would be paid on the annual average, $\bar{x}$. From Jensen's inequality, $\frac{1}{T}\sum_{t=1}^{T} t(x_t) > t(\bar{x})$. Lambert (1993, p. 195) shows how various equally distributed equivalent income measures can be used to define the progressivity of $t(x)$.

[4] It is sometimes defined using $(G_y - C_y)/2G_y$: see Jenkins (1988).

effect can be decomposed into vertical, horizontal and reranking components of a tax system. They showed that when the population is divided into N groups, such that within each group individuals have similar pre-tax incomes, y_k, for $k = 1, \ldots, N$, and groups are ranked in ascending order $(y_1 < y_2 \ldots < y_N)$

$$L = (G_y - G_0) - \sum_{k=1}^{N} \theta_k G_k - R \qquad (3)$$

where G_0 is the between-groups Gini measure of post-tax income obtained by replacing every post-tax income within each group by the arithmetic mean; θ_k is the product of the population share and the post-tax income share of those in the kth group; and G_k is the Gini measure of inequality of post-tax income of those in the kth group. The first two terms measure vertical redistribution, V, and horizontal inequity, H, respectively, where the latter arises from the unequal treatment of equals. Hence

$$L = V - H - R \qquad (4)$$

and the horizontal inequity and reranking effects both reduce the redistributive effect of the tax structure. This decomposition extends that produced by Kakwani (1984), who showed that $L = \{g/(1-g)\}K - R$, where $K = C_t - G_y$ and C_t is the tax concentration index. Hence K is a measure of the disproportionality of tax payments which combines the horizontal and vertical effects.

In practice few exact pre-tax equals are observed in survey data, so the decomposition in (3) cannot be applied directly. If groups of 'near-equals' are used, this decomposition must be modified. For example in the first term it is necessary to replace G_y with a corresponding between-groups measure. This is obtained, like G_0, by replacing individual values in each group of near-equals with their arithmetic mean value.

Further complications arise with the measure of horizontal inequity. This issue was examined in detail by van de Ven et al. (1998). Their analysis, supported by carefully constructed simulation experiments, found that the measured vertical effect initially increases towards its true value as the class width is increased, and then falls after reaching a maximum. This suggests a strategy whereby the class width used to combine individuals into groups of near-equals is chosen to maximise the estimated vertical effect. The estimate of the vertical effect consequently obtained is thus closest to the 'true value'. The reranking measure, R, can of course be obtained directly from equation (2) using the ungrouped values and is therefore not affected by the choice of class width. The horizontal effect can then be obtained using $H = V - R - L$.

III. The Simulation Model

This Section provides a brief description of the structure of the simulation model; for further details see Creedy and van de Ven (1999) and van de Ven (1998). The model is designed to examine the lifetime experience of a cohort of males and, where relevant, their nuclear families. The simulated cohort does not attempt to reflect the full heterogeneity of the population. A highly parsimonious structure has been adopted for the model so that the characteristics of the simulated population can be varied by adjusting a few easily interpreted parameters. For the analysis undertaken, the simulated cohort reflects the Australian population. This approach contrasts with that used, for example, by Harding (1994) and Falkingham and Hills (1995) which makes extensive use of transition matrices.

Simulation of pre-tax incomes over the life cycle

The model encompasses family formation, births, labour force participation of both male and female household members, and income dynamics over the life cycle. The heterogeneity among individuals is restricted to the following six characteristics in each year: marital status; age of spouse, where relevant; number and age of dependant children; employment status of males between the ages of 20 and 69 (who are either employed full-time or unemployed); employment status of females between the ages of 18 and 64 (who are either employed full-time, employed part-time or unemployed) and; labour incomes of males and females, when employed.

In any given year, these characteristics are determined following a sequence of calculations, or a 'linear' process. For any combination of calendar year and age, the first consideration involves the marital status of each male, which is assumed to be set at the beginning of the year. Simulated marital status is based upon marital status in the previous year and the probability of changing status.[5] Where marriage takes place, a random selection is made from the conditional distribution of the age of bride, given the age of groom.

Births are determined according to conditional probabilities, given the age of the wife and the previous number of births. No births are allowed after females reach the age of 44, and no births are allowed prior to marriage. Hence, single parents arise only from marriage break-up, in which case children are considered as dependents of the male.[6] In calculating taxes and transfers, each child is assumed to be dependant for 16 years.

Male employment status is determined using a probit analysis and depends on marital status and age. All males are either unemployed, retired or fully employed; this assumption is warranted by the observed distributions of hours worked by men, which reveal little part-time employment.[7] The model can allow for the probability of unemployment to be influenced by the individual's previous experience of unemployment. Self-employment is not modelled and all males are retired at age 69 if they have not retired earlier.

The probit equation used to simulate male employment status is consequently restricted compared with the standard models analysed in the literature, a characteristic that is a direct consequence of the objective of parsimony underlying the model's construction. However, the impact of this restriction on the results obtained is limited by feedback effects that are included in the model. In particular, individual-specific characteristics such as education, that are usually included in probit equations of employment but are omitted in the current model, have a persistent effect throughout the life of an individual. This persistence is captured by the inclusion of past unemployment as an element that determines the probability of future employment.

A model of age-earnings profiles, containing a stochastic process to generate relative

---

[5] Individuals are not allowed to re-marry and marriage can only take place up to a critical age, after which break-ups occur; these include divorce and deaths combined. Deaths of males are not modelled, so all males are assumed to survive until age 70.
[6] In view of the structure of the model, the focus is not on sole parents and in a simulated population of 5,000 males, there are no sole parents with dependant children.
[7] The various Australian Income Distribution Surveys provide details of the number of hours worked by each individual. Part-time employed males were excluded from the regression of the associated probit equation.

changes from year to year, is then used to determine the annual income of individuals who are identified as being employed. The model for males has a quadratic profile of mean log-earnings with age and a Gibrat process of year-to-year changes, involving random proportionate changes.

Similarly, female employment status, which may be retired, part-time, full-time, or unemployed, is determined using a probit analysis and depends on age, number of children below the age of 17 and the husband's net relative income. In the model, all females are married, so single women were excluded when carrying out the probit analyses. All females are retired at age 64 if they have not already retired. This specification means that female labour force participation is responsive to the nature of the tax and transfer system insofar as it affects the husband's net income. The annual income of females is determined using a model of age-income profiles which allows for a degree of correlation between the stochastic processes of male and female family members. The model for females has a cubic profile of mean log-earnings with age. The income simulation models can allow for productivity growth over the life of the cohort.

Taxes and transfers

This paper examines the effects of taxes and transfers applied during March 1998. Brief details of these schemes are given in the Appendix. The taxes include income taxation and the Medicare levy. Transfer payments (either administered directly or through the income tax system) include the Parenting Allowance, Partner Allowance, Newstart (unemployment benefit), Family Payment, Family Tax Initiative, Low Income Earner Rebate and the Dependant Spouse Rebate.[8] The transfer payments included are a selection of the programmes administered by the taxation and redistribution system in Australia; in particular the complexities of superannuation savings and the Age Pension are excluded from consideration.[9] However, they comprise about 70 per cent of social security expenditure, excluding social security pensions for the retired.[10]

The simulation model assumes that all individuals receive the transfers to which they are entitled, and therefore makes no allowance for non-take-up of benefits. The analysis consequently focusses upon the redistribution implied by the formal rules and regulations of the tax and transfer programmes. In practice, the main group for which take-up rates are less than 100 per cent includes those who, under income-tested schemes, are only entitled to small amounts which do not outweigh the costs of applying. Hence it is unlikely that the distributional effects are substantially distorted.

Equivalence scales

Before calculating inequality measures, it is necessary to specify a set of equivalence scales for deflating household incomes. Many alternative scales are available, but the approach used here is to adopt a flexible specification. Let n_a and n_c denote respectively the number of adults and children in the household. Equivalence scales, z, are expressed as

---

[8] Given that sole parents are not the focus of the analysis undertaken in this paper, the Sole Parent Pension and the Sole Parent Rebate are not modelled.

[9] On superannuation in Australia see Atkinson *et al.* (1996).

[10] This proportion is based on 'total outlays' of various programmes as given in the 1996–7 DSS Annual Report.

$$z = (n_a + \Phi n_c)^\theta \qquad (5)$$

This formulation has been used by, for example, Cutler and Katz (1992), Banks and Johnson (1994) and Jenkins and Cowell (1994). If y is total household income, equivalent adult income is equal to y/z. Suitable choice of the parameters, for $0 \leqslant (\Phi, \theta) \leqslant 1$, can produce an approximation to a wide range of the equivalence scales currently in use, even though the age and gender of each household member is ignored. The value of Φ affects the weight given to children relative to adults and θ is a measure of economies of scale, which are increased as θ is reduced. Values of $\theta = 1$ and $\Phi = 0.5$ were used below unless otherwise specified.

IV.   SIMULATION RESULTS

Inequality of alternative distributions

Gini inequality measures of annual income distributions are displayed in Figure 1 and Table I; the latter gives annual averages over five year periods. The corresponding lifetime income distribution measures are reported in Table II. Lifetime incomes are obtained as the sum of incomes over the period between male ages of 20 and 65.[11] The distributions are pre-tax-and-transfer incomes and post-tax-and-transfer incomes for males, households and

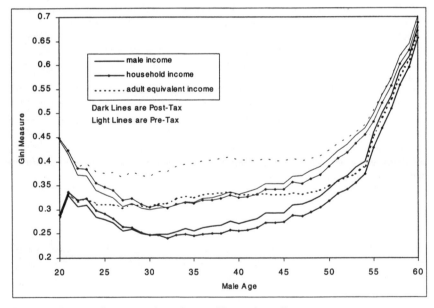

Figure 1.   Pre-tax and post-tax-and-transfer annual income inequality

---

[11] Alternative lifetime income concepts are examined in Creedy (1997).

Table I   Cross-sectional income inequality

| | Gini Coefficient | | | | | |
| | Male | | Household | | Adult Equivalent | |
Age	pre-tax	post-tax	pre-tax	post-tax	pre-tax	post-tax
20–24	0.3888	0.3027	0.3995	0.3131	0.4064	0.3140
25–29	0.3157	0.2635	0.3285	0.2707	0.3740	0.3095
30–34	0.3067	0.2519	0.3087	0.2462	0.3819	0.3166
35–39	0.3263	0.2656	0.3214	0.2505	0.4031	0.3322
40–44	0.3440	0.2828	0.3338	0.2640	0.4025	0.3323
45–49	0.3727	0.3123	0.3578	0.2895	0.4055	0.3355
50–54	0.4368	0.3724	0.4209	0.3452	0.4486	0.3680
55–59	0.5742	0.5401	0.5586	0.5121	0.5765	0.5317
60–64	0.7950	0.7783	0.7825	0.7606	0.7928	0.7721
65–69	0.9634	0.9604	0.9577	0.9533	0.9606	0.9565

Table II   Lifetime income inequality

| | Gini Coefficient | |
	Pre-tax	Post-tax
Males	0.2232	0.1743
Households	0.2129	0.1708
Equivalent Adults	0.2229	0.1684

equivalent adults. As can be seen from Table II, all of the lifetime inequality measures are less than the smallest associated annual income measures. This result is partially due to the inclusion of the unemployed, which causes periods of high income variability for individuals from one year to the next as employment status fluctuates. Since simulated individuals are typically unemployed for few years of their total working lives, taking a lifetime measure of income results in lower inequality. The results also demonstrate that the lifetime redistributive effect of the tax and transfer system is less than the average redistributive effect on annual incomes.[12]

The method used to simulate incomes implies that if all individuals were employed throughout their lives, an approximately linear trend with age would be observed for each of the inequality measures based upon annual income. Since the relationships between each of the inequality measures and age shown in Figure 1 are nonlinear, it can be inferred that the inequality analysis based upon annual incomes is strongly influenced by inclusion of the unemployed. This conclusion is supported by the close relationship between the probability of not being employed and annual inequality in each age group. Specifically, as the unemployment rate increases, the total income of the simulated population is distributed among fewer individuals, which raises the associated measures of inequality.

Figure 1 and the corresponding data of Table I, also show a close relationship between

[12] The effects of individual taxes and transfers are examined in detail in Creedy and van de Ven (1999).

male and household inequality measures based upon annual income distributions, where
male inequality is slightly greater than household inequality after the male ages of 33 and 30
respectively for pre-tax-and-transfer and post-tax-and-transfer distributions. The close
relationship suggests that household income inequality is driven by male income inequality,
a result that is to be expected since the simulation is based upon a cohort of males and their
nuclear families. The fact that male inequality is greater than household inequality for the
majority of the simulated working life is consistent with the findings of earlier studies. This
equalising effect of wives' earnings arises despite the existence of a positive correlation
between the earnings of wives and husbands in each year.[13]

Decomposition results

The estimates derived from the decomposition method applied to lifetime incomes
indicated that the effect of H on the redistributive effect of the tax and transfer payments
was negligible. The values derived for the horizontal effect ranged between one one-
hundreth and six one-hundreths of a per cent of the associated redistributive effect. It may be
thought that these low values arise because of the limited extent of heterogeneity in the
population, but low values of horizontal inequity have also been reported in annual contexts
by other researchers. For example, Aronson *et al.* (1994) and Wagstaff and Doorslaer (1997)
found that horizontal inequity formed only about one per cent of the overall redistribution.
Furthermore, these authors used arbitrary class widths in carrying out the computations,
which is likely to distort the measure of horizontal inequity; see van de Ven *et al.* (1998).

Estimates of reranking, R, were calculated using both the annual and lifetime measures of
equivalent adult income using the Atkinson-Plotnick measure, and were converted into
percentages of the associated redistributive effect, L. Figure 2 illustrates the reranking effects
calculated from the pre-tax-and-transfer and post-tax-and-transfer income distributions
assuming equivalence scale parameters of $\theta = 1$ and $\Phi = 0.5$, as before.

Reranking measures the extent to which the ranking of individuals switches when moving
from the pre-tax to the post-tax income distribution. The inclusion of the unemployed has
only a small impact on the reranking effect based upon annual data. This is because of the
large pre-tax income gap that exists between employed and unemployed households. In a
lifetime context, inclusion of the unemployed has a smaller impact on the decomposition
components due to the associated effect of averaging.[14]

The age profile of the reranking effect based on annual measures of income, depicted in
Figure 2, is driven by a large number of factors. Reranking is increased as the income
disparity between unequals falls. This is because less inequity in the tax and transfer system
is required to generate switching between the pre-tax-and-transfer and post-tax-and-transfer
incomes. Reranking also increases with demographic heterogeneity since it inflates the
effects of any disparity between the equivalence scaling factor used and that implied by the
tax system. Another characteristic that increases the reranking effect is the employment rate,
because high unemployment implies that more individuals are defined as pre-tax equals,
which reduces the pool from which reranking is generated. The discontinuity exhibited at

---

[13] For a recent empirical study of this issue using US data, and further references, see Cancian and
Reed (1998).
[14] At any given age, the unemployed form the largest group of pre-tax equals, and it is possible that
some horizontal inequity arises in the annual context.

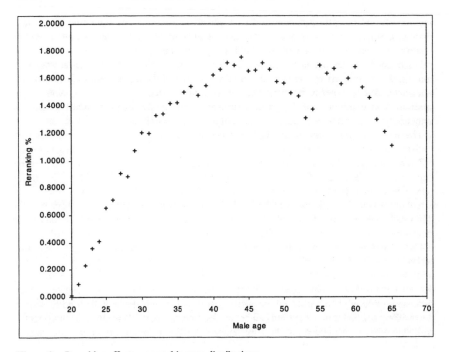

Figure 2. Reranking effects – annual income distributions

Table III Reranking effects: lifetime incomes

θ	Φ	Reranking
0.00	–	9.2375
0.33	0.00	6.6272
0.33	0.33	5.1432
0.33	0.66	4.3575
0.33	1.00	3.8684
0.66	0.00	3.5410
0.66	0.33	1.7382
0.66	0.66	1.3141
0.66	1.00	1.2969
1.00	0.00	1.6887
1.00	0.33	0.7903
1.00	0.66	1.2431
1.00	1.00	1.8316

the male age of 55 arises because unemployed males after the age of 54 may be identified as retired by the simulation model, and consequently ineligible for Newstart payments.

As suggested in the introduction to this paper, reranking is expected to be larger in a lifetime compared with an annual context. The reranking observed here is indeed larger than has been found in earlier studies based on annual incomes.[15] The reranking of lifetime incomes is substantially larger than that of annual incomes because of the income variability over the life cycle, combined with the nonlinearity of the tax system.

Furthermore, reranking is larger, the larger is the difference between the treatment of household composition by the tax and transfer system and the adjustment used to produce equivalent adult incomes in measuring inequality. Since the tax system tends to favour larger families, it is expected that the equal treatment of all family members when measuring inequality would produce the highest measured degree of reranking.

The extent of reranking in lifetime incomes was therefore calculated for a range of equivalence scale parameters and the results are depicted in Table III. The scales reflect different value judgements and views regarding 'needs', so it seems appropriate to report the implications of a range of values. The contribution of reranking clearly depends on the equivalence scale used. The scales using $\theta = 1.00$ and $\Phi = 0.33$ give rise to the lowest extent of measured reranking, whereby $100R/L = 0.79$. This scale simply equates each child in a family to one third of an adult. This is close to the value used in generating the earlier results for annual incomes that can therefore be interpreted as close to 'minimum values'.

Care needs to be taken in interpreting such a set of reranking-minimising equivalence scales. Consider, for example, a government that designs tax and transfer policy so as to minimise reranking and horizontal inequity, subject to some exogenous assessment error, desired net revenue, progressivity and beliefs regarding individual needs. The impact on measured reranking and horizontal inequity of varying the equivalence scale used to analyse the resultant tax and transfer system can be divided into two parts. One effect relates directly, while the other is orthogonal, to the government's procedure for specifying tax and transfer policy.

Specifically, adjusting the equivalence scale away from the scale that relates most closely to the government's beliefs regarding individual needs implies that the relative positions of individuals in the associated pre- and post-tax-and-transfer adult equivalent income distributions are likely to depart from the associated rankings that the government would (implicitly) make. Given that the government designs the tax and transfer system in relation to its beliefs regarding individual needs, the direct effect of moving away from the government's implicit scale is consequently likely to increase measured reranking and horizontal inequity.

Alternatively, the orthogonal effect arises due to the impact that the equivalence scale has on tax and transfer progressivity. Whereas the government designs the tax and transfer system for a given measure of progressivity, varying the equivalence scale used to examine redistribution affects the measured extent of progressivity. The precise effect that varying the equivalence scale has on measured progressivity is determined by the extent to which the adult equivalent income of the wealthy is affected relative to the poor. It is evident that varying the equivalence scale will have a similar distorting effect on the associated measures of horizontal inequity and reranking.

Hence, although the direct effect is likely to increase horizontal inequity and reranking as the equivalence scale departs from the scale implicitly underlying the beliefs of the government, the impact of the orthogonal effect is unknown *ex ante*. Consequently, given that the relative magnitudes of the two effects are unknown, it is not possible to state

---

[15] Decompositions in the context of indirect taxation, using short-period expenditure concepts, have also found more reranking than annual income analyses. This arises from substantial differences in expenditure patterns among households with the same total expenditure. On the decomposition in the context of indirect taxes, see Decoster *et al.* (1997a, b) and Creedy (1998).

conclusively that the equivalence scale which minimises measured reranking and horizontal inequity corresponds to the scale that most closely reflects the associated value judgements made by policy makers. However, it is possible to argue that the equivalence scale implicitly adopted by policy makers will be in the neighbourhood of the scale that minimises horizontal inequity and reranking, due to the direct effect.

V. CONCLUSIONS

This paper has used a dynamic cohort microsimulation model in order to examine and decompose the redistributive effect on annual and lifetime inequality of a range of taxes and transfers in Australia. The model allows for family formation, births, labour force participation of males and females, along with income dynamics.

First, the basic inequality properties of the simulations may be summarised. Lifetime inequality, measured by the Gini coefficient of income over the male ages 20 to 65, was found to be lower than in any single year for males, households and equivalent households, with respect to both pre-tax and post-tax incomes. This result is in part attributed to the inclusion of the unemployed in the simulated population in each period.[16] Equivalent adult lifetime pre-tax incomes were found to be only slightly more unequal than household incomes (and were less than that of male incomes) while post-tax-and-transfer equivalent adult lifetime incomes were less unequal than household incomes. The inequality reducing effect of the taxes and transfers examined was found to be smaller in the lifetime than in the annual context. This result is consistent with other simulation studies.[17]

The earnings of wives were found to have an equalising effect on unadjusted household annual income inequality, which was lower than that of males after the male age of about 30 years. Equivalent household annual incomes were found to be substantially more unequal than male incomes, particularly during the middle years of the life cycle.

The redistributive effects of taxes and transfers were then decomposed, in cross-sectional and lifetime contexts, using the technique proposed in van de Ven *et al.* (1998) to deal with the need to group observations into classes of 'near equals'. Horizontal inequities in the tax and transfer system – the unequal treatment of equals – were found to be negligible. However, reranking – the unequal treatment of unequals – was observed in annual and lifetime distributions. The extent of reranking was substantially greater in the lifetime than in the annual context. This arises partly because of the combination of fluctuating incomes over the life cycle with a tax system having a progressive rate structure.

The degree of measured reranking was found to be significantly affected by the equivalence scales used to adjust household incomes for the purpose of inequality measurement. If no adjustment is made to household incomes, reranking is about nine per cent of the reduction in lifetime inequality. However, if each child is counted as equivalent to one-third of an adult, reranking is less than one per cent. The relationship between equivalent scales and reranking appears to warrant further study.

---

[16] It would not be possible to include zero pre-tax annual incomes in an Atkinson measure of inequality.
[17] For example, see Fullerton and Rogers (1993) and literature cited there. However, it does not necessarily arise, and care must be taken in interpreting the result in view of the difference between the pre-tax-and-transfer distributions being examined.

APPENDIX: TAXES AND TRANSFER PAYMENTS

This appendix provides a brief description of the taxes and transfers examined. The regulations allow for considerably more complexity than is described below, but only the elements that are relevant to the simulations are presented. All individuals are, for simplicity, assumed to remain resident in Australia during each year of their working life. The schemes are described as follows.[18]

Newstart, NS, is an unemployment benefit available to individuals between the ages of 18 and 65, at which time men become eligible for the Age Pension. Recipients must be capable of, available for, and actively seeking employment, or temporarily incapacitated.[19] All simulated adults under the age of 60 who are identified as not working and otherwise eligible for Newstart payments are assumed to fulfil these criteria. For an unemployed person the basic Newstart rate is $240 per fortnight if single and $290.10 per fortnight if married. This basic rate is paid subject to income and assets tests and is taxable.

The *Partner Allowance, PA,* is paid to an individual who is not employed, and whose spouse receives Newstart payments. The Partner Allowance has the same income test, assets test, and benefits as Newstart, but does not require the recipient to be in the labour force. Consequently, the effects of both *NS* and *PA* payments are aggregated in the following simulation analysis, where the aggregate is referred to as Newstart alone.

The *Parenting Allowance, P_gA,* is paid to one member of a married couple with at least one dependant child under the age of 16.[20] It is paid in two parts, a basic rate and an additional rate: these two parts sum to $290.10 per fortnight, which equals the *NS* payment made to married individuals. Both parts of the P_gA are subject to income and assets tests. The income test applied to the P_gA scheme is more generous than for *NS*, with less severe reductions in payments for earned income, and only the additional component of the payment is taxable.

Family payments, FP, are paid where there are dependants aged 16 years and younger.[21] The amount paid depends on the number and ages of children, with fortnightly payments of $96.40 for each child younger than 13 years of age, $125.40 for each child between the ages of 13 and 15, and $60.20 for each 16 year old child. A large-family supplement of $7.70 per fortnight is also paid for the fourth and each subsequent child. The payments are non-taxable and subject to an income and an assets test. Benefits are given to the spouse with the lower income.

Income taxation is imposed on individual rather than joint incomes. The income tax function takes the standard multi-step form with five marginal rates varying between 0 for

---

[18] See Creedy and van de Ven (1999) for a more detailed description.

[19] Recipients may do training and voluntary work, and must be willing to enter into an Activity Agreement if required. There are also Australian residence requirements. It is possible to be working in casual or part-time employment and to receive NS payments so long as income earned is less than a threshold and individuals can prove that they are actively seeking employment. Simulated individuals classified as working are assumed not to be seeking employment elsewhere and so do not receive NS payments.

[20] In the following simulations this is interpreted as less than or equal to 16, for consistency with the age limit regarding other taxes and benefits. The recipient must be an Australian resident and present in Australia, except that it can be paid for up to 13 weeks of temporary absence if the person was resident for at least 13 weeks before departure. It is available to new migrants after 104 weeks in Australia.

[21] From 1 April 1998 Family Payments became known as Family Allowances. Family Payments can be received for dependant children under the age of 16 and up to the age of 18 in relation to full-time secondary students. There are also residence requirements.

income earned up to $5400 and 47 per cent for income over $50,000. In addition to the standard marginal tax rates charged under the income taxation system, income is also deducted for the *Medicare levy, ML*.[22] The proportion of income paid under the Medicare levy varies between 0 and 2.5 per cent depending on income and family composition, with different rules applying for single people without dependants and multiple member families.

The *Family Tax Initiative* is a scheme designed to support households with dependant children. It is comprised of two parts. Family Tax Assistance, *FTA*, provides an increase in the tax-free threshold for one of the supporting parents of dependant children and is consequently administered by the Australian Taxation Department. Low-income families who are unable to take advantage of *FTA* are eligible for a Family Tax Payment, *FTP*, which is administered by the Department of Social Security. For families who satisfy the eligibility criteria of both *FTA* and *FTP* programmes, any payment received under *FTP* reduces the effective benefit received from *FTA* dollar for dollar.[23] The *FTA* and *FTP* schemes both comprise two parts. Part *A* provides an effective annual payment of $200.00 per child to the parent receiving the payment. Part *B*, which is additional to Part *A*, is paid only to families with at least one dependant child under the age of 5 and provides an annual payment of $500.00 which is unaffected by the number of dependant children. These payments are not taxable.

The *Dependant Spouse Rebate, DSR*, is given to married individuals when the spouse earns a sufficiently low 'separate net income', *SNI*, as defined by the Australian Taxation Department. For the purposes of the current analysis, *SNI* is the sum of wages from employment and all benefits described above that are taxable. The basic *DSR* received is $1324 if there are no dependant children or $1452 if there are children. It is subject to an income test.

The *Low Income Rebate, LIR*, of $150 is received by individuals with annual taxable incomes less than $20,700, and is reduced linearly at the rate of four cents for each dollar in excess of $20,700 earned.

The complexities of the various transfer payment schemes relate to their eligibility conditions, particularly with respect to the arrangements for means testing. Typically, both income and assets tests are applied. However, with the exception of Newstart Payments where the assets test is designed specifically to exclude the short term unemployed, it is the income test that is relevant for the vast majority of practical cases. Consequently, since the simulation model does not include wealth accumulation and home ownership, a 'pseudo assets test' has only been applied for Newstart payments, where two-thirds of the income earned in the previous year is applied to the standard Newstart income test to determine eligibility.

REFERENCES

Aronson, J.R. and Lambert, P.J. 1994, 'Decomposing the Gini Coefficient to Reveal Vertical, Horizontal and Reranking Effects of Income Taxation', *National Tax Journal*, vol. 47, pp. 273–294.

[22] The amount depends on whether the individual is covered by private health insurance, but the following analysis assumes that there is no private insurance.
[23] Consequently, for the following simulations, families are assumed only to receive benefits from one of the programmes in any given year.

Aronson, J.R., Johnson, P. and Lambert, P.J. 1994, 'Redistributive Effect and Unequal Income Tax Treatment', *Economic Journal*, vol. 104, pp. 262–270.

Atkinson, A.B. 1979, 'Horizontal Equity and the Distribution of the Tax Burden', In *The Economics of Taxation* (ed. by H.J. Aaron and M.J. Boskins). The Brookings Institution, Washington.

Atkinson, M.E., Creedy, J. and Knox, D. 1996, 'Alternative Retirement Income Strategies: A Cohort Analysis of Lifetime Redistribution', *Economic Record*, vol. 72, pp. 97–106.

Banks, J. and Johnson, P. 1994, 'Equivalence Scale Relativities', *Economic Journal*, vol. 104, pp. 883–890.

Cancian, M. and Reed, D. 1998, 'Assessing the Effects of Wives' Earnings on Family Income Inequality', *Review of Economics and Statistics*, vol. 80, pp. 73–79.

Creedy, J. 1997, 'Lifetime Inequality and Tax Progressivity with Alternative Income Concepts', *Review of Income and Wealth*, vol. 43, pp. 283–295.

Creedy, J. 1998, 'Non-uniform Indirect Taxation, Horizontal Inequity and Re-ranking', *University of Melbourne Department of Economics Research Paper*, no. 647.

Creedy, J. and van de Ven, J. 1999, 'The Effects of Selected Australian Taxes and Transfers on Annual and Lifetime Inquality', *Australian Journal of Labour Economics*, vol. 3, pp. 1–22.

Cutler, D.M. and Katz, L. 1992, 'Rising Inequality? Changes in the Distribution of Income and Consumption in the 1080s', *American Economic Review*, vol. 82, pp. 546–551.

Decoster, A., Schokkaert, E. and Van Camp, G. 1997a, 'Is Redistribution Through Indirect Taxes Equitable?', *European Economic Review*, vol. 41, pp. 599–608.

Decoster, A., Schokkaert, E. and Van Camp, G. 1997b, 'Horizontal Neutrality and Vertical Redistribution with Indirect Taxes', *Research on Economic Inequality*, vol. 7, pp. 219–239.

Falkingham, J. and Hills, J. (eds) 1995, *The Dynamic of Welfare: The Welfare State and The Life Cycle*, Prentice Hall, London.

Fullerton, D. and Rogers, D.L. 1993, *Who Bears the Lifetime Tax Burden?*, The Brookings Institution, Washington, DC.

Harding, A. 1994, 'Lifetime vs Annual Income Distribution in Australia', In *Taxation, Poverty and Income Distribution* (ed. by J. Creedy), pp. 104–139. Edward Elgar, Aldershot.

Jenkins, S.P. 1988, 'Empirical Measurement of Horizontal Inequity', *Journal of Public Economics*, vol. 37, pp. 305–329.

Jenkins, S.P. and Cowell, F.A. 1994, 'Parametric Equivalence Scales and Scale Relativities', *Economic Journal*, vol. 104, pp. 891–900.

Kakwani, N.C. 1984, 'On the Measurement of Tax Progressivity and Redistributive Effect of Taxes with Applications to Horizontal and Vertical Equity', *Advances in Econometrics*, vol. 3, pp. 191–213.

Lambert, P.J. 1993, *The Distribution and Redistribution of Income: A Mathematical Analysis*, Manchester University Press, Manchester.

Plotnick, R. 1981, 'A Measure of Horizontal Inequity', *Review of Economics and Statistics*, vol. 63, pp. 283–87.

Reynolds, M. and Smolensky, E. 1977, *Public Expenditures, Taxes and the Distribution of Income: The United States 1950, 1961, 1970*. Academic Press, New York.

van de Ven, J. 1998, 'A Dynamic Cohort Microsimulation Model', *University of Melbourne Department of Economics Research Paper*

van de Ven, J., Creedy, J. and Lambert, P.J. 1998, 'The Redistributive Effect of Taxes Revisited', *University of Melbourne Department of Economics Research Paper*, no. 657.

Wagstaff, A. and Doorslaer, E. van 1997, 'Progressivity, Horizontal Equity and Reranking in Health Care Finance: A Decomposition Analysis for the Netherlands', *Journal of Health Economics*, vol. 16, pp. 499–516.

[10]

Taxation, Reranking and Equivalence Scales

John Creedy and Justin van de Ven
The University of Melbourne

Abstract

This paper considers the relationship between equivalence scales and the reranking effects of taxation. The impact on reranking of varying an equivalence scale is divided into two effects. The first, referred to as the direct effect, increases reranking as the equivalence scale used departs from the scale that implicitly underlies the tax system. The second, referred to as the indirect effect, increases reranking as measures of adult equivalent income increase. It is argued that the equivalence scale that underlies a tax system is likely to be in the neighbourhood of the scale that minimises reranking. Household data from Australia and the UK are analysed.

1   Introduction

Tax and transfer payments are often determined with reference to non-income characteristics of tax units, such as their size and demographic composition. This implies that the rank order of pre-tax incomes is usually different from that of the post-tax distribution. The extent to which tax systems lead to reranking of income is of interest from a distributional perspective due to the association of reranking with equity.[1] The interpretation of observed reranking is, however, complicated by the extent to which it is a deliberate objective of policy makers in response to perceived, but implicit, views regarding differences in the needs of tax units.

---

[1] As stressed by Musgrave (1959, p.160), 'The requirements of horizontal and vertical equity are but different sides of the same coin'; see also van de Ven *et al.* (2001).

The aim of this paper is to consider the relationship between equivalence scales and the reranking effects of taxation. Given that equivalence scales evaluate the needs of different tax units, this relationship provides a useful means of interpreting observed measures of reranking. The paper also examines the conditions under which an implicit set of scales contained in the tax and transfer system may be identified from variations in the measured reranking of adult equivalent incomes.[2] If it is thought that policy makers design tax and transfer systems in terms of adult equivalent incomes, then it is reasonable to expect that policy makers would consider any reranking of (their perceived) adult equivalent incomes as undesirable. Within this framework, it may therefore seem logical to infer implicit scales by selecting the set that produces the minimum amount of measured reranking.[3] However, it is shown below that such an argument must be qualified.

Some earlier studies have used equivalence scales based on a limited part of the tax system; for example, Seneca and Taussig (1971) used scales implicit in income tax allowances, and Nolan (1987), following the Royal Commission on the Distribution of Income and Wealth, used scales based on Supplementary Benefit rates.[4] However, individual tax and transfer schemes often appear to suggest quite different scales; see, for example, Nolan (1987, p.284), Banks and Johnson (1993), and Coulter *et al.* (1992, p.100). If a scale is unrepresentative of the entire tax and transfer system, it is likely to be unrepresentative for the entire population. As Coulter *et al.* (1992 pp.100-101) argued, 'since social assistance benefits aim to provide minimum "safety net" incomes, it is not clear their relativities are appropriate for distributional assessments concerning the whole income distribution rather than

---

[2]A related issue concerns the aversion to inequality. Attempts to impute a value of inequality aversion implicit in government tax decisions include Christiansen and Jansen (1978) and Stern (1977); see also Mera (1969), Moreh (1981) and Brent (1984).

[3]The suggestion was mentioned briefly in Creedy and van de Ven (2001); see also Nolan (1987).

[4]This is a rare study looking at the effect of using adult equivalent incomes on reranking, and is discussed further below.

2

just the bottom tail.' Hence, caution needs to be exercised when analysing measures of reranking obtained using scales that are inferred from subsets of the tax system.

Section 2 begins by describing the basic framework of analysis and considers the way in which observed reranking can arise. The question of whether a reranking-minimising set of equivalence scales can be interpreted as the scales used by policy makers is examined analytically in section 3. Section 4 reports simulation analyses. An application using UK and Australian tax structures is reported in section 5. Conclusions are in section 6.

2 Taxation and Reranking

This section presents a general framework for considering the relationship between equivalence scales and reranking. Tax and transfer systems are necessarily specified in terms of observable characteristics of the tax unit. However, it is appropriate to regard the redistributive objectives of the government as being framed in terms of income per equivalent adult.[5] In general, values in adult equivalent terms, as measured by the government, are denoted by a * superscript. Let a_i^* denote the number of equivalent adults in tax unit i. Each a_i^* can be regarded as a function of a set of q observable variables of the tax unit, $u_i = u(u_{i1}, ..., u_{iq})$, so that:

$$a_i^* = a^*(u_i) \tag{1}$$

Let x_i and y_i denote the pre-tax and post-tax income of tax unit i. Hence, $x_i^* = x_i/a_i^*$ and $y_i^* = y_i/a_i^*$ are respectively pre-tax and post-tax income per equivalent adult. An assumption of equal sharing of tax unit (adult equivalent) income is made.

Given a population distribution of x_i^*, the government is considered to attempt to impose a tax structure that is capable (subject to a budget con-

---

[5]In practice neither the objectives nor the equivalence scales are made explicit.

3

straint) of achieving its distributional aims. This involves a tax function, $T^*(x_i^*)$, so that the net adult equivalent income of unit i is:

$$y_i^* = x_i^* - T^*(x_i^*) \tag{2}$$

This relationship would be expected to avoid reranking of adult equivalent incomes, since reranking frustrates the redistributive objective of the system.[6] In terms of observed incomes, (2) translates to:

$$y_i = x_i - a_i^* T^*\left(\frac{x_i}{a_i^*}\right) \tag{3}$$

Consider the special case where the government's desired redistribution policy involves the linear function:

$$T^*(x_i^*) = t_1 x_i^* - \beta \tag{4}$$

In this case:

$$a_i^* T^*\left(\frac{x_i}{a_i^*}\right) = t_1 x_i - \beta a_i^* \tag{5}$$

Hence the applicable tax function is also linear in terms of observed incomes. There is a single transfer payment, β, adjusted according to the government's equivalence scales.[7] Substituting (5) into (3):

$$y_i = (1 - t_1) x_i + \beta a_i^* \tag{6}$$

---

[6] It may not be possible for the government to impose its desired tax function. Suppose that the various rates and thresholds used depend on a vector of m characteristics of the units, $v_i = v(v_{i1}, ..., v_{im})$. The closest practical approximation to the desired tax function is written as $T(x_i, v_i)$. There may, in addition, be a stochastic term arising from various measurement or administrative errors, or imperfect take-up of benefits. If $T(x_i, v_i) \neq a^*(u_i) T^*(x_i^*)$, the government has to accept some undesired reranking in terms of adult equivalent incomes. A desire to increase the progressivity associated with $T^*(x_i^*)$ may involve a trade-off whereby reranking (in terms of adult equivalent incomes) increases. Hence, the government may not necessarily wish to reduce reranking to zero, given its distributional objectives and the administrative constraints imposed.

[7] It can be seen that the introduction of a non-linear term in (4), such as $t_2 x_i^{*2}$, involves the addition of a term $\{t_2/a_i^*\} x_i^2$ in (5) so that the tax rate applied to the square of income also depends on equivalent household size.

4

This expression shows that reranking of untransformed incomes can easily arise; that is, for some pairs (i,j), $x_i > x_j$ while $y_i < y_j$. However, this reranking is a deliberate aim of those designing the tax and transfer system.

Suppose that an independent judge wishes to examine the redistributive effect of this tax system using, instead of the government's equivalence scales, an alternative set of scales, say a'_i. The corresponding measured adult equivalent incomes, x'_i and y'_i, are related by:

$$y'_i = (1 - t_1) x'_i + \beta \frac{a^*_i}{a'_i} \tag{7}$$

Hence, reranking is observed unless a'_i is distributionally equivalent to a^*_i such that $a^*_i/a'_i = c$, where c is a constant. The next section examines in further detail the relationship between reranking and the equivalence scales used.

3 Equivalence Scales and Reranking

This section considers the question of how measured reranking varies when the equivalence scales applied differ from those used by policy makers. To generalise the linear case discussed above, suppose that the government imposes a polynomial tax function, such that:

$$T^* (x^*_i) = \sum_{j=0}^{K} \beta_j (x^*_i)^j \tag{8}$$

This function is increasing and convex with a slope less than 1. Consider the effect on measured reranking of adopting an equivalence scale, a'_i, that is possibly different from the scale, a^*_i, used by the government. The aim here is to examine how measured reranking varies as the proportional difference between a^* and a' varies.

Substituting these assumptions into (2), and multiplying throughout by a^*_i/a'_i gives:

$$y'_i = x'_i - \frac{a^*_i}{a'_i} \sum_{j=0}^{K} \beta_j (x^*_i)^j \tag{9}$$

5

which may be compared with (7). Write the proportional difference between the two sets of scales as:

$$\frac{a_i^* - a_i'}{a_i^*} = \mu + \phi_i \tag{10}$$

where $E(\phi_i) = 0$. After some rearrangement, using $x_i^* = x_i' a_i'/a_i^*$, it can be shown that:

$$y_i' = x_i' - \sum_{j=0}^{K} \beta_j x_i'^j (1 - \mu - \phi_i)^{j-1} \tag{11}$$

Rewrite (11) by adding and subtracting a term $(1-\mu)^{j-1}$ to $(1-\mu-\phi_i)^{j-1}$ so that:

$$
\begin{aligned}
y_i' &= x_i' - \frac{1}{(1-\mu)} \sum_{j=0}^{K} \beta_j \left\{ x_i' (1-\mu) \right\}^j - \tau_i \\
&= x_i' - \frac{1}{(1-\mu)} T^* \left(x_i' (1-\mu) \right) - \tau_i
\end{aligned}
\tag{12}
$$

In (12), all of the individual-specific effects, ϕ_i, are gathered in τ_i, where:[8]

$$\tau_i = \sum_{j=0}^{K} \beta_j x_i'^j \left[(1 - \mu - \phi_i)^{j-1} - (1 - \mu)^{j-1} \right] \tag{13}$$

Thus if $a_i^*, a_i' > 0$, and $\phi_i = 0$ for all i, then no reranking of x_i' and y_i' arises.[9] In this case, the scales a' and a^* embody the same value judgements and are analytically equivalent for the measurement of relative inequality. However, when $\phi_i \neq 0$, so that $\tau_i \neq 0$, for some i, reranking of x_i' and y_i' takes place.

Consider the effect on measured reranking of adjusting a' toward a^*. This adjustment implies that the relative positions of individuals in the associated pre-tax and post-tax equivalent income distributions approach the rankings that the government implicitly makes. The extent of this convergence is directly related to the variance of ϕ_i. As the variance of ϕ_i tends toward zero, it can be seen from (13) that τ_i, and hence observed reranking, also

---

[8] For the simple linear function discussed in section 2 it can be seen that $y_i' = x_i' - [\beta_0 + \beta_1 x_i' (1 - \mu)] / (1 - \mu) - [\beta_0 \phi_i / \{(1 - \mu)(1 - \mu - \phi_i)\}]$

[9] If $a_i^*, a_i' > 0$ for all i, then $\mu < 1$.

tend toward zero. This result is unrelated to the size of μ, since μ enters τ_i only through cross product terms with ϕ_i, and $E(\phi_i) = 0$ by assumption.

Equation (12) reveals that measured reranking is a function of the variance of τ_i. If the variance falls, observed reranking (for large populations) is reduced. As the general magnitude of the a_i's increase, corresponding measures of adult equivalent income fall, and hence, from equation (13), there is a tendency for the variance of τ_i to be reduced. In addition, from (10), as the general magnitude of a_i' increases, μ is decreased. The impact on measured reranking of μ is, however, likely to be small, particularly when a_i' is (distributionally) close to a_i^*. Increasing the magnitude of the a_i's therefore tends to reduce measured reranking.

Consequently, the impact on measured reranking of varying the equivalence scales used can be divided into two effects. The direct effect relates to the variance of ϕ_i, and tends to increase measured reranking as the equivalence scale used departs from the government's implicit scale. The indirect effect tends to decrease measured reranking as the magnitude of the scales used increases. The impact on measured reranking of the indirect effect may oppose that of the direct effect and, since the relative strength of the two is unknown, it is not possible to tell which dominates.[10] These results suggest that the scale that minimises reranking is not necessarily associated with the equivalence scale implicitly adopted by policy makers. The following section considers these features in more detail using a simulation analysis.

4   A Simulation Analysis

This section examines the relationship between reranking and equivalence scales using a number of simulation analyses. Equivalence scales are assumed to depend on the number of persons in the tax unit, n_i. All simulations assume

---

[10]This conclusion is true unless observed reranking varies directly with the magnitude of a', in which case the direct effect must dominate.

that x_i and n_i are jointly lognormally distributed as:

$$\Lambda \left(x_i, n_i \,|\, \mu_x, \mu_n, \sigma_x^2, \sigma_n^2, \rho_{x,n} \right) \tag{14}$$

where $\mu_x = 10.4$ and $\mu_n = 0.7$ denote the mean of logarithms of x and n, $\sigma_x^2 = 0.3$ and $\sigma_n^2 = 0.25$ denote their respective variance of logarithms, and $\rho_{x,n}$ is the correlation coefficient between the logarithms of x_i and n_i.[11]

Post-tax income is calculated from x_i and a_i^* using the simple linear tax function given in equation (4), where $t_1 = 0.45$. The value of β is adjusted endogenously, using $\beta = 0.35 \exp(\mu_{x^*})$, in order to limit the impact of different a_i^* values on the progressivity of the equivalent tax function.

Reranking is measured using the Atkinson-Plotnick measure, R.[12] This is based on the Lorenz curve and the concentration curve of post-tax (adult equivalent) income. The former is obtained by ranking individuals according to y' while the latter ranks by x'. The concentration curve gives rise to the concentration index, $C_{y'}$, that takes the same basic form as a Gini measure, except for the different ranking. The Gini inequality measure, $G_{y'}$, is based on the Lorenz curve. Hence:

$$R = G_{y'} - C_{y'} \tag{15}$$

When the ordering of individuals by y' is the same as the ordering by x', it is clear that $G_{y'} = C_{y'}$ and R is zero.

4.1   A Simple Specification of Equivalence Scales

In order to focus on a limited number of variables, suppose initially that a_i^* depends simply on n_i, such that:

$$a_i^* = n_i^\theta \tag{16}$$

---

[11]The parameter values used here correspond approximately to Australian data, for which the assumption of joint log-normality provides a reasonable fit.
[12]See Atkinson (1979) and Plotnick (1981).

This specification was used by Buhmann *et al.* (1988), who showed that adjusting θ provided an approximation to a wide range of scales in use. Consider the case where the scale used by an independent observer to calculate progressivity and reranking takes a similar form:

$$a'(n_i) = n_i^{\hat{\theta}} \tag{17}$$

The only difference between the equivalence scale that underlies the tax system, a^*, and a' is consequently the value adopted for $\hat{\theta}$.

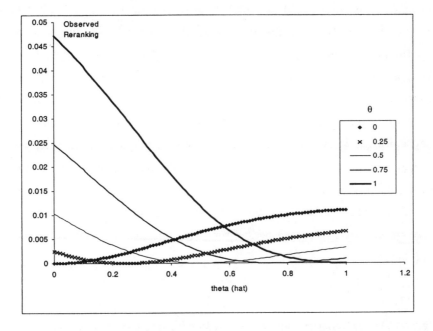

Figure 1: Observed Reranking versus $\hat{\theta}$ - Varying θ

A simulated population of 10,000 tax units was drawn from the joint distribution in (14), with the correlation between n_i and x_i set to 0. Figure 1 displays the relation between observed reranking and assumed $\hat{\theta}$, for five alternative values of θ. This figure shows that the shape of the relation between $\hat{\theta}$ and observed reranking displays a distinct minimum at the point where $\hat{\theta} = \theta$ for each of the five values of θ considered. As θ is increased, measures of reranking, obtained for deviations from the government's scale, increase.

These results are consistent with equation (7), which indicates that measured reranking is zero when $\hat{\theta} = \theta$. Larger measures of reranking were obtained for higher values of θ for two reasons. First, despite the endogenous specification of β, the progressivity of the tax function (as measured by the difference between the Gini inequality measures of pre-tax and post-tax adult equivalent income) increases from 0.1168 when $\theta = 0$, to 0.1541 when $\theta = 1$. This increase is equivalent to an increase in the tax function coefficients for a given pre-tax (equivalent) income distribution. From (13), an increase in the tax function coefficients increases measured reranking. This factor accounts for most of the observed variation between the magnitude of the series displayed in Figure 1.[13] Second, for values of $\hat{\theta} < \theta$, both the direct and indirect effects tend to increase observed reranking. In contrast, when $\hat{\theta} > \theta$, the direct effect tends to increase, while the indirect effect decreases measured reranking. Hence, the reranking measures obtained for values of $\hat{\theta} < \theta$ are greater than those where $\hat{\theta} > \theta$. The impact of this effect can be seen by comparing the measures of reranking obtained for values of $\hat{\theta}$ above and below θ, where $\theta = 0.5$.

As the parameters of a scale are varied, the impact on the magnitude of x_i' (and hence the indirect effect) depends on the relationship between x_i and the tax unit characteristics included in a_i'. In addition, the relationship between x_i' and ϕ_i also depends on how x_i relates to the characteristics included in a_i'. These observations imply that the relation between a_i' and x_i affects the intensity of both the direct and indirect effects. The effect of relating a_i' to x_i is considered by varying the correlation coefficient between n_i and x_i.

---

[13]Simulations which held the progressivity of the tax system constant by generating x^* exogenously were also undertaken. These displayed substantially less variation between the magnitude of the reranking measures obtained for the series displayed in Figure 1.

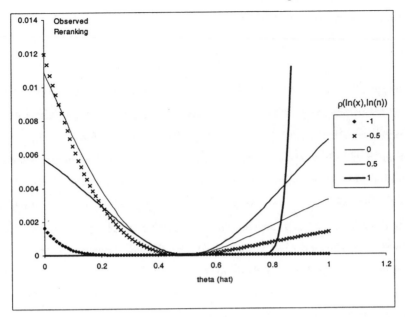

Figure 2: Observed Reranking versus $\hat{\theta}$ - Varying $\rho_{x,n}$.

The results derived for five correlation coefficients, between -1 and +1, are displayed in Figure 2, where $\theta = 0.5$.

Each of the series displayed in Figure 2 share a minimum where $\hat{\theta} = \theta$. Comparisons between the five series indicate that the correlation between x_i and n_i affects the relation between observed reranking and $\hat{\theta}$ in two important ways.[14] First, the curvature of the relation is affected; the rate of change of observed reranking with $\hat{\theta}$ decreases below, and increases above, θ as the correlation between x_i and n_i increases. This effect is most evident when comparing the $\rho_{x,n} = 0$ and $\rho_{x,n} = 0.5$ series in Figure 2.

The impact on reranking of the relationship between n_i and x_i can be

---

[14]Like the analysis of the previous figure, comparisons between the series displayed in Figure 2 are complicated by differences in the progressivity of taxation.

viewed in practical terms by noting that, for the scales specified:

$$x'_i = x^*_i n_i^{\left(\theta - \hat{\theta}\right)} \tag{18}$$

Consequently, when $\left(\theta - \hat{\theta}\right) > 0$, x'_i is an increasing function of both x^*_i and n_i. This implies that when x^*_i is positively correlated with n_i, the ranking associated with the distribution of x^*_i is likely to be reinforced in the distribution of x'_i. A positive relation between x'_i and n_i consequently tends to reduce observed reranking as the correlation between x^*_i and n_i increases. Conversely, when $\left(\theta - \hat{\theta}\right) < 0$, x'_i is a decreasing function of n_i, which implies that, when x^*_i is positively correlated with n_i, the ranking associated with the distribution of x^*_i is likely to be weakened in the distribution of x'_i, leading to increased observed reranking.

The relationship between x_i and n_i affects the relationship between x^*_i and n_i. When x_i and n_i are negatively correlated, a large x_i is likely to be associated with a low n_i, resulting in a large x^*_i. When x_i and n_i are positively correlated, the relationship between n_i and x^*_i depends on the equivalence scale. For the case considered, it is shown in the appendix that x^*_i is positively correlated with n_i if and only if:

$$\frac{\rho_{x,n}\sigma_x}{\sigma_n} > \theta \tag{19}$$

which means that the regression coefficient, in the joint distribution of x and n, must exceed the government's scale parameter.

The second effect of $\rho_{x,n}$ on the relationship between observed reranking and $\hat{\theta}$ displayed in Figure 2 is the possibility that reranking may be minimised by a range of $\hat{\theta}$ values. This effect is closely related to the first. Consider the case where the correlation between x^*_i and n_i is equal to one, such that $x^*_i = A + B n_i$, with $B > 0$. Substituting this specification for x^*_i into equation (18), and taking the first derivative with respect to n_i, gives:

$$\frac{\partial x'_i}{\partial n_i} = A \left(\theta - \hat{\theta}\right) n_i^{\left(\theta - \hat{\theta} - 1\right)} + \left(1 + \theta - \hat{\theta}\right) B n_i^{\left(\theta - \hat{\theta}\right)} \tag{20}$$

12

This partial derivative is greater than zero so long as:

$$\hat{\theta} < \theta + \frac{Bn}{A + Bn} \tag{21}$$

Since $Bn > 0$ and $A + Bn = x^* > 0$, any value of $\hat{\theta}$ up to a limit that is greater than θ produces a distribution of x' that has the same ranking as x^*. This result is reflected in Figure 2. The indeterminacy is perhaps not surprising: as the correlation between income and the equivalence scale tends toward either $+1$ or -1 the need for an equivalence scale is reduced since any required adjustment can be inferred directly from income and incorporated into the tax function.

4.2   An Alternative Specification of Equivalence Scales

Consider the case where other unspecified considerations enter into the government's scale, so that a_i^* is defined as:

$$a_i^* = \left(n_i^\theta\right)^\kappa (\xi_i)^{(1-\kappa)} \tag{22}$$

Hence a_i^* is considered to be a weighted geometric mean of the scale used earlier, n_i^θ, and the term, ξ_i, with weights κ and $(1 - \kappa)$ respectively. The closest approximation to (22) that can be achieved by the scale $a_i' = n_i^{\hat{\theta}}$ is to set $\hat{\theta} = \theta\kappa$. Indeed, (22) is equivalent to having a multiplicative error term on the previous scale, since a_i^* can be written as $a_i^* = n_i^\alpha u_i$, where $\alpha = \theta\kappa$ and $u_i = \xi^{1-\kappa}$.

The variable ξ_i is assumed to be distributed log-normally as:

$$\Lambda\left(\xi_i | \mu_\xi, \sigma_\xi^2\right) \tag{23}$$

Hence:

$$a_i^* \text{ is } \Lambda\left(a_i^* | \mu_{a^*}, \sigma_{a^*}^2\right) \tag{24}$$

where:

$$\mu_{a^*} = \theta\kappa\mu_n + (1 - \kappa)\,\mu_\xi \tag{25}$$

13

$$\sigma_{a^*}^2 = (\theta\kappa)^2 \sigma_n^2 + 2\theta\kappa(1-\kappa)\rho_{n,\xi}\sigma_n\sigma_\xi + (1-\kappa)^2\sigma_\xi^2 \qquad (26)$$

The parameters of ξ_i are specified to keep the mean and variance of a_i^* constant at the values $\theta\mu_n$ and $\theta^2\sigma_n^2$, irrespective of the value of κ.[15] This framework enables the relative importance of n_i and ξ_i in determining a_i^* to be exogenously specified by adjusting the parameter κ.

It was mentioned in section 2 that if the ratio a'/a^* is constant, then a_i' is distributionally equivalent to a_i^*. The coefficient of variation of the ratio (a_i'/a_i^*), can consequently be used to evaluate how closely an equivalence scale, $a_i' = n_i^{\hat\theta}$, reflects the scale a_i^*.

Three populations, each of 10,000 tax units, were simulated for alternative assumptions about the correlations between the relevant variables. For each population, results were obtained using a range of values of θ and κ. Table 1 shows the values of $\hat\theta$ that minimise observed reranking, $\hat\theta_R$, and the coefficient of variation, $\hat\theta_{CV}$. In practice, it would obviously not be possible to compute the coefficient of variation; these are useful here for evaluating $\hat\theta_R$.

The three cases considered in Table 1 assume $\rho_{x,n} = 0$, so that n_i, and therefore a_i', is independent of x_i. Focusing on the measures obtained when $\rho_{n,\xi} = \rho_{x,\xi} = 0$, the values of $\hat\theta_{CV}$ are all approximately equal to $\theta\kappa$, as expected given the specification of a_i^*. The values of $\hat\theta$ that minimise reranking are greater than those that minimise the coefficient of variation; this result applies to all three populations considered in Table 1.[16] This result is expected given that the indirect effect tends to increase observed reranking as $\hat\theta$ decreases. Where the indirect effect does not dominate (where $\hat\theta_R \neq 1$), the values obtained for $\hat\theta_R$ are in the vicinity of $\hat\theta_{CV}$.

The results for $\hat\theta_R$ indicate that the indirect effect is larger where θ is high. This arises due to the impact of a^* on the progressivity of the tax function.

---

[15] $\mu_\xi = \theta\mu_n$ and σ_ξ is obtained by solving the appropriate quadratic.

[16] The small disparity associated with the case where $\theta = 0.3$ and $\kappa = 0.1$ can be attributed to differences in the weights applied by the coefficient of variation and the Gini.

Table 1: Measures of $\hat{\theta}$ that Minimise Observed Reranking and CV

κ	θ	$\rho_{x,\xi} = 0$ $\rho_{n,\xi} = 0$		$\rho_{x,\xi} = 0.5$ $\rho_{n,\xi} = 0$		$\rho_{x,\xi} = 0$ $\rho_{n,\xi} = 0.5$	
		$\hat{\theta}_R$	$\hat{\theta}_{CV}$	$\hat{\theta}_R$	$\hat{\theta}_{CV}$	$\hat{\theta}_R$	$\hat{\theta}_{CV}$
0.1	0.1	0.01	0.01	0.01	0.01	0.06	0.06
0.1	0.3	0.03	0.04	0.03	0.03	0.19	0.18
0.1	0.5	0.08	0.06	0.08	0.05	0.36	0.29
0.1	0.7	0.09	0.06	1.00	0.06	1.00	0.42
0.1	0.9	1.00	0.08	1.00	0.08	1.00	0.53
0.3	0.1	0.03	0.03	0.03	0.03	0.08	0.08
0.3	0.3	0.10	0.09	0.11	0.09	0.25	0.23
0.3	0.5	0.19	0.14	0.23	0.14	0.47	0.39
0.3	0.7	0.39	0.21	1.00	0.21	1.00	0.55
0.3	0.9	1.00	0.26	1.00	0.27	1.00	0.69
0.5	0.1	0.05	0.05	0.05	0.05	0.09	0.09
0.5	0.3	0.16	0.15	0.18	0.15	0.29	0.27
0.5	0.5	0.29	0.25	0.38	0.25	0.54	0.47
0.5	0.7	0.57	0.34	1.00	0.35	1.00	0.66
0.5	0.9	1.00	0.45	1.00	0.47	1.00	0.85
0.7	0.1	0.07	0.07	0.07	0.07	0.11	0.10
0.7	0.3	0.22	0.21	0.24	0.21	0.33	0.31
0.7	0.5	0.40	0.35	0.48	0.36	0.58	0.53
0.7	0.7	0.64	0.47	0.99	0.49	0.95	0.74
0.7	0.9	1.00	0.64	1.00	0.63	1.00	0.95
0.9	0.1	0.09	0.09	0.09	0.09	0.11	0.11
0.9	0.3	0.27	0.27	0.29	0.27	0.34	0.34
0.9	0.5	0.47	0.45	0.52	0.45	0.58	0.56
0.9	0.7	0.70	0.63	0.81	0.63	0.86	0.79
0.9	0.9	0.99	0.81	1.00	0.81	1.00	1.00

15

Table 2: Values of $\hat{\theta}$ that Minimise Reranking and CV: $\rho_{x^*,n} = 0$

κ	θ	$\rho_{x^*,\xi} = 0$ $\rho_{n,\xi} = 0$		$\rho_{x^*,\xi} = 0$ $\rho_{n,\xi} = 0.5$		$\rho_{x^*,\xi} = 0.5$ $\rho_{n,\xi} = 0$	
		$\hat{\theta}_R$	$\hat{\theta}_{CV}$	$\hat{\theta}_R$	$\hat{\theta}_{CV}$	$\hat{\theta}_R$	$\hat{\theta}_{CV}$
0.1	0.1	0.01	0.01	0.01	0.01	0.06	0.06
0.1	0.3	0.03	0.03	0.04	0.03	0.17	0.17
0.1	0.5	0.05	0.05	0.05	0.05	0.29	0.29
0.1	0.7	0.08	0.07	0.08	0.06	0.40	0.41
0.1	0.9	0.08	0.10	0.09	0.09	0.55	0.54
0.3	0.1	0.03	0.03	0.03	0.03	0.08	0.08
0.3	0.3	0.09	0.09	0.09	0.09	0.23	0.23
0.3	0.5	0.14	0.15	0.15	0.15	0.39	0.39
0.3	0.7	0.21	0.21	0.20	0.20	0.52	0.54
0.3	0.9	0.30	0.26	0.26	0.26	0.69	0.72
0.5	0.1	0.05	0.05	0.05	0.05	0.09	0.09
0.5	0.3	0.15	0.15	0.15	0.15	0.28	0.28
0.5	0.5	0.25	0.25	0.25	0.25	0.46	0.47
0.5	0.7	0.36	0.35	0.38	0.36	0.64	0.66
0.5	0.9	0.47	0.45	0.46	0.45	0.82	0.84
0.7	0.1	0.07	0.07	0.07	0.07	0.11	0.11
0.7	0.3	0.21	0.21	0.21	0.21	0.32	0.32
0.7	0.5	0.35	0.35	0.35	0.35	0.52	0.52
0.7	0.7	0.51	0.50	0.48	0.48	0.74	0.74
0.7	0.9	0.63	0.61	0.63	0.62	0.96	0.95
0.9	0.1	0.09	0.09	0.09	0.09	0.11	0.11
0.9	0.3	0.27	0.27	0.27	0.27	0.33	0.34
0.9	0.5	0.45	0.45	0.45	0.45	0.56	0.56
0.9	0.7	0.64	0.63	0.63	0.63	0.78	0.78
0.9	0.9	0.81	0.81	0.81	0.81	1.00	1.00

16

As mentioned with regard to Figure 1, despite the endogenous specification adopted for β, increasing a^* increases the progressivity of the tax function. This is equivalent to increasing the coefficients of the tax function for a given pre-tax income distribution. From (13), it is evident that increasing the coefficients increases the impact of the indirect effect, consistent with the results obtained. The effects of holding the progressivity of taxation constant are examined below.

Where $\rho_{x,\xi} = 0.5$, the values of $\hat{\theta}_{CV}$ are also approximately equal to $\theta\kappa$, consistent with the specification of a^*. In this case the indirect effect is larger where θ is high, as before, and where κ is low. This relationship with κ may be considered in terms of the impact that n_i has on a_i^*. When $\kappa = 1$, a_i^* is entirely determined by n_i, which diminishes the indirect effect associated with varying $\hat{\theta}$. As κ decreases, the impact on a_i^* of n_i is reduced and hence the relationship between measured reranking and $\hat{\theta}$ is driven by the indirect effect. Comparing the values of $\hat{\theta}_{CV}$ with $\hat{\theta}_R$ indicates that the indirect effect has a more pronounced impact when $\rho_{x,\xi} = 0.5$ than for the case where $\rho_{x,\xi} = 0$. This result is driven by the varying progressivity of the tax function, as explored below.

When $\rho_{n,\xi} = 0.5$, $\hat{\theta}_{CV} > \theta\kappa$, unlike the other two populations considered in Table 1. This arises because a_i^* is determined, for any $\kappa \neq 1$, by both n_i and ξ_i. If ξ_i is positively correlated with n_i, a stronger relation exists between n_i and a_i^* than if n_i and ξ_i were uncorrelated. The effect of $\rho_{n,\xi}$ on $\hat{\theta}_{CV}$ and $\hat{\theta}_R$ can be considered as a form of omitted variable bias, and may lead to unexpected results. If, for example, n_i and ξ_i are negatively correlated and κ is low, an inverse relation may be observed between a_i^* and n_i, and hence a negative value obtained for $\hat{\theta}_{CV}$ and $\hat{\theta}_R$. The apparent effect of increasing the correlation between n_i and ξ_i on the impact of the indirect effect is driven by associated differences in the progressivity of taxation.

The results in Table 1 were obtained for given distributions of x and n, which are of particular interest because they can be observed in practice.

17

However, the endogenous nature of x^* implies that the progressivity of taxation varies with the specification of a^*. This complicates comparison of the various series due to the associated impact of the indirect effect. To avoid this contamination, the simulation analysis was modified to generate the distribution of x^* exogenously (where associated values of x were obtained by calculating x^*a^*). Corresponding results are displayed in Table 2.

As can be seen from Table 2, the modified simulation procedure has no significant effect on the values obtained for $\hat{\theta}_{CV}$. This result reflects the fact that the values of $\hat{\theta}_{CV}$ are independent of tax progressivity and the indirect effect. Comparison of the $\hat{\theta}_R$ values displayed in Tables 1 and 2 reveals that the impact of the indirect effect is substantially reduced when the progressivity of taxes (in terms of adult equivalent incomes) is held constant for many of the cases considered. In fact, the close correspondence between $\hat{\theta}_R$ and $\hat{\theta}_{CV}$ displayed in Table 2 suggests that the indirect effect has a minor impact on measured reranking relative to the direct effect when progressivity is held constant at a level that is consistent with observed data. This result supports the previous discussion, and the proposition that the scale which minimises measured reranking is likely to be in the neighbourhood of the government's implicit scale.

The effects of correlation between x_i and n_i are considered in Table 3, where $\rho_{x,n}$ takes the values 0.2 and -0.2. The measures of $\hat{\theta}$ displayed in Table 3 follow directly from the associated discussion undertaken where $\kappa = 1$. Specifically, it was mentioned with regard to Figure 2 that when a positive correlation exists between n_i and x_i, measured reranking falls below θ and increases above θ. This relation tends to decrease the value of $\hat{\theta}_R$, particularly for higher values of θ.

These simulation results indicate that, if the characteristics that underlie the equivalence scale used to measure reranking are uncorrelated with income, it is likely that the scale that minimises reranking will closely reflect, from a distributional perspective, the scale that underlies the tax and trans-

18

Table 3: Values of $\hat{\theta}$ that Minimise Observed Reranking and CV: $\rho_{x,\xi} = \rho_{n,\xi} = 0$

κ	θ	$\rho_{x,n} = 0.2$		$\rho_{x,n} = -0.2$	
		$\hat{\theta}_R$	$\hat{\theta}_{CV}$	$\hat{\theta}_R$	$\hat{\theta}_{CV}$
0.1	0.1	0.01	0.01	0.01	0.01
0.1	0.3	0.01	0.03	0.05	0.03
0.1	0.5	0.00	0.04	0.14	0.04
0.1	0.7	0.00	0.09	1.00	0.07
0.1	0.9	0.00	0.10	1.00	0.10
0.3	0.1	0.03	0.03	0.03	0.03
0.3	0.3	0.07	0.08	0.12	0.09
0.3	0.5	0.13	0.14	0.27	0.15
0.3	0.7	0.21	0.22	1.00	0.21
0.3	0.9	1.00	0.29	1.00	0.26
0.5	0.1	0.05	0.05	0.05	0.05
0.5	0.3	0.15	0.15	0.17	0.15
0.5	0.5	0.26	0.25	0.37	0.26
0.5	0.7	0.43	0.35	1.00	0.34
0.5	0.9	1.00	0.46	1.00	0.47
0.7	0.1	0.07	0.07	0.07	0.07
0.7	0.3	0.21	0.21	0.23	0.21
0.7	0.5	0.36	0.35	0.44	0.35
0.7	0.7	0.58	0.50	1.00	0.50
0.7	0.9	1.00	0.63	1.00	0.62
0.9	0.1	0.09	0.09	0.09	0.09
0.9	0.3	0.27	0.27	0.28	0.27
0.9	0.5	0.47	0.46	0.49	0.45
0.9	0.7	0.68	0.64	0.74	0.63
0.9	0.9	0.93	0.81	1.00	0.81

19

fer system. Interpretation of such a scale is, however, complicated by any correlation that may exist between the characteristics of the scale used to measure reranking and those of the scale that (implicitly) underlies the tax system. When the characteristics of the scale used to measure reranking are correlated with income, the scale that minimises reranking is likely to depart from the scale that underlies the tax system. The extent of this departure is dependent on the scale used, the degree of correlation, and the associated intensity of the direct and indirect effects. To consider these issues in an applied context, the next section examines the relation between the equivalence scale and reranking using Australian and UK data.

5   An Application

This section explores the effect on measured reranking of varying the parameters of a given equivalence scale using household data for Australia and the UK. First the data sources are briefly described, after which empirical results are reported.

5.1   The Data

Australian data were obtained from the 1993 Household Expenditure Survey (HES), the most recent edition produced by the Australian Bureau of Statistics (ABS). This survey provides data for a representative cross-section of 8,389 households, including the age of household members, total household income, government benefits, implicit taxes (both direct and indirect taxes), and expenditure.[17] Households are used as the unit for analysis due to the shared expenditure that exists between household members. The raw sample was edited to remove any households not including at least one member over the age of 17 years, those with negative net income or expenditure, or where

---

[17]Indirect taxes were imputed by the ABS from household income and expenditure data.

the data exhibited inconsistencies. This provided a clean sample of 7,825 households.

The UK data were obtained from the 1993 Family Expenditure Survey (FES), produced by the Central Statistical Office (CSO).[18] The FES provides similar household data to the HES, with the exception that indirect taxes are not included. Indirect taxes were imputed by assuming, a 17.5 per cent Value Added Tax (VAT) imposed on tax-inclusive expenditure (excluding food and domestic fuel), a 5 per cent VAT on domestic fuel, a 22 per cent *ad valorum* Excise duty on tobacco, and a 13 per cent *ad valorum* tax Excise duty on alcohol.[19] The FES provides data for 6,979 households, from which 23 households were omitted due to data deficiencies.

5.2   Empirical Results

Measures of household income were adjusted for family size and composition using a variant of the equivalence scale examined in section 4. Let $n_{d,i}$ and $n_{c,i}$ refer respectively to the number of adults and children in tax unit i, and:

$$a'_i = (n_{d,i} + \Phi n_{c,i})^\theta \qquad (27)$$

where $0 \leq (\theta \text{ and } \Phi) \leq 1$. This formulation was used by, for example, Cutler and Katz (1992), Banks and Johnson (1994) and Jenkins and Cowell (1994).

To obtain a detailed picture of the effect of selecting different combinations of θ and Φ on reranking, the unit square including all conceivable combinations of θ and Φ was divided into a grid of 31 intervals per coefficient. The values of R associated with the intersections of the grid are plotted as surface projections for Australia and the UK respectively in Figures 3 and 5. Figures 4 and 6 provide the associated topographic maps, which divide the observed variation into forty equally spaced iso-reranking lines.

---

[18]The CSO is now called the Office of National Statistics (ONS).

[19]Tax schedules were derived from an on-line report by the Institute for Fiscal Studies (IFS). The 13 per cent tax on alcohol is an estimate derived from the associated per unit excise.

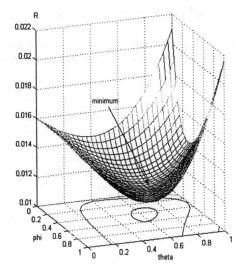

Figure 3: Surface Plot of Measured Reranking by Equivalence Scale Parameters: Australia

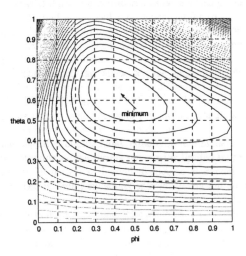

Figure 4: Topographic Plot of Measured Reranking by Equivalence Scale Parameters: Australia

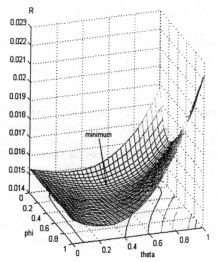

Figure 5: Surface Plot of Measured Reranking by Equivalence Scale Parameters: UK

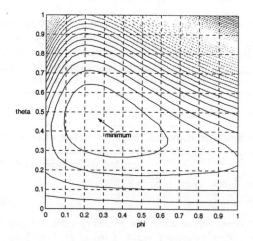

Figure 6: Topographic Plot of Measured Reranking by Equivalence Scale Parameters: UK

Comparing Figure 3 with 5, the range of reranking measures associated with the various equivalence scale parameters considered is similar for the Australian and UK data. In both figures, the corners of the unit square all form local maxima. The shape of the relations displayed in Figures 3 to 6 explains the result obtained by Nolan (1987), who expressed surprise on finding that adult equivalent incomes derived using 1977 FES data and equivalence scales based on 1977 Support Benefit rates showed more reranking than unadjusted incomes. In fact a large set of combinations of θ and Φ lead to higher measures of reranking than the case were $\theta = \Phi = 0$, particularly for the UK data. The equivalence scale that most accurately reflects the benefits system may be defined within this set due principally to the value of θ.

Specifically, the value of θ that most accurately reflects the benefits system is likely to be greater than the value that minimises measured reranking, for two reasons. First, given that the benefits system focuses on the low end of the income distribution, it is likely that the associated scales over-state the impact of family size compared with the entire tax and transfer system. Second, positive correlation between household size and income implies that the coefficients that minimise measured reranking are likely to depart from those that most accurately reflect the scales implicit in the entire tax and transfer system.

To examine how measured reranking is likely to be affected by correlation between income and the characteristics of the scales in equation (27), it is useful to adopt the framework used to analyse the series displayed in Figure 2. For the scales analysed here, (18) becomes:

$$x_i' = x_i^* \frac{(n_{d,i} + \Phi^* n_{c,i})^{\theta^*}}{(n_{d,i} + \Phi' n_{c,i})^{\theta'}} \tag{28}$$

By taking the partial derivative with respect to $n_{d,i}$, it can be shown from (28) that x_i' is increasing in $n_{d,i}$ if:

$$\theta^* (n_{d,i} + \Phi' n_{c,i}) > \theta' (n_{d,i} + \Phi^* n_{c,i}) \tag{29}$$

Similarly, it can be shown that x_i' is increasing in $n_{c,i}$ if:

$$\Phi^* \left(\theta^* - \theta'\right) n_{c,i} > \left(\theta' - \frac{\Phi^*}{\Phi'}\theta^*\right) n_{d,i} \tag{30}$$

The correlation between n_d and x based on the Australian data is 0.4340, while the correlation between n_c and x is 0.1193. The correlations derived from UK data are also both positive, taking the values of 0.3621, and 0.0964 respectively. These observations make it likely that x^* is positively correlated with both n_d and n_c. When x^* is positively correlated with n_d and n_c, (29) and (30) imply (as in section 4) that measured reranking is likely to be reduced where $\theta^* > \theta'$, and $\Phi' > \Phi^*$. Hence the parameter values that minimise reranking are likely to understate θ^* and overstate Φ^*.

As indicated by Figures 3 to 6, measured reranking tends to increase more slowly from the global minimum as scale parameters are altered toward, rather than away from, the $\theta = 0$ axis. Since both of the effects described above imply that the value of θ that most accurately reflects the benefits system is greater than the value that minimises reranking, it is possible (and, it may be said, likely) that the scale that underlies the benefits system is associated with higher measured reranking than the unadjusted income distribution.

The global minimum is at the point where $\theta = 0.6333$ and $\Phi = 0.4333$ for Australian data, and $\theta = 0.4667$ and $\Phi = 0.2667$ for the UK. The scale that minimises measured reranking based on the Australian data consequently makes a larger adjustment for household size and composition than the scale calculated for UK data. The question arises as to what, if anything, this result implies regarding the scales implicit in the respective tax and transfer systems.

It is evident from the above discussion that one of the primary considerations associated with using Figures 3 to 6 to make inferences regarding the scales that implicitly underlie the Australian and UK tax and transfer systems is the correlation between income and household size. It was found above that the values of θ and Φ that minimise reranking are likely to be, respectively, less than, and greater than, the values that most closely reflect the associated tax and transfer systems. However, it is not possible to infer the extent of the departure between the scales that underlie the tax and transfer system, and those that minimise reranking.

Specifically, although the correlation measures between income and household size derived from Australian data are greater than those for the UK, equation (28) indicates that it is the correlation between equivalent income, x^*, and household size that is of primary relevance. While the correlation between x and household size provides an indication of the associated correlation between x^* and household size, it provides no definitive information, as discussed in section 4.

Consider, for example, the case where the values of θ and Φ that most accurately reflect the Australian tax and transfer system are, respectively, 0.68 and 0.18. For the UK, let the same parameters take the values 0.72 and 0.16.[20] Under these conditions, the correlation between x^* and n_d, based on Australian data is 0.1452, while the correlation between x^* and n_c is 0.0243. Both of these correlations are *less* than those derived from the UK data, which equal, respectively, 0.1506 and 0.0255.

Since it is not possible to measure the correlation between x^* and the characteristics that underlie the equivalence scale used to measure reranking, it is not possible to infer the expected magnitude of the indirect effect. This implies that any conclusions about the equivalence scale that underlies a tax and transfer system that is derived from an analysis of the relationship between equivalence scales and reranking must be qualified.

The issue of comparing the scales that implicitly underlie two different tax and transfer systems is further complicated by differences in the profile observed between equivalence scale and reranking. Comparison of the Aus-

---

[20]These values are consistent with the expectation that $\theta^* > \theta'$ and $\Phi^* < \Phi'$ described previously.

tralian and UK profiles displayed in Figures 3 to 6, for example, reveals that the Australian profile exhibits more curvature about the global minimum. This is highlighted by the larger areas defined by the iso-reranking lines that surround the global minimum in the topographic map calculated from UK as opposed to Australian data. The observation implies that a larger indirect effect is required to motivate a given difference between the scale that minimises measured reranking, and the scale that underlies the tax system, for the Australian data compared with the UK.

Thus no definitive comparison can be made between the scales that implicitly underlie the Australian and UK tax and transfer systems, based on the analysis presented here. However, the analysis provides a means of understanding and interpreting the observed relationship between equivalence scales and the reranking effects of taxation. Furthermore, the framework enables inferences to be drawn regarding the properties of the scales that implicitly underly a tax system.

6   Conclusions

This paper has examined the relationship between equivalence scales and the reranking effects of taxation, based on measures of equivalent income. In undertaking this study, the related issue of identifying an equivalence scale that underlies tax and transfer policy has also been explored.

Two separate, but related, effects were identified analytically as contributing to the impact on reranking of varying the equivalence scale. The first, referred to as the direct effect, increases reranking as the equivalence scale used for measurement departs from the scale that underlies tax and transfer policy. The second, referred to as the indirect effect, tends to increase reranking as the magnitude of the scales used decreases. Since these effects may oppose one another, it is not possible to identify the scale that minimises reranking as the scale that underlies a tax and transfer system.

The associated simulation analyses undertaken were found to be consistent with the analytical conclusions. Specifically, the simulation results indicate that the scale that minimises reranking closely reflects the scale that underlies the tax and transfer system if the characteristics that underlie the equivalence scale used to measure reranking are uncorrelated with income. When the characteristics of the scale used to measure reranking are correlated with income, the relation between the scale that minimises reranking and the scale that underlies the tax system depends on the scale used, the degree of correlation, and the associated intensity of the direct and indirect effects.

The analysis was applied to interpret the relationships between the equivalence scales and reranking observed for Australian and UK household data. This analysis has shed some light on the previously unexpected distributional results of Nolan (1987) and has provided inferences regarding the properties of the equivalence scales that underlie the Australian and UK tax and transfer systems.

Appendix: Covariance Between Adult Equivalent Income and Number of Persons

Consider the following question. If the income per equivalent adult is given by $x_i^* = x_i/n_i^\theta$, what is the covariance between x_i^* and n_i? Suppose that income and the number of persons in the income unit are jointly log-normally distributed as:

$$\Lambda\left(x_i, n_i\right) = \Lambda\left(x_i, n_i \mid \mu_x, \mu_n, \sigma_x^2, \sigma_n^2, \rho_{x,n}\right) \tag{31}$$

First, note that for any log-normal distribution $\Lambda\left(x \mid \mu, \sigma^2\right)$, the following properties hold:

$$E\left(x\right) = \exp\left(\mu + \sigma^2/2\right) \tag{32}$$

and:

$$x^\alpha \text{ is } \Lambda\left(x^\alpha \mid \alpha\mu, \alpha^2\sigma^2\right) \tag{33}$$

For two variables $\Lambda\left(x, y \mid \mu_x, \mu_y, \sigma_x^2, \sigma_y^2, \rho_{x,y}\right)$:

$$\frac{x}{y} \text{ is } \Lambda\left(\frac{x}{y} \middle| \mu_x - \mu_y, \sigma_x^2 + \sigma_y^2 - 2\rho_{x,y}\sigma_x\sigma_y\right) \tag{34}$$

The covariance between x^* and n is by definition:

$$\mathrm{Cov}\left(x^*n\right) = E\left(\frac{x}{n^{\theta-1}}\right) - E\left(\frac{x}{n^\theta}\right) E\left(n\right) \tag{35}$$

Hence, using (33), (34) and (32) the average adult equivalent income is given by:

$$E\left(\frac{x}{n^\theta}\right) = \exp\left\{\mu_x - \theta\mu_n + \frac{1}{2}\left(\sigma_x^2 + \sigma_n^2 - 2\rho_{x,n}\theta\sigma_x\sigma_n\right)\right\} \tag{36}$$

A similar result holds for $E\left(\frac{x}{n^{\theta-1}}\right)$. It can be shown, after some manipulation, that $\mathrm{Cov}(x^*n)$ takes the form:

$$\mathrm{Cov}\left(x^*n\right) = \left(\exp A\right)\left(\exp B - 1\right) \tag{37}$$

where:

$$A = \mu_x + \left(\theta - 1\right)\mu_n + \frac{1}{2}\left\{\sigma_x^2 + \left(1 + \theta^2\right)\sigma_n^2 - 2\rho_{x,n}\theta\sigma_x\sigma_n\right\} \tag{38}$$

29

and:

$$B = \rho_{x,n}\sigma_x\sigma_n - \theta\sigma_n^2 \tag{39}$$

Thus the covariance is positive if $\exp B - 1 > 0$, or if $B > 0$. Hence there is a positive correlation between adult equivalent income and the number of adults if:

$$\rho_{x,n}\frac{\sigma_x}{\sigma_n} > \theta \tag{40}$$

This condition is therefore simply interpreted in terms of the size of the regression coefficient in the linear regression relationship between logarithms of n and x.

References

Atkinson, A.B. (1979), Horizontal equity and the distribution of the tax burden. In *The Economics of Taxation*. Edited by H. J. Aaron and M. J. Boskins. Washington DC: Brookings Institution.

Banks, J. & Johnson, P. (1993), *Children and household living standards*. Institute of Fiscal Studies.

Banks, J. & Johnson, P. (1994), "Equivalence scale relativities revisited", *Economic Journal*, 104, pp. 883-890.

Brent, R. J. (1984), "On the use of distributional weights in cost-benefit analysis: a survey of schools", *Public Finance Quarterly*, 12, pp. 213-230.

Buhmann, B., Rainwater, L., Schmaus, G. & Smeeding, T. M. (1988), "Equivalence scales, well-being, inequality, and poverty: Sensitivity estimates across ten countries using the Luxembourg income study (LIS) database", *Review of Income and Wealth*, 34, pp. 115-142.

Christiansen, V. & Jansen, E.S. (1978), "Implicit social preferences in the Norwegian system of social preferences". *Journal of Public Economics*, 10, pp. 217-245.

Coulter, F. A. E., Cowell, F. A. & Jenkins, S. P. (1992), "Differences in needs and assessment of income distributions", *Bulletin of Economic Research*, 44, pp. 77-124.

Creedy, J. & van de Ven, J. (2001), "Decomposing redistributive effects of taxes and transfers in Australia: annual and lifetime measures", *Australian Economic Papers*, (forthcoming).

Cutler, D. M. & Katz, L. (1992), "Rising inequality? Changes in the distribution of income and consumption in the 1980s", *American Economic Review*, 82, pp. 546-551.

Jenkins, S. P. & Cowell, F. A. (1994), "Parametric equivalence scales and scale relativities", *Economic Journal*, 104, pp. 891-900.

Mera, K. (1969), "Experimental determination of relative marginal utilities". *Quarterly Journal of Economics*, 83, pp. 464-477.

Moreh, J. (1981) "Income inequality and the social welfare function". *Journal of Economic Studies*, 8, pp. 25-37.

Musgrave, R. A. (1959), *The Theory of Public Finance*. London: McGraw-Hill.

Nolan, B. (1987), "Direct taxation, transfers and reranking: some empirical results for the UK". *Oxford Bulletin of Economics and Statistics*, 49, pp. 273-290.

Plotnick, R. (1981), "A measure of horizontal inequity", *Review of Economics and Statistics*, 63, pp. 283-288.

Seneca, J. J. & Taussig, M. K. (1971), "Family equivalence scales and personal income tax exemptions for children", *Review of Economics and Statistics*, 53, pp. 253-262.

Stern, N. (1977) Welfare weights and the elasticity of the marginal valuation of income. In Artis, M. and Nobay,R. (eds.) *Studies in Modern Economic Analysis*. Oxford: Basil Blackwell.

van de Ven, J., Creedy, J, & Lambert, P.J. (2001), "Close equals and calculation of the vertical, horizontal and reranking effects of taxation". *University of Melbourne Department of Economics Research Paper*.

[11]

The GST and Vertical, Horizontal and Reranking Effects of Indirect Taxation in Australia[*]

John Creedy

The University of Melbourne

Abstract

This paper decomposes the redistributive effect of indirect taxation into vertical, horizontal inequity and reranking effects. The latter two effects arise because households with the same total expenditure have different expenditure patterns. The pre- and post-GST structures in Australia are examined. The results show that an important role is played, in particular, by reranking.

1   Introduction

The purpose of this paper is to examine the orders of magnitude of three different components of redistribution in the context of indirect taxation. The changes in these components, resulting from the reform of the tax structure in Australia associated with the introduction of a Goods and Services Tax (GST), are considered.[1] Use is made of a decomposition of the reduction in inequality, as measured by the difference in the Gini coefficient of pre- and

---

[*]I should like to thank Glenys Harding for obtaining the budget shares from the Household Expenditure Survey, and Rosanna Scutella for providing the effective tax rates used here.

[1]It can be argued that separate taxes should not be examined in isolation, since it is the overall effect of all taxes and transfers that ultimately matters. However, the importance of indirect taxes in policy debates means that a special focus on them is warranted.

1

post-tax measures of total expenditure, into vertical, horizontal and rerank-ing effects. The vertical component measures the redistributive effect of the 'effective tax schedule', which is derived from the actual tax schedule by al-locating to each household the average tax paid by respective pre-tax equals. Horizontal inequity relates to the 'unequal treatment of equals', whereby those with equal total expenditures pay different amounts of tax. Reranking refers to the 'unequal treatment of unequals', where the rank-order of house-holds with different pre-tax total expenditures is reversed as a result of the indirect tax system. The effective redistribution is reduced by horizontal and reranking effects.

The decomposition was first produced by Aronson *et al.* (1994) in the context of income taxation.[2] Its only application to indirect taxes appears to be by Decoster *et al.* (1997a, 1997b), who examined taxation in Belgium. A serious practical problem with these uses of the decomposition is that, to overcome the fact that exact pre-tax equals are not observed in sample data, arbitrary class-widths for combining individuals into groups of near-equals were used. However, this strategy was examined by van de Ven *et al.* (2001), who showed that it can produce highly misleading results. This paper applies the alternative strategy suggested by van de Ven *et al.* (2001).

In the context of income taxation, horizontal and reranking effects arise because of the existence of various allowances and deductions depending on non-income characteristics of tax units. Non-uniform indirect taxes give rise to these effects because households with the same total expenditure do not necessarily have the same budget shares for all goods. There is in fact much heterogeneity in the consumption patterns of households with similar total expenditures, even where household composition is similar. The use of equiv-alent adult scales can also play a role, as with income taxation, in adjusting total expenditure for household size and composition.

---

[2] It was examined further by Lambert and Ramos (1997a, 1997b).

2

The indirect tax structure operating in Australia before July 2000 was highly differentiated and opaque. Reforms to the system, involving the introduction of a new goods and services tax (GST), have introduced greater uniformity, as well as raising extra revenue, although the indirect tax system as a whole is still not transparent. The GST is the most visible of the indirect taxes and therefore receives most public attention. There are some exemptions, largely introduced for distributional reasons.[3] In particular, most food is exempt from taxation, as it is in many of those countries which have a general consumption tax such as a value added tax. The question arises of whether this has affected the extent of horizontal inequities and reranking.

The decomposition method is described briefly in section 2. The pre- and post-reform indirect tax structures are described in section 3. Results are obtained for the proposed system, which included a GST on all food, as well as the actual GST system introduced in 2000. The empirical results are given in section 4. The redistributive effect of indirect taxation is measured in terms of the difference between the Gini inequality of total expenditure and that of expenditure measured net of indirect taxes; the latter is taken to represent consumption. Decompositions are obtained for separate demographic groups distinguished by household composition, as well as for the distribution of expenditure per equivalent adult. The implications of using alternative equivalence scales are examined. The approach measures the *impact* effects of the indirect tax structure; that is, the budget shares are assumed to be fixed when the tax structure is varied.[4] Brief conclusions are given in section 5.

---

[3] There are of course efficiency reasons for non-uniformity. In the standard optimal tax literature, uniformity of indirect taxes requires strong assumptions; see Stern (1990). Furthermore, as soon as some goods cannot be taxed, second-best problems arise. It is sometimes argued that the information about preferences is not available (with sufficient accuracy) in order to deal with the efficiency aspects of non-uniform taxes, while the information required to examine the distributional aspects is more widely available. Certainly, more emphasis has been given to distributional issues in public debates.

[4] It is necessary to use the full detail regarding the differences in budget shares, so estimated demand functions cannot be used in this context.

2   Summary Measures

The redistributive impact of a tax structure may be judged by the degree to which it reduces the Gini measure of inequality when moving from pre-tax to post-tax total household expenditure. In the case of the distribution of pre-tax expenditure, y, the Gini measure, G_y, is expressed in terms of the following covariance:

$$G_y = \left(\frac{2}{\bar{y}}\right) Cov\,(y, F(y)) \tag{1}$$

where $F(y)$ is the distribution function of household expenditure, so that $F(y)$ represents the proportion of individuals with expenditure less than or equal to y, and $\bar{y}$ is the arithmetic mean pre-tax expenditure. On such covariance expressions, see Jenkins (1988).

Suppose that the tax and transfer system is such that net or post-tax expenditure, x, is given by:

$$x = y - T(y) \tag{2}$$

The redistributive effect of the tax system the difference between the two Gini measures, L, so that:

$$L = G_y - G_x \tag{3}$$

This is referred to as the Reynolds-Smolensky (1977) measure.

The concentration index, C_x, of x is similar to the Gini inequality measure. If the ranking of individuals by y is maintained:

$$C_x = \left(\frac{2}{\bar{x}}\right) Cov\,(x, F(y)) \tag{4}$$

The possibility of reranking of individuals, when moving from the pre-tax to the post-tax expenditure distribution, introduces an 'unequal treatment of unequals' which is contrary to the vertical redistribution intended by the form of the tax function. Following Atkinson (1979) and Plotnick (1981), reranking, R, can be measured using:[5]

$$R = G_x - C_x \tag{5}$$

The concentration measure, C_x, involves ranking by y and the Gini inequality measure, G_x, involves ranking by x, so an absence of reranking implies that $R = 0$.

2.1 The Decomposition

Aronson *et al.* (1994) showed that the redistributive effect can be decomposed into vertical, horizontal and reranking components of a tax system. They showed that when the population is divided into N groups, such that within each group individuals have similar pre-tax values of y, y_k for $k = 1, ..., N$, and groups are ranked in ascending order ($y_1 < y_2 ... < y_N$):

$$L = (G_y - G_0) - \sum_{k=1}^{N} \theta_k G_k - R \tag{6}$$

where G_0 is the between-groups Gini measure of post-tax expenditure obtained by replacing every post-tax expenditure within each group by the arithmetic mean; θ_k is the product of the population share and the post-tax expenditure share of those in the kth group; and G_k is the Gini measure of inequality of post-tax expenditure of those in the kth group. The first two terms measure vertical redistribution, V, and horizontal inequity, H, respectively, where the latter arises from the 'unequal treatment of equals'. Hence $L = V - H - R$ and the horizontal inequity and reranking effects both reduce the redistributive effect of the tax structure.[6]

---

[5]It is sometimes defined using $(G_y - C_y)/2G_y$.

[6]This decomposition extends that produced by Kakwani (1977), who showed that $L = \{g/(1-g)\} K - R$, where $K = C_t - G_y$ and C_t is the tax concentration index, obtained by substituting the arithmetic mean amount of tax paid, $\overline{T}$ for $\bar{x}$ and $T(y)$ for x in (4), so that $C_t = \left(\frac{2}{\overline{T}}\right) Cov(T(y), F(y))$. Hence K is a measure of the disproportionality of tax

In practice exact pre-tax equals are not observed in survey data, so the decomposition in (6) cannot be applied directly. If groups of near-equals are used, this decomposition must be modified; for example in the first term it is necessary to replace G_y with a corresponding between-groups measure obtained, like G_0, by replacing individual values in each group of near-equals with the mean value. Further complications arise with the measure of horizontal inequity.

This issue was examined in detail by van de Ven *et al.* (2001). The use of an arbitrary class width to measure near-equals, as in earlier applications, was found to produce misleading results. However, analysis shows that as the class width is increased, the measured vertical effect initially increases and then falls after reaching a maximum. This maximum is closest to the true value, which suggests a strategy whereby the class width used to combine individuals into groups of near-equals is chosen as the value that maximises the estimated vertical effect. The reranking measure, R, can of course be obtained directly from (5) using the ungrouped values and is therefore not affected by the choice of class width. The horizontal effect can then be obtained using $H = V - R - L$.

3   Alternative Tax Structures

Many indirect taxes operate in Australia. Before July 2000 these included wholesales sales tax, excise tax, financial institutions duty, payroll tax, land tax, stamp duties, municipal rates and primary production tax; see Johnson *et al.* (1997, pp.14-17, 22-24) and Sood and Scutella (1997) for further details. The final effect of these taxes on consumer prices is the result of a complex process, particularly as different taxes are imposed at different stages of the production and distribution process and some taxes are unit taxes while

---

payments which combines the horizontal and vertical effects. For further treatment of the impact effect of taxes, see Lambert (1993a, 1993b).

Table 1: Effective Indirect Tax Rates

No.	Description	Pre-GST	GST-P	Post-GST
1	Current housing costs	0.1363	0.1791	0.1988
2	Fuel and Power	0.0872	0.1634	0.1697
3	Food and Non Alcoholic Beverages	0.1142	0.1753	0.1015
4	Alcohol	0.2969	0.3332	0.3046
5	Tobacco products	0.6826	0.8959	0.9025
6	Clothing and footwear	0.0681	0.1476	0.1548
7	Furnishings and equipment	0.1072	0.1382	0.1493
8	Services and Operation	0.0903	0.1176	0.1183
9	Medical Care and Health	0.0569	0.0362	0.0462
10	Transport	0.2381	0.1977	0.2039
11	Recreation and entertainment	0.1436	0.1930	0.1927
12	Personal care	0.1259	0.1360	0.1138
13	Miscellaneous goods and services	0.1411	0.1241	0.1566
14	Other Capital Housing	0.1147	0.1462	0.1622

others are *ad valorem*. The effective rates on different commodity groups depend on the extent to which taxes are shifted forward at each production stage and on the nature of inter-industry transactions.

Estimates of the effective indirect tax rates arising from the pre-GST system were reported by Johnson *et al.* (1999, p.12) for 14 commodity groups used by the Household Expenditure Survey. Johnson *et al.* also reported the price changes for the proposed GST system which included food; this system is referred to here as GST-P. The effective rates are shown in Table 1, after converting the price changes into tax rates using the result that if the tax rate changes from t_1 to t_2, the price increase is given by $\dot{p} = (t_2 - t_1) / (1 + t_1)$, so that $t_2 = t_1 + (1 + t_1) \dot{p}$.[7] The GST that was eventually introduced involved several modifications to the proposals, the most important of which was the exemption of most food from the GST. The post-GST indirect tax rates are

---

[7]Johnson *et al.* (1999) reported values to just one decimal point, but more detailed values were kindly provided by Rosanna Scutella.

shown in the final column of Table 1.[8] The values reported in the table are effective tax-exclusive *ad valorem* rates, calculated using the method devised by Scutella (1997). This involves tracing the incidence through the input-output matrix, assuming full shifting at each stage. It can be seen that there is a considerable degree of non-uniformity in the effective rates.[9]

The commodity groups in Table 1 are those used by the Household Expenditure Survey, so it was necessary to carry out a certain amount of consolidation from the more than 100 rates obtained for the categories in the input-output matrix. Hence the rates shown can only be regarded as approximate rates obtained under strong shifting assumptions. Indeed, a serious problem is the lack of transparency of the tax structure; most consumers appear to be aware only of the GST.

4   Empirical Results

This section applies the alternative indirect tax structures to households in the 1993 Australian Household Expenditure Survey. The budget shares for each of the 14 commodity groups were calculated for each household, along with total household expenditure. If w_i represents the budget share of the ith good, for $i = 1, ..., n$, and t_i is the *ad valorem* tax-exclusive rate, the tax-inclusive rate is $t_i' = t_i / (1 + t_i)$ and the total consumption tax, T, paid by a household with total expenditure of y is given by:

$$T = y \sum_{i=1}^{n} t_i' w_i \qquad (7)$$

Hence total consumption net of indirect taxation is $y \left(1 - \sum_{i=1}^{n} t_i' w_i\right)$.

It has been mentioned that horizontal inequities and reranking arise through differences in expenditure patterns of households with the same total

---

[8]These are the same as those used by Johnson (1999).

[9]Potential general equilibrium effects of indirect taxes on factor prices were ignored in calculating these rates. The two sets of rates clearly do not generate the same amount of revenue from indirect taxes.

Table 2: Redistributive Effect for Household Groups

	Household Type	no.	G_y	SE		$G_y - G_x$	
					Pre-	GST-P	Post-
1	All households	7590	0.3581	0.0030	-0.0005	-0.0018	-0.0001
	Couples without children						
2	No one retired	1430	0.3151	0.0063	-0.0009	-0.0018	0.0007
3	≥ 1 person ret'd	450	0.3024	0.0153	0.0017	-0.0003	0.0026
	Couples with children						
4	1 dep. child	586	0.2707	0.0097	-0.0006	-0.0021	-0.0003
5	2 dep. child	790	0.2718	0.0077	-0.0006	-0.0017	0.0004
6	≥ 3 dep. child	540	0.2836	0.0111	-0.0015	-0.0026	-0.0001
	Sole parents						
7	1 dep. child	190	0.2587	0.0174	-0.0003	-0.0024	-0.0008
8	≥ 2 dep. child	187	0.2984	0.0237	-0.0007	-0.0041	-0.0011
	Single Persons						
9	not retired	1000	0.3627	0.0103	-0.0019	-0.0038	-0.0017
10	retired	620	0.2973	0.0121	0.0023	-0.0007	0.0016

expenditure and household structure, as well as the use of equivalent adult scales when households of different composition are combined. Hence it is useful first to provide a separate analysis of different household types, where scales are not required.

4.1 Results for Different Household Types

The sample was divided into a range of household types; the demographic groups considered are shown in the second column of Table 2. Group 1 includes all the households, irrespective of their size and composition. The separate household types, listed as groups 2 to 9 in the table, comprise about three quarters of all households in the Household Expenditure Survey. These household types represent the major demographic groups found in the HES; the sample size restricts the analysis to these groups as there are too few households in other categories.

The final three columns of Table 2 show the inequality reductions, us-

9

ing the Reynolds-Smolensky measure, that results from each of the tax systems. The negative values for the current system indicate that it is slightly inequality-increasing, except for household types 3 and 10 (containing retired persons). The Reynolds-Smolensky measure is also negative for the GST-P system, indicating that it is also slightly inequality increasing for all household types; the extent of this is slightly greater than in the pre-GST structure. The post-GST structure is inequality-reducing for four of the household types, and for others the increase in the Gini is smaller, as a result of the treatment of food. Table 2 also shows the Gini measure of total expenditure, G_y, for each demographic groups, along with the standard error obtained using the method proposed by Kakwani *et al.* (1997). It is clear that the changes in inequality resulting from each of the tax systems are not statistically significant (being all below one standard deviation from the sample Gini).

The decomposition of the redistributive effect of indirect taxes into vertical, horizontal and reranking effects was computed for the three tax structures and the results are presented in Table 3. This table lists the three components of the reduction in the Gini inequality measure resulting from the indirect tax structures, along with the percentage contribution of each. In cases where the indirect taxes produce positive redistribution $(L > 0)$, the percentage contribution of vertical redistribution must exceed 100. For each tax structure and demographic group, the class width used in grouping households into near-equals was selected following the procedure suggested by van de Ven *et al.* (2001): the required width varied between $20 and $40 per week.

For the retired housholds, types 3 and 10, it can be seen that, without the negative effects of horizontal inequity and reranking, the pre-GST sytem would have produced a reduction in the Gini of about 14 per cent more. The effect of the proposed system GST-P for these household types is to cause a slight increase in inequality (of post-tax consumption compared with total

10

expenditure). This arises, in the case of household type 3, entirely from reranking (which contributes to about 80 per cent of the inequality increase) and horizontal inequity. For household type 10, reranking also increases substantially for GST-P. For household type 3, the GST produces a small proportional contribution from reranking, and the overall effect is inequality reducing. Reranking is also lower for household type 10 compared with the structure that taxes all food. For all households, it is the reranking that largely contributes to the negative Reynolds-Smolensky measure.

The results in Table 3 demonstrate that for other household types there are substantial differences in the proportional contributions of vertical redistribution, horizontal inequity and reranking, particularly under the pre-GST indirect tax structure. Horizontal inequity generally contributes few percentage points to the inequality change, but reranking is substantial. For household type 7, single parents with one dependent child, horizontal inequity and reranking are largest (contributing 17 and 63 per cent of the increase in inequality) for the pre-GST. These inequities are much lower for the proposed system GST-P. Reranking and horizontal inequity are both relatively higher for the post-GST compared with GST-P. The absolute values are of course relatively small, given the small amount of redistribution involved. However, the results show that the heterogeneity in expenditure patterns, among households with similar demographic characteristics and total expenditure levels, plays an important but neglected role.

4.2 Expenditure per Equivalent Adult

The above results relate to separate household types, where no adjustment for differences in composition within each group were required. The approach adopted in this subsection is to evaluate the redistributive effects of the three tax systems in terms of the distribution of total expenditure per equivalent adult. For this purpose a set of adult equivalent scales is required. Several

11

Table 3: Decomposition of Redistribution for Alternative Tax Structures

HH type	V	per cent	$100H$	per cent	$100R$	per cent
		Pre-GST Indirect Taxes				
1	-0.0003	69.30	0.0005	1.12	0.0143	29.57
2	-0.0007	81.82	0.0005	0.60	0.0159	17.58
3	0.0019	114.29	0.0029	1.75	0.0208	12.55
4	-0.0004	71.98	0.0013	2.09	0.0160	25.92
5	-0.0004	73.27	0.0007	1.26	0.0140	25.47
6	-0.0013	89.13	0.0026	1.72	0.0136	9.15
7	-0.0001	19.45	0.0049	17.34	0.0178	63.21
8	-0.0005	72.97	0.0068	9.19	0.0131	17.84
9	-0.0017	86.40	0.0045	2.34	0.0218	11.26
10	0.0026	113.69	0.0079	3.43	0.0237	10.26
		GST-P Indirect Taxes				
1	-0.0017	92.71	0.0016	0.89	0.0116	6.40
2	-0.0017	92.81	-0.0003	0.19	0.0132	7.38
3	0.0000	9.14	0.0035	11.70	0.0236	79.16
4	-0.0020	93.41	0.0006	0.30	0.0133	6.28
5	-0.0015	92.84	0.0007	0.43	0.0111	6.74
6	-0.0024	94.55	0.0025	0.97	0.0115	4.48
7	-0.0022	91.00	0.0043	1.77	0.0176	7.24
8	-0.0039	95.44	0.0067	1.63	0.0120	2.93
9	-0.0036	93.87	0.0040	1.06	0.0192	5.07
10	-0.0004	57.46	0.0042	5.90	0.0259	36.64
		Post-GST Indirect Taxes				
1	0.0000	22.98	0.0012	11.09	0.0117	111.89
2	0.0009	120.16	0.0015	2.09	0.0130	18.07
3	0.0028	110.26	0.0035	1.36	0.0229	8.91
4	-0.0002	50.25	0.0015	4.87	0.0137	44.88
5	0.0005	136.54	0.0014	3.86	0.0115	32.69
6	0.0000	8.28	0.0015	10.62	0.0116	81.10
7	-0.0006	70.51	0.0041	5.21	0.0191	24.27
8	-0.0009	82.24	0.0071	6.22	0.0132	11.54
9	-0.0015	87.94	0.0014	0.85	0.0187	11.22
10	0.0020	121.49	0.0095	5.84	0.0254	15.65

12

Table 4: Adult Equivalent Household Size

Household Type	Johnson *et al.*	$\Phi = 0.5$ $\theta = 0.5$	$\Phi = 0.3$ $\theta = 0.4$	$\Phi = 0.4$ $\theta = 0.6$
Couple: no children	1.6	1.4142	1.3195	1.5157
Couple: no children, ≥ 1 ret'd	1.6	1.4142	1.3195	1.5157
Couple: 1 dependent child	1.9	1.5811	1.3951	1.6909
Couple: 2 dependent child	2.2	1.7321	1.4655	1.8548
Couple: ≥ 3 dependent child	2.6	1.9365	1.6521	2.0840
1 parent: 1 dependent child	1.3	1.2247	1.1107	1.2237
1 parent: ≥ 2 dependent child	1.7	1.5	1.2509	1.5157
Single person, not retired	1	1	1	1
Single person, retired	1	1	1	1

scales are use here. First, a simple adjustment is used, following Johnson *et al.* (1995), whereby the first adult is given a weight of 1, the second adult is given a weight of 0.6 and each child is given a weight of 0.3.

Second, let n_d and n_c refer respectively to the number of adults and children in a household. The number of adult equivalents, a, is given by:

$$a = (n_d + \Phi n_c)^\theta \qquad (8)$$

where $0 \leq \theta$ and $\Phi \leq 1$. This formulation has been used by, for example, Cutler and Katz (1992), Banks and Johnson (1994) and Jenkins and Cowell (1994). Three pairs of values for the parameters are used here. Table 4 shows the resulting values of adult equivalent household size for the different scales.

Table 5 shows the redistributive effects arising from the use of these scales, when using values of consumption per adult equivalent person.[10] For both pre-GST and GST-P systems, the redistributive effect of indirect taxes is small but negative, and is higher for the GST-P system. The post-GST structure shows a small reduction in the Gini measure, as a result of the exemption of most food. However, the standard error of the pre-tax Gini measure of

---

[10]Remember that household types 2 to 10 together form about three quarters of the households in the HES. Hence the difference between these values and those obtained for 'all households' above reflects the differing samples as well as the use of the equivalent household size adjustment.

Table 5: Redistributive Effects

Equiv Scales	G_y	SE(G_y)	Pre-GST	GST-P	Post-GST
			$G_y - G_x$	$G_y - G_x$	$G_y - G_x$
Johnson *et al.*	0.3334	0.0038	-0.0001	-0.0017	0.0007
$\Phi = 0.5; \theta = 0.5$	0.3360	0.0036	-0.0003	-0.0019	0.0005
$\Phi = 0.3; \theta = 0.4$	0.3407	0.0035	-0.0004	-0.0020	0.0003
$\Phi = 0.4; \theta = 0.6$	0.3334	0.0034	-0.0002	-0.0018	0.0005

Table 6: Distribution of Equivalent Household Expenditure

Structure	V	per cent	$100H$	per cent	$100R$	per cent
Pre-GST						
Johnson *et al.*	0.0001	115.71	0.0016	19.44	0.0165	196.27
$\Phi = 0.5; \theta = 0.5$	-0.0001	39.40	0.0012	4.36	0.0158	56.24
$\Phi = 0.3; \theta = 0.4$	-0.0003	63.55	0.0003	0.65	0.0154	35.80
$\Phi = 0.4; \theta = 0.6$	-0.0001	28.14	0.0006	2.47	0.0166	69.39
GST-P						
Johnson *et al.*	-0.0015	90.04	0.0021	1.22	0.0150	8.74
$\Phi = 0.5; \theta = 0.5$	-0.0017	92.06	0.0011	0.60	0.0137	7.34
$\Phi = 0.3; \theta = 0.4$	-0.0018	92.74	0.0009	0.46	0.0133	6.81
$\Phi = 0.4; \theta = 0.6$	-0.0017	91.79	0.0008	0.42	0.0144	7.79
Post-GST						
Johnson *et al.*	0.0009	122.33	0.0012	1.62	0.0154	20.71
$\Phi = 0.5; \theta = 0.5$	0.0006	132.26	0.0012	2.42	0.0143	29.84
$\Phi = 0.3; \theta = 0.4$	0.0004	148.25	0.0003	0.90	0.0136	47.35
$\Phi = 0.4; \theta = 0.6$	0.0007	132.43	0.0029	0.23	0.0149	27.20

consumption shows that (as with changes within each demographic group) the changes in the Gini are not statistically significant.

The decompositions are shown in Table 6 for each of the indirect tax structures and the alternative adult equivalent scales. For the pre-GST structure, reranking in particular contributes a substantial proportion of the inequality change. In the case of the Johnson *et al.* (1995) scales, the extent of this is such that it reverses a small degree of positive vertical redistribution. The relative importance of reranking is substantially reduced by the GST-P structure. As with the previous results, the exemption of food introduces positive

14

bution, and vertical equity. However, the redistribution would be greater, were it not for the higher proportional negative impact of reranking, reflecting considerable heterogeneity in budget shares for food.

5   Conclusions

This paper has examined the decomposition of the redistributive effect of indirect taxation into vertical, horizontal inequity and reranking effects. The fact that households with the same total expenditure have different consumption patterns introduces reranking and horizontal inequity effects. The pre- and post-GST indirect tax structures were examined, along with the proposed scheme that included GST imposed on food.

For the pre-GST and GST-P systems, it was found that indirect taxes generates, for all household types except those with a retired person under the pre-GST structure, a small increase in the Gini measure of inequality when moving from the distribution of gross expenditure to that of expenditure net of indirect taxes. The GST implies a reduction in the Gini for some household types. A similar result was obtained in terms of the complete distribution of expenditure per equivalent adult for pre-GST and GST-P systems. However, there is a reduction in inequality when using consumption per equivalent adult.

A substantial proportional contribution to the redistributive effect was found to arise from reranking. The GST was found, except for retired households, to reduce the percentage contribution of horizontal inequity and reranking to the overall redistributive effect of the indirect tax structure. This arises because of a general flattening of the effective indirect tax structure. Under the GST Reranking is generally smaller than the pre-GST but is greater than for the GST-P system, The existence of some negative effects of horizontal inequity and reranking are of course inevitable in an indirect tax system with non-uniform tax rates.

15

It is suggested that the calculation of these neglected effects of indirect taxes provides useful additional information about the tax structure. However, the question remains of precisely how these components of redistribution are to be viewed, and of course the issue inevitably involves value judgements. Some judges may, for example, only be interested in the overall redistributive effect of the tax structure, attaching little weight to the component parts. On the other hand, others may object to such 'unintended' consequences of non-uniformity and may wish to attempt to design a tax structure that achieves overall distributional objectives while minimising horizontal inequities and reranking. These welfare issues warrant further consideration.

References

[1] Aronson, J. R., Johnson, P. and Lambert, P. J. (1994) Redistributive effect and unequal income tax treatment. *Economic Journal,* 104, pp. 262-270.

[2] Atkinson, A.B. (1979) Horizontal equity and the distribution of the tax burden. In *The Economics of Taxation* (ed. by H.J. Aaron and M.J. Boskins). Washington: The Brookings Institution.

[3] Banks, J. and Johnson, P. (1994) Equivalence scale relativities revisited. *Economic Journal,* 104, pp. 883-890.

[4] Cutler, D.M. and Katz, L. (1992) Rising inequality? Changes in the distribution of income and consumption in the 1980s. *American Economic Review,* 82, pp. 546-551.

[5] Decoster, A., Schokkaert, E. and Van Camp, G. (1997a) Is redistribution through indirect taxes equitable? *European Economic Review,* 41, pp. 599-608.

[6] Decoster, A., Schokkaert, E. and Van Camp, G. (1997b) Horizontal neutrality and vertical redistribution with indirect taxes. *Research on Economic Inequality,* 7, pp. 219-239.

[7] Jenkins, S.P. (1988) Calculating income distribution indices from microdata. *National Tax Journal,* XLI, pp. 139-142.

[8] Jenkins, S.P. and Cowell, F. A. (1994) Parametric equivalence scales and scale relativities. *Economic Journal,* 104, pp. 891-900.

[9] Johnson, D. (1999) The impact of new tax legislation on households. *Family Matters,* 54, pp. 55-59.

17

[10] Johnson, D., Manning, I. and Hellwig, O. (1995) *Trends in The Distribution of Cash Income and Non-cash Benefits.* Canberra: AGPS.

[11] Johnson, D., Freebairn, J., Creedy, J., Scutella, R. and Cowling, S. (1997) *A Stocktake of Taxation in Australia.* Melbourne: Melbourne Institute of Applied Economic and Social Research.

[12] Johnson, D., Freebairn, J., Creedy, J., Scutella, R., Cowling, S. and Harding, G. (1998) *Indirect Taxes: Evaluation of Options for Reform.* Melbourne: Melbourne Institute of Applied Economic and Social Research

[13] Johnson, D., Freebairn, J. and Scutella, R. (1999) *Evaluation of the Government's Tax Package.* Melbourne: Melbourne Institute of Applied Economic and Social Research.

[14] Kakwani, N.C. (1977) Measurement of tax progressivity: an international comparison. *Economic Journal,* 87, pp. 71-80.

[15] Kakwani, N., Wagstaff, A. and van Doorslaer, E. (1997) Socioeconomic inequalities in health: measurement, computation and statistical inference. *Journal of Econometrics,* 77, pp. 87-103.

[16] Lambert, P.J. (1993a) *The Distribution and Redistribution of Income: A Mathematical Analysis.* Manchester: Manchester University Press.

[17] Lambert, P.J. (1993b) Evaluating impact effects of tax reforms. *Journal of Economic Surveys,* 7, pp. 205-242.

[18] Lambert, P.J. and Ramos, X. (1997a) Horizontal inequity and reranking. *Research on Economic Inequality,* 7, pp. 1-18.

[19] Lambert, P.J. and Ramos, X. (1997b) Horizontal inequity and vertical redistribution. *International Tax and Public Finance,* 4, pp. 25-37.

18

[20] Plotnick, R. (1981) A measure of horizontal inequity. *Review of Economics and Statistics,* 63, pp. 283-87.

[21] Reynolds, M. and Smolensky, E. (1977) *Public Expenditures, Taxes and the Distribution of Income: The United States 1950, 1961, 1970.* New York: Academic Press.

[22] Scutella, R. (1997) The incidence of indirect taxes on final demand in Australia. *Melbourne Institute of Applied Economic and Social Research Working Paper,* no. 18/97.

[23] Sood, R. and Scutella, R. (1997) Description of the current Australian indirect tax system. *Melbourne Institute of Applied Economic and Social Research Working Paper,* no. 19/97.

[24] Stern, N. (1990) Uniformity versus selectivity in indirect taxation. *Economics and Politics,* 2, pp. 83-102.

[25] van de Ven, J., Creedy, J. and Lambert, P. (2001) Close equals and calculation of the vertical, horizontal and reranking effects of taxation. *Oxford Bulletin of Economics and Statistics* (forthcoming).

[12]

Non-uniform Consumption Taxes: A 'Blunt Redistributive Instrument'?

John Creedy
The University of Melbourne

Abstract

This paper examines the question of the extent to which redistribution can be achieved using a structure of consumption taxes with differential rates and exemptions. A local measure of progression, that of liability progression (equivalent to the revenue elasticity) is examined. Results are obtained for the Australian indirect tax structure and forms in which only those commodity groups with total expenditure elasticities greater than 1 are taxed. Comparisons are also made using equivalent variations, and inequality measures of a money metric welfare measure are reported.

1 Introduction

This paper considers the question of how redistributive it is possible to make consumption taxes, by using a non-uniform set of rates. It is sometimes suggested that indirect taxes provide a 'blunt instrument' for redistribution; for example, see Stern (1990, p.103) and Chisholm *et al.* (1990, p.150). It is not easy to provide a simple measure of the redistributive potential of a general tax structure. Sah (1983) considered the use of commodity taxes and subsidies (negative taxes) in order to improve the welfare of the worst-off individual, subject to the government budget constraint. He obtained an upper limit in terms of the maximum budget share of the worst-off as a ratio of the minimum average budget share in the economy. However, concern is

1

generally with measures of tax progressivity or redistribution. The issue is examined here by considering the nature of, and implications for inequality, of 'extreme' forms of indirect taxation.

In the context of income taxation, it is in principle possible to specify a tax function (involving income and a range of non-income variables) that can achieve precisely the type of income redistribution required.[1] The fundamental 'limits to redistribution' are imposed by labour supply incentive effects and population heterogeneity. But in practice, tax functions are specified in terms of a set of income thresholds, between which marginal tax rates are constant, and a limited range of non-income variables relating to household size and composition (which influence deductions[2]). Some 'errors' (or deviations from the desired schedule) are therefore inevitable, and a practical income tax scheme is likely to have various (unintended) horizontal inequities that reduce the intended vertical redistribution.

A greater range of constraints is imposed on the ability of non-uniform consumption taxes to reduce the inequality of consumption, measured in terms of total expenditure minus the indirect tax paid. Indirect tax rates are by their nature set independently of individuals' income levels and other characteristics used in specifying an income tax structure. One obvious limitation is that virtually all broad commodity groups are consumed by all types of households at all income levels; thus, for example, the exemption of food from a general consumption tax benefits all income groups, while it is motivated by a desire to introduce progressivity. There are strong administrative constraints on the number of separate indirect tax rates that could be used. It may be possible to find certain 'luxury' goods which are most likely to be consumed only by high-income households but, like extremely high marginal income tax rates at very high incomes, these are not likely to

---

[1] The term 'redistribution' is used, even if there are no explicit transfers, to describe the reduction in inequality from pre-tax to post-tax distributions.

[2] There are usually other endogenous, and often complex, deductions.

2

produce much revenue or have much overall impact on inequality. Differentiation by very narrow commodity groups or brand names would of course involve considerable administrative problems.

A consumption tax imposed at a uniform rate on *all* goods and services has no redistributive effect since the real incomes of all households are reduced by the same proportion.[3] This paper starts from the basic idea that a progressive tax is one for which the marginal tax rate is greater than the average tax rate at all total expenditure levels. The ratio of the marginal rate to the average rate provides a measure of liability progression. In section 2, this is used to extend the simple view that a consumption tax is most progressive, or inequality reducing, if it taxes most heavily those goods which form a systematically higher proportion of the budgets of high-income households. Profiles of liability progression are examined for several indirect tax structures in Australia along with alternatives designed to introduce more redistribution.

Section 3 extends the analysis to consider welfare changes at different total expenditure levels. In addition, social evaluations, based on the use of alternative social welfare functions which reflect distributional value judgements, are presented. Brief conclusions are in section 4.

2   Liability Progression

This section examines the behaviour of a measure of progressivity, that of liability progression, in the context of indirect taxation. The definitions and basic properties are presented in subsection 2.1. A crucial role is played by budget shares and their variation with household total expenditure. Such variations are examined using Australian Household Expenditure Survey data in subsection 2.2. Subsection 2.3 goes on to examine liability progres-

---

[3]Here, indirect taxes are judged in terms of their tax base, total expenditure, rather than income. Issues relating to the use of income in examining indirect taxes, and the role of savings, are discussed in Creedy (1998).

sion in Australia before and after the introduction of a goods and services tax, the GST, in 2000. The subsection also considers hypothetical structures which are substantially more selective.

2.1   Basic Properties

Let w_i represent the budget share of the ith good, for $i = 1, ..., n$. If t_i is the *ad valorem* tax-exclusive rate on good i, the tax-inclusive rate is $t_i' = t_i / (1 + t_i)$ and the total consumption tax revenue, T, paid by an individual with total expenditure of y, is given by:

$$T = y \sum_{i=1}^{n} t_i' w_i \tag{1}$$

The ratio of the marginal tax rate, dT/dy, to the average tax rate, T/y, is equivalent to the elasticity of tax revenue with respect to total expenditure, $\eta = \frac{dT/T}{dY/y}$. This provides an indication of the progressivity of the tax system; it is the Musgrave-Thin measure of liability progression. Writing:

$$\frac{dT}{dy} = \sum_{i=1}^{n} t_i' w_i + y \sum_{i=1}^{n} t_i' \frac{dw_i}{dy} \tag{2}$$

The revenue elasticity becomes:

$$\eta = 1 + \frac{\sum_{i=1}^{n} t_i' w_i \left(\frac{dw_i}{dy} \frac{y}{w_i} \right)}{\sum_{i=1}^{n} t_i' w_i} \tag{3}$$

This can be expressed in terms of the total expenditure elasticities, e_i. Given that $w_i = p_i q_i / y$, where p_i and q_i are the price and quantity of good i, it can be seen that:

$$\frac{y}{w_i} \frac{dw_i}{dy} = \frac{y}{q_i} \frac{dq_i}{dy} - 1 = e_i - 1 \tag{4}$$

Hence:[4]

$$\eta = 1 + \frac{\sum_{i=1}^{n} t_i' w_i (e_i - 1)}{\sum_{i=1}^{n} t_i' w_i} \tag{5}$$

---

[4] In Creedy and Gemmell (2001), the revenue elasticity with respect to gross income, x, can be shown to be $(1 - t_k) x \sum_{i=1}^{n} t_i' w_i e_i / \left(y \sum_{i=1}^{n} t_i' w_i \right)$, where t_k is the relevant marginal income tax rate. For a progressive income tax, this elasticity is less than 1 for a uniform consumption tax system, unlike the elasticity considered above.

Using the adding-up conditions that $\sum_{i=1}^{n} w_i e_i = \sum_{i=1}^{n} w_i = 1$, (5) shows that $\eta = 1$ at all total expenditure levels when taxes are uniform, that is when all $t_i = t$.

A tax structure is more progressive than another if it has higher values of η at all y. The property of an increasing budget share is equivalent to $e_i > 1$. The above argument that, for progression, goods which form a higher proportion of the budgets of poorer households should be taxed at a lower rate translates into the statement that goods with total expenditure elasticities greater than 1 should be taxed most heavily. However, a degree of progressivity can be obtained even if taxes are imposed on some goods for which $e_i < 1$ at some income levels. In practice taxes are of course likely to be imposed on such goods for non-distributional reasons (including merit good arguments and revenue requirements).

For any demand system, the total expenditure elasticities tend to unity as total expenditure increase (though this tendency may not be monotonic); hence η tends to 1 as y tends to ∞, whatever the nature of the tax structure. A further implication of the convergence of the total expenditure elasticities towards unity is that, in those cases for which $e_i > 1$ at all levels of y, the elasticity declines as y increases, though again this may not necessarily be monotonic. This provides a further constraint on the progressivity of an indirect tax structure.

Consider a two-rate system in which goods are ordered such that the first s goods are taxed at a uniform rate. From (5) the revenue elasticity becomes:

$$\eta = \frac{\sum_s w_i e_i}{\sum_s w_i}$$

$$= 1 + \frac{\sum_s w_i \eta_{w_i, y}}{\sum_s w_i} \tag{6}$$

where $\eta_{w_i, y}$ denotes the elasticity of the budget share with respect to total expenditure. In this case the revenue elasticity is independent of the uniform rate imposed on taxed goods. The tax rate can therefore be set only in order to satisfy a revenue requirement. This independence of η from the common indirect tax rate means that the government has only one policy variable, the value of s, with which to influence progression in such a system. This is a serious limitation on the ability to design a progressive consumption tax structure. An income tax with a single marginal rate above a tax-free threshold has, in comparison, considerable scope.

From (6), the revenue elasticity depends in a clear way on the extent to which the tax base changes as total expenditure increases.[5] Compared with an income tax system (where the average tax rate at low incomes can be made very low by suitably setting the tax-free income threshold), it is much harder to impose an indirect tax structure that achieves a high revenue elasticity (liability progression) at low income levels. Furthermore, in a direct tax system, the marginal rate can easily be increased at higher income thresholds, enabling the liability progression to increase by discrete 'jumps', whereas indirect taxes are imposed on goods independently of the circumstances of the purchasers.

The expression in (6) can be related to the earlier general suggestion that progression requires higher rates to be imposed on goods for which $e_i > 1$. In a system with uniform taxation on a selection of goods, liability progression is maximised (at a given total expenditure level) by taxing only the good with maximum $e_i \geqslant 1$. This requirement of extreme selectivity to achieve maximum progressivity is clearly not a practical policy option. The revenue requirement is likely to imply an unrealistically high tax rate. Furthermore, in practice the tax changes are likely to affect the budget shares, providing a further restriction on the ability to impose high tax rates. With a maximum feasible tax rate, other goods need to be taxed to satisfy a revenue requirement. In general, the rule for maximising progressivity is simply to start

---

[5] A similar result applies for an income tax system in which allowances are endogenous, whereby if allowances increase in the same proportion as income, the revenue elasticity is 1. In a multi-step income tax function, the revenue elasticity is independent of tax rates only for those in the first tax bracket; see Creedy and Gemmell (2001).

by ranking commodity groups in decreasing order of expenditure elasticity. Then start with the group having the highest expenditure elasticity, and add further groups as required in order to meet the revenue requirement, bearing in mind the practical constraints on the maximum tax rate that can be imposed on each group. In order for the revenue elasticity to exceed the corresponding value under a uniform tax on those goods subject to a non-zero rate, it is necessary to set $t_i > t_j$ where $e_i > e_j$.

If negative taxes, or subsidies, are allowed, it is possible to achieve substantially higher values of liability progression at lower levels of total expenditure. Furthermore, the imposition of negative taxes on some goods implies a progressivity maximising structure in which all goods are taxed, including those which have total expenditure elasticities less than 1 but are not subsidised. However, subsidies are typically not part of the consumption tax structures of industrialised countries. On the other hand, they are sometimes used for redistributive purposes in developing countries which rely on indirect taxes rather than having an income tax and transfer system.

2.2   Variations in Budget Shares

In practice, the relationship observed in cross-sectional surveys between average budget shares and total household expenditure displays substantial variability. Hence the calculation of elasticities based on such shares would result in a number of negative values and excessive variability. It is therefore useful to estimate the parameters of a specified functional form. Let w_i denote the average budget share of good i for households with total expenditure of y. It is found that the following specification provides a good description of the variation in the budget shares:

$$w_i = a_i + b_i \log{(y)} + \frac{c_i}{y} \qquad (7)$$

Eliminating the term in c_i/y gives the form used in the 'almost ideal demand system' proposed by Deaton and Muellbauer (1980). The results of estimat-

7

ing (7) for each of the 14 commodity groups used in the Australian 1993 Household Expenditure Survey are shown in Table 1, where values of y are measured in cents per week.[6]

Differentiating (7) gives:

$$\frac{dw_i}{dy} = \frac{b_i y - c_i}{y^2} \tag{8}$$

so that w_i unequivocally falls as y rises if $b_i < 0$ and $c_i > 0$; or if $c_i < 0$, so long as $y > c_i/b_i$. Hence the budget shares fall for Australian households over the relevant range of incomes in the cases of: current housing costs; electricity, gas and other fuels; food and non-alcoholic beverages; postal and telephone charges; health services; and personal care products. The above discussion has shown that any attempt to make the indirect tax structure as progressive as possible would therefore not tax these commodity groups.

Alternatively, the shares rise as income rises in the case of: clothing and footwear; furniture and appliances; motor vehicles and parts; recreational items; miscellaneous; and house building payments. These groups would therefore be taxed in any system attempting to introduce progressivity. In the cases of alcohol and tobacco the budget shares initially rise before falling in the higher-income groups, so that the overall effects of taxes on these commodity groups are more ambiguous.

2.3 Alternative Tax Structures

This subsection examines the variation in revenue elasticities with total expenditure for a range of alternative tax structures, using the budget shares obtained from the regression equations reported in the previous subsection.[7] First, the Australian indirect tax systems before and after the introduction

---

[6]The results are for all households, with no adjustment made for size and composition.

[7]The estimation guarantees that the predicted budget shares always add to 1. However, they do not guarantee that all $w > 0$ at all total expenditure levels; a small number of minor adjustments were therefore made at the lower levels of y.

Table 1: Budget Shares: All Households Combined

Commodity Group	a_i	b_i	c_i	$\overline{R}^2$
Current housing costs	0.8439	-0.0628	-311.4117	0.9603
Electricity, gas and other fuels	0.1688	-0.0130	328.4054	0.9874
Food and beverages	0.9671	-0.0697	-495.8344	0.9773
Spirits, beer and wine	0.1546	-0.0078	-431.7199	0.5450
Tobacco	0.2110	-0.0169	-335.5932	0.9281
Clothing and footwear	-0.0570	0.0096	-91.8081	0.8194
Furniture and appliances	-0.1774	0.0204	124.5691	0.8643
Postal and telephone charges	0.2572	-0.0185	64.6643	0.9580
Health services	0.2507	-0.0180	-395.9763	0.8101
Motor vehicles and parts	-0.0151	0.0153	-751.3042	0.8265
Recreational items	0.0937	0.0039	-826.4007	0.8096
Personal care products	0.0653	-0.0041	-67.4465	0.5269
Miscellaneous	-0.0782	0.0133	-200.5533	0.8326
House building payments	-1.6847	0.1514	3390.4360	0.8099

of the goods and services tax (GST) are considered. This is followed by consideration of hypothetical cases.

Many indirect taxes operated in Australia before July 2000. These included wholesales sales tax, excise tax, financial institutions duty, payroll tax, land tax, stamp duties, municipal rates and primary production tax; see Johnson *et al.* (1997, pp.14-17, 22-24) and Sood and Scutella (1997) for further details. The final effect of these taxes on consumer prices is the result of a complex process, particularly as different taxes are imposed at different stages of the production and distribution process and some taxes are unit taxes while others are *ad valorem*. The effective rates on different commodity groups depend on the extent to which taxes are shifted forward at each production stage and on the nature of inter-industry transactions.

Estimates of the effective indirect tax rates arising from the pre-GST system were reported by Johnson *et al.* (1999, p.12) for 14 commodity groups used by the Household Expenditure Survey. They also reported the price changes for the proposed GST system which included food; this system is

9

Table 2: Effective Indirect Tax Rates

No.	Description	Pre-GST	GST-P	Post-GST
1	Current housing costs	0.1363	0.1791	0.1988
2	Fuel and Power	0.0872	0.1634	0.1697
3	Food and Non Alcoholic Beverages	0.1142	0.1753	0.1015
4	Alcohol	0.2969	0.3332	0.3046
5	Tobacco products	0.6826	0.8959	0.9025
6	Clothing and footwear	0.0681	0.1476	0.1548
7	Furnishings and equipment	0.1072	0.1382	0.1493
8	Services and Operation	0.0903	0.1176	0.1183
9	Medical Care and Health	0.0569	0.0362	0.0462
10	Transport	0.2381	0.1977	0.2039
11	Recreation and entertainment	0.1436	0.1930	0.1927
12	Personal care	0.1259	0.1360	0.1138
13	Miscellaneous goods and services	0.1411	0.1241	0.1566
14	Other Capital Housing	0.1147	0.1462	0.1622

is referred to here as GST-P. The effective rates are shown in Table 2.[8] The GST that was eventually introduced involved several modifications to the proposals, the most important of which was the exemption of most food from the GST. The post-GST indirect tax rates are shown in the final column of Table 2.[9] The values reported in the table are effective tax-exclusive *ad valorem* rates, calculated using the method devised by Scutella (1997). This involves tracing the incidence through the input-output matrix, assuming full shifting at each stage. It can be seen that there is a considerable degree

---

[8] Johnson *et al.* (1999) reported values to just one decimal point, but more detailed values were kindly provided by Rosanna Scutella. In addition, the rates are obtained after converting the price changes into tax rates using the result that if the tax rate changes from t_1 to t_2, the price increase is given by $\dot{p} = (t_2 - t_1)/(1 + t_1)$, so that $t_2 = t_1 + (1 + t_1)\dot{p}$.

[9] These are the same as those used by Johnson (1999). Potential general equilibrium effects of indirect taxes on factor prices were ignored in calculating these rates. For example, a tax imposed on a good which comprises a high proportion of total expenditure of low-wage households may involve, through output and factor substitution effects and depending on relative factor intensities, a compensating rise in the incomes of those households. The two sets of rates clearly do not generate the same amount of revenue from indirect taxes.

10

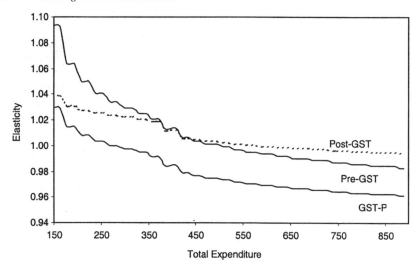

Figure 1: Elasticity Profiles for Australian Tax Structure

of non-uniformity in the effective rates.[10]

Profiles of the revenue elasticity are shown in Figure 1.[11]   It can be seen that the pre-GST system has measures of liability progression that are slightly above 1 only for total expenditure levels below about $500 per week. For the GST-P structure, it falls below 1 after about $250 per week. The post-GST system is only slightly more progressive, at all total expenditure levels, than the proposed system that included a GST on food. While the post-GST system has lower values of liability progression at the lower total expenditure levels, these are closer to 1 at the higher expenditure levels. However, the differences are very small and the flatness of the profiles sug-

---

[10]It was necessary to carry out a certain amount of consolidation from the more than 100 rates obtained for the categories in the input-output matrix. Hence the rates shown can only be regarded as approximate rates obtained under strong shifting assumptions.

[11]These profiles are not smooth because of the use of total expenditure groups (those used to obtain average budget shares for the regressions), within which the budget shares are assumed to be constant.

11

Table 3: Alternative Tax Structures

No.	Description	A	B	C
1	Current housing costs			0.25
2	Electricity, gas and other fuels			0.35
3	Food and beverages			0.45
4	Spirits, beer and wine			
5	Tobacco			
6	Clothing and footwear	0.30	0.30	
7	Furniture and appliances	0.30	0.30	
8	Postal and telephone charges			0.20
9	Health services			0.25
10	Motor vehicles and parts	0.30	0.40	
11	Recreational items	0.30	0.20	
12	Personal care products			0.20
13	Miscellaneous	0.30	0.20	
14	House building payments	0.30	0.40	

gests that, despite the non-uniformity involved, their overall effect differs little from a uniform system.[12]

Consider alternative structures designed to produce a larger amount redistribution. Based on the earlier discussion, the following analysis considers hypothetical tax structures shown in Table 3. Instead of imposing the extreme structure based on taxing the good with the highest total elasticity, cases A and B taxes those goods whose budget shares rise with income (that is, have an elasticity greater than one). Case A has a uniform tax imposed on a selection of goods, so that liability progression does not actually depend on the rate used. Case B has relatively higher taxes imposed on those groups for which the shares increase relatively faster with income: motor vehicles and parts (category 10) and house building payments (category 14) have the highest tax rate of 40 per cent, while a lower rate is imposed on recreational items (category 11) and miscellaneous (category 13). These systems obviously have far more selectivity than has been suggested in practice. For

---

[12]This is confirmed by examination of the Gini measure of inequality of total expenditure net of indirect taxation; these were found to be not statistically significantly different.

12

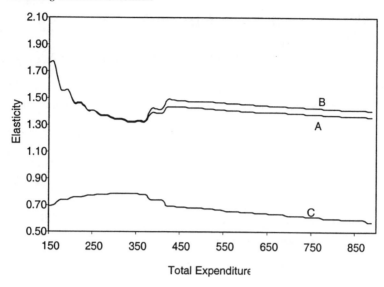

Figure 2: Elasticity Profiles for Alternative Tax Structures

contrast, case C has a regressive structure involving non-uniform taxes on a selection of goods, for which the budget shares fall as income rises.

The profiles of the revenue elasticities (liability progression) are shown in Figure 2. Cases A and B are, expected, quite similar, and give values that are higher than the actual tax structure at all the relevant total expenditure levels. Nevertheless, the highest elasticity values, at the lower total expenditure levels, are substantially below those achieved by a progressive income tax structure. The non-monotonic variation in the revenue elasticity arises because of the non-monotonic variations in the income elasticities as total expenditure varies. The profiles are also based on average budget shares within total expenditure groups. In practice the heterogeneity in consumption patterns between households with similar levels of total expenditure is likely to introduce horizontal inequities and reranking effects that militate against the attempt to increase redistribution.

13

3   Welfare Change Measures

The above discussion concentrated on 'local' measures of tax progression. This section considers the effects of the alternative 'extreme' indirect tax structures on measures of welfare change and on overall evaluations using a social welfare function. The welfare changes were obtained using the method described in Creedy (1999), which involves the use of strong assumptions regarding preferences. In particular, it is assumed that, within each total expenditure group, households have similar additive utility functions. Equivalent variations are calculated for each of a range of total expenditure groups, using separate estimates of the linear expenditure function for each group. Price changes, $\dot{p}_i$, are regarded as arising from the indirect tax structure, so that $\dot{p}_i = t_i$.

Use is also made of a money metric welfare measure which, following King (1983), is often known as 'equivalent income'. This is defined as the value of total expenditure, y_e, that, at some reference set of prices, p_r, gives the same utility as the actual total expenditure and prices.[13] When pre-change prices are used as reference prices, the change in equivalent income is the equivalent variation, so that equivalent income is given by $y_e = y - EV$, since pre-change equivalent income is simply y. The proportionate change in equivalent income following a set of price changes is EV/y. If this ratio is the same for all households, any relative measure of inequality of equivalent income is unchanged as a result of the tax change. The overall effects of a tax change can also be evaluated using a social welfare function specified in terms of equivalent incomes.

---

[13]In terms of the indirect utility function, y_e is therefore defined by $V(p_r, y_e) = V(p, y)$. Using the expenditure function gives $y_e = E(p_r, V(p, y))$. Crucially, it is invariant with respect to monotonic variations in the utility function.

14

Table 4: Ratio of Equivalent Variations to Total Expenditure

y	A	B	C
200	0.078	0.075	0.189
400	0.102	0.098	0.163
600	0.118	0.116	0.146
800	0.129	0.128	0.133
1000	0.138	0.138	0.123
1200	0.145	0.147	0.115
1400	0.157	0.160	0.100

3.1   Equivalent Variations

The equivalent variations for the alternative tax structures, for a range of levels of weekly total expenditure (in dollars), are shown in Table 4. In order to place the total expenditure levels, y, in perspective, the median value is $556.35; the lower and upper quartiles are $335.92 and $845.02; and the first and ninth deciles are $204.62 and $1227.36.

Under cases A and B it can be seen that the ratio, EV/y, increases as y increases, which is consistent with an inequality reducing effect.[14] For B, the ratio EV/y increases more rapidly as y increases, but this difference is very small. Structure C gives rise, as expected, to a reduction in EV/y as y increases, consistent with an increase in inequality.

3.2   Abbreviated Social Welfare Functions

An overall evaluation of a tax change can be made using a social welfare or evaluation function expressed in terms of the distribution of equivalent incomes. The abbreviated social welfare function associated with Atkinson's inequality measure is given by:

$$W_A = \bar{y}_e \left(1 - A\left(\varepsilon\right)\right) \tag{9}$$

---

[14]For a uniform system the ratio is constant. For example, with a uniform rate of $t_i = 0.15$ for all i, then $\dot{p}_i = \dot{p} = 0.15$ for all i, and $EV/y = \dot{p}/\left(1 + \dot{p}\right) = 0.13$ for all values of y.

15

where W_A is welfare per person, ε is the degree of constant relative inequality aversion, $\bar{y}_e$ is the arithmetic mean equivalent income and $A(\varepsilon)$ is Atkinson's inequality measure.[15] The same form of welfare function can be used with the Gini inequality measure (or the extended Gini, $G(v)$, for $v \geq 1$).[16] On abbreviated welfare functions, see Lambert (1993).

The approach adopted here is to evaluate alternative welfare functions specified in terms of the distribution of equivalent income per equivalent adult, using a very simple adjustment, whereby the first adult is given a weight of 1, the second adult is given a weight of 0.6 and each child is given a weight of 0.3.[17] Households were divided into 9 separate groups, described in Table 5. These groups cover about 75 per cent of all households in the Household Expenditure Survey. For groups 2 to 10, the number of equivalent adults were set respectively to [1.6, 1.6, 1.9, 2.2, 2.6, 1.3, 1.7, 1, 1]. In computing the welfare effects, separate elasticities and parameters of the utility functions were obtained for each household type and total expenditure level.

Values of inequality and social welfare, based on equivalent incomes per equivalent adult, are shown in Table 6. These are compared with a uniform structure that has no redistributive effect.[18] It can be seen that structures A and B give rise to lower values of inequality *and* higher social welfare. The inequality reduction therefore outweighs the reduction in average equivalent income per equivalent adult as the tax becomes more progressive. However, for all degrees of inequality aversion, the reduction in inequality is small, considering the substantial differences between the tax structures.

---

[15] A 1 per cent increase in equality is viewed as being equivalent to a 1 per cent increase in mean income, bearing in mind that the measure of equality increase depends on the value of ε.

[16] The extended Gini is $G(v) = -\frac{v}{\bar{y}}\mathrm{Cov}\{y, (1-F(y))^{v-1}\}$, where F denotes the distribution function, and the standard Gini is $G(2)$.

[17] See Johnson *et al.* (1995) for discussion of alternative scales used in Australia.

[18] The uniform tax rate was set at 0.15, which is approximately revenue neutral.

16

Table 5: Household Groups

No.	Household Type	number
1	All households	7590
2	Couple: no children	1430
3	Couple: no children, ≥ 1 retired	450
4	Couple: 1 dependant child	586
5	Couple: 2 dependant children	790
6	Couple: ≥ 3 dependant children	540
7	1 parent: 1 dependant child	190
8	1 parent: ≥ 2 dependant children	187
9	Single person, not retired	1000
10	Single person, retired	620

Table 6: Equivalent Income per Equivalent Adult

ε	W_A	$A(\varepsilon)$	v	$G(v)$	W_G
		Uniform Taxes			
0.10	562.08	0.0212	1.10	0.0646	537.17
1.60	394.33	0.3133	2.60	0.4472	317.48
		Tax Structure A			
0.10	562.95	0.0195	1.10	0.0615	538.84
1.60	406.59	0.2919	2.60	0.4313	326.54
		Tax Structure B			
0.10	563.01	0.0193	1.10	0.0611	539.03
1.60	407.57	0.2901	2.60	0.4295	327.52

17

4 Conclusions

This paper has examined the question of the extent to which redistribution can be achieved using a structure of consumption taxes with differential rates and exemptions. Although redistribution can be achieved by taxing most heavily those goods for which the income elasticity exceeds unity (for which the budget shares increase as income increases), there are strong limitations in view of the fact that virtually all households consume some goods in each commodity group (given a broad classification) and elasticities ultimately tend to unity as income rises.

The issue was examined by considering a local measure of progression, that of liability progression which is equivalent to the revenue elasticity with respect to total expenditure. Progressivity was found to be maximised when only one commodity group, that having the largest total expenditure elasticity, is taxed. Where further commodity groups need to be taxed to meet revenue requirements, the tax rate should fall as the total expenditure elasticity falls. With a uniform structure, where some goods are exempt from a consumption tax, the liability progression is independent of the level of the tax rate. The Australian indirect tax structure was examined along with alternative forms involving the taxation of only those groups for which the expenditure elasticity exceeds unity at all total expenditure levels. Budget shares and income elasticities were based on the Household Expenditure Survey for 1993. In addition, comparison were made of equivalent variations, for a range of levels of total expenditure, resulting from the imposition of indirect taxes. Inequality measures of the distribution of household equivalent income (a money metric welfare measure) per equivalent adult were computed. It was found that even extreme forms of differentiation in indirect taxes have a relatively small effect on liability progression and inequality. The results confirm the initial suggestion that consumption taxes provide only a 'blunt redistributive instrument'.

18

References

[1] Chisholm, A., Freebairn, J. and Porter, M. (1990) A goods and services tax for Australia. *Australian Forum*, 7, pp. 127-190.

[2] Creedy, J. (1998) Are consumption taxes regressive? *Australian Economic Review,* 31, pp. 107-116.

[3] Creedy, J. (1999) Indirect tax reform in Australia: the welfare effects on different demographic groups. *Australian Economic Papers*, 38, pp. 367-392.

[4] Creedy, J. and Gemmell, N. (2001) The built-in flexibility of taxation. *Journal of Economic Surveys,* (forthcoming).

[5] Deaton, A.S. and Muellbauer, J. (1980) *Economics and Consumer Behaviour.* Cambridge: Cambridge University Press.

[6] Johnson, D. (1999) The impact of new tax legislation on households. *Family Matters*, 54, pp. 55-59.

[7] Johnson, D., Manning, I. and Hellwig, O. (1995) *Trends in The Distribution of Cash Income and Non-cash Benefits.* Canberra: AGPS.

[8] Johnson, D., Freebairn, J., Creedy, J., Scutella, R. and Cowling, S. (1997) *A Stocktake of Taxation in Australia.* Melbourne: Melbourne Institute of Applied Economic and Social Research.

[9] Johnson, D., Freebairn, J. and Scutella, R. (1999) *Evaluation of the Government's Tax Package.* Melbourne: Melbourne Institute of Applied Economic and Social Research.

[10] King, M. A. (1983) Welfare Analysis of Tax Reforms Using Household Data. *Journal of Public Economics*, 21, pp. 183-214.

[11] Lambert, P.J. (1993) *The Distribution and Redistribution of Income: A Mathematical Analysis.* Manchester: Manchester University Press.

[12] Sah, R.K. (1983) How much redistribution is possible through indirect taxes. *Journal of Public Economics*, 12, pp. 83-102.

[13] Scutella, R. (1997) The incidence of indirect taxes on final demand in Australia. *Melbourne Institute of Applied Economic and Social Research Working Paper*, no. 18/97.

[14] Sood, R. and Scutella, R. (1997) Description of the current Australian indirect tax system. *Melbourne Institute of Applied Economic and Social Research Working Paper*, no. 19/97.

[15] Stern, N. (1990) Uniformity versus selectivity in indirect taxation. *Economics and Politics,* 2, pp. 83-102.

[13]

Bayesian Estimation of Social Welfare and Tax Progressivity Measures.

Duangkamon Chotikapanich and John Creedy*

1 Introduction

Measures of social welfare, income inequality and tax progressivity are used in comparing tax systems in different countries and time periods, as well as alternative (actual or hypothetical) tax systems within a country. However, the vast majority of empirical studies report only sample values or point estimates, without measures of their precision. One approach to describe the precision of an estimate is by the use of the posterior probability density function for the corresponding parameter. This paper investigates Bayesian methods for examining posterior distributions of several inequality, concentration, tax progressivity and social welfare measures.

Several approaches to the Bayesian estimation of the Gini inequality measure were used by Chotikapanich and Griffiths (2000) to produce posterior distributions for a sample of households in Bangkok. In obtaining the likelihood function, which is derived from a multinomial distribution, Chotikapanich and Griffiths (2000) explored explicit income distribution assumptions and alternative assumptions regarding the arithmetic mean within each income group. In view of the use of the multinomial distribution, these methods are necessarily applied

*School of Economics and Finance, Curtin University of Technology, Perth, and Department of Economics, University of Melbourne. This research was supported by a Melbourne University Faculty of Economics and Commerce Research Grant. We should like to thank Bill Griffiths and two referees for comments on an earlier draft.

1

to grouped income distributions rather than individual data.[1]

Extending the Bayesian approaches to the examination of tax progressivity measures raises the need to deal with three related distributions; these are pre-tax and post-tax income distributions and the distribution of tax payments. Furthermore, it is necessary to obtain concentration measures in addition to Gini measures. The concentration measures involve cumulative distributions of post-tax income and tax payments, where the ranking of individuals is according to pre-tax incomes. This ranking is typically different from the other distributions in view of the reranking caused by the tax system.

In examining the concentration and progressivity measures, it is necessary to have individual data. Separate grouped distributions, of pre-tax and post-tax incomes and tax payments, are insufficient because of the need to have measures ranked by alternative variables. In extending the Chotikapanich and Griffiths (2000) methods to the present context, the question of the appropriate choice of grouping method therefore immediately arises. This issue involves the choice regarding the type of income class as well as that of the number of groups. However, one cost of the use of some form of grouping is that it substantially reduces the extent of measured reranking.

The summary measures investigated are described briefly in section 2; these included the Reynolds-Smolensky measure of redistribution, the Kakwani measure of tax progressivity and the abbreviated social welfare function based on the Gini inequality measure. The computation of alternative measures using grouped data is discussed in section 3. Section 4 presents the three alternative methods used to derive posterior distributions; these methods assume that the pre-tax income distribution follows the two-parameter lognormal form, that the income-group means are equal to their sample values, and that, within each group, the income-group means follow a triangular distribution. Section 5 reports numerical results of applying the approaches, including the analysis of alternative grouping

---

[1]Kakwani and Podder (1973, 1976) employed an approximate linear model framework and grouped data to obtain a sampling theory estimate of the Gini coefficient. A multinomial framework for sampling theory estimation of the parameters of a variety of income distributions was used by Kloek and van Dijk (1978) and van Dijk and Kloek (1980), and for the Pareto distribution by Aigner and Goldberger (1970).

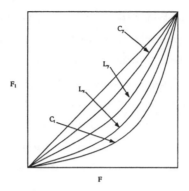

Figure 1: Lorenz and Concentration Curves

methods. Conclusions are in section 6.

2   Summary Measures

The summary measures of inequality and progressivity used here are based on Lorenz and concentration curves.[2] First, rank individuals in ascending order according to their pre-tax incomes, x_i, for $i = 1, ..., N$, so that $x_i > x_j$ for $i > j$. As i is increased from 1 to N, the Lorenz curve is defined as the relationship between the proportion, $F(x_i)$, of people with income less than or equal to x_i, and the associated proportion, $F_1(x_i)$, of total income obtained by those individuals. Hence, for a continuous distribution it is the relationship between the distribution function, $F(x) = \int_0^x dF(u)$, and the first moment distribution function, $F_1(x) = \int_0^x u\,dF(u) / \int_0^\infty u\,dF(u)$. Writing $\pi = F(x)$ and $\eta = F_1(x)$, the Lorenz curve is defined as:

$$\eta = \eta(\pi) \tag{1}$$

A Lorenz curve of pre–tax income is shown in Figure 1 as the line L_x. The tax system transforms pre-tax income, x_i, into post-tax income, y_i, the Lorenz curve of which is illustrated in Figure 1 as the line L_y. The Gini measure of inequality

---

[2]For further discussion of these concepts see, for example, Lambert (1993) and Creedy (1996).

is defined as twice the area contained by the Lorenz curve and the line of equality and is thus given by:

$$G = 1 - 2 \int_0^1 \eta(\pi) \, d\pi \tag{2}$$

The absolute difference between pre- and post-tax Ginis, G_x and G_y, is the Reynolds-Smolensky (1977) measure of redistributive effect, L, so that:

$$L = G_x - G_y \tag{3}$$

The concentration curve of post-tax income is obtained by ranking individuals according to their pre-tax incomes, and relating the proportion of people to the corresponding proportion of total post-tax income. An example is shown in Figure 1 as C_y. If there is any reranking of individuals when moving from the pre-tax to the post-tax distribution, the concentration curve must lie inside the Lorenz curve of y over some of its range. The concentration index, C_y, is similar to the Gini inequality measure.

In addition, a tax concentration curve is shown in Figure 1. This is defined as the proportion of people plotted against the corresponding proportion of total tax paid by those individuals, when they are ranked according to pre-tax incomes. This gives rise to a tax concentration index, C_t. If the tax system is proportional, the four curves coincide and $L_y = C_y = C_t = L_x$. The curves differ if there is some disproportionality in the tax system. If the tax system is progressive, the average tax rate increases and the proportions of total tax paid must be less than the corresponding $F_1(x)$. Hence, the concentration curve of taxation shows more inequality than the Lorenz curve of pre-tax income, as illustrated in Figure 1.

Kakwani's (1977) measure of progressivity, K, is the difference between the tax concentration index and the Gini measure of x, so that:

$$K = C_t - G_x \tag{4}$$

The possibility of reranking of individuals when moving from the pre-tax to the post-tax income distribution arises from the existence of tax-relevant non-income differences between individuals. Without reranking, G_y and C_y are equal, and

4

the Atkinson (1979)-Plotnick (1981) reranking index, R, is:

$$R = G_y - C_y \tag{5}$$

The Gini measure can be related to explicit value judgements. Although it is not consistent with an individualistic social welfare function, Sen (1973) showed that it can be derived from a 'pairwise maximin' criterion. According to this, the welfare level of any pair of individuals is equal to the income of the poorest of the two. The average welfare of all pairs is equal to:

$$W = \bar{y}\,(1 - G) \tag{6}$$

which gives the abbreviated social welfare function expressed in terms of arithmetic mean income and its equality (one minus inequality). The following section discusses how these measures can be computed using grouped data.

3   Computation of Alternative Measures

This section describes the computation of alternative measures using grouped data and introduces the notation used in the following section. Suppose the sample of pre-tax incomes is ranked such that $x_1 < x_2 < ... < x_N$ and divided into M groups, with lower and upper limits of $x_{L,i}$ and $x_{U,i}$ respectively, and frequencies, n_i, for $i = 1, ..., M$. Let p_i be the probability that an individual chosen randomly has income in class i and let μ_i be the mean income within the ith class. The proportions, π_i and η_i, for each class can be expressed as:

$$\pi_i = \sum_{j=1}^{i} p_j \tag{7}$$

$$\eta_i = \frac{\sum_{j=1}^{i} p_j \mu_j}{\sum_{j=1}^{M} p_j \mu_j} \tag{8}$$

A Lorenz curve based on grouped data has linear segments, assuming that there is no inequality within each income class. Computing the area between each linear segment and the 45^0 line, and aggregating over segments, leads to the Gini expression:

$$G_x = \sum_{i=1}^{M-1} \eta_{i+1} \pi_i - \sum_{i=1}^{M-1} \eta_i \pi_{i+1} \tag{9}$$

5

Sample values based on (9), are necessarily lower than the sample value based on the original individual incomes. The extent of the difference depends on the grouping method used and the number of groups. This issue is examined in more detail in section 5.

In practice, p_i can be calculated as n_i/N, where $N = \sum_{i=1}^{M} n_i$. For μ_i, if the group arithmetic means, $\overline{x}_i$, are known, then $\mu_i = \overline{x}_i$. For this case, the proportions corresponding to the distribution function and first moment distribution, π_i and η_i, are defined as:

$$\pi_i = \frac{1}{N} \sum_{j=1}^{i} n_j \tag{10}$$

$$\eta_i = \frac{1}{\overline{x}} \sum_{j=1}^{i} n_j \overline{x}_j \tag{11}$$

If $\overline{x}_i$ are not known, the group mid-point is often used as μ_i. The values of p_i and μ_i are normally treated as being known with certainty. However, Chotikapanich and Griffiths (2000) argue that they are not known with certainty and they suggest several ways of capturing uncertainty using posterior probability density functions; their approaches are summarised in the next section.

The expression for the Gini measure in equation (9) can be modified to produce concentration measures of post-tax income and taxation. Those in group i have an arithmetic mean post-tax income of $\overline{y}_{x,i}$, where the first subscript, x, indicates that the ranking is by pre-tax incomes. The minimum and maximum values of post-tax income in group i are $y_{L,i}$ and $y_{U,i}$.

The arithmetic mean tax payment in group i is denoted $\overline{T}_{x,i}$, where again the first subscript indicates the variable used to rank the individuals. There is a possibility that some of the class limits of post-tax income overlap, so that, for example, $y_{U,i} > y_{L,i+1}$. However, the grouping of the data reduces this possibility. For the pre-tax, post-tax and tax distributions, the number of observations in group i may not necessarily be the same, but these are chosen here to be the same as n_i to make computation more straightforward.

For the post-tax concentration curve, the values of η_i are:

$$\eta_i = \frac{1}{\overline{y}} \sum_{j=1}^{i} n_j \overline{y}_{x,j} \tag{12}$$

6

while the corresponding π_i are as in (10). The concentration measure, C_y, is obtained by appropriate substitution into equation (9). The tax concentration measure is obtained in a similar way, using:

$$\eta_i = \frac{1}{\overline{T}} \sum_{j=1}^{i} n_j \overline{T}_{x,j} \tag{13}$$

This approach to grouped data produces sample values and, in view of the assumption of within-group equality, they generally understate the corresponding sample values that are based on individual observations. The computation of posterior distributions is considered in the following section.

4   Posterior Densities

Posterior densities are used to reflect the uncertainties in p_i and μ_i. The first subsection below considers the posterior density for p_i, while the second subsection considers two approaches to the μ_i.

4.1   Posterior Density For p_i

Let n and p respectively denote vectors of observed group frequencies n_i, and the p_i ($i = 1, ..., M$). Using Bayes's Theorem, the posterior pdf for p is:

$$f(p|n) \propto f(p) f(n|p) \tag{14}$$

where $f(p)$ is the prior distribution and $f(n|p)$ is the likelihood function. A possible noninformative prior takes the form:[3]

$$f(p) \propto \prod_{i=1}^{M} p_i^{-1} \tag{15}$$

The likelihood function, $f(n|p)$, follows the multinomial distribution, whereby:

$$f(n|p) \propto \prod_{i=1}^{M} p_i^{n_i} \tag{16}$$

---

[3]See, for example, Gelman *et al.* (1995, p.399)

Combining this prior and the likelihood function, the posterior probability density function for p is:

$$f(p|n) \propto \prod_{i=1}^{M} p_i^{n_i-1} \tag{17}$$

This is a Dirichlet distribution from which random observations can be drawn and which reflects the uncertainty about the p_is.

4.2 Information about μ_i

In this subsection, two approaches for reflecting uncertainty about the μ_is are examined. First, an explicit functional form is assumed and, secondly, assumptions are made about the group means.

4.2.1 Lognormal Distribution of Pre-tax Income

The lognormal distribution has a long history in theoretical and empirical studies of income distribution, since the seminal work of Aitchison and Brown (1957). It has been found to provide an approximation to many observed distributions and is therefore a natural candidate for use here. Suppose that x is distributed lognormally as $\Lambda\left(x|\mu,\sigma^2\right)$, where μ and σ^2 are respectively the mean and variance of the logarithms of pre-tax income. Hence:

$$\Lambda(x) = N\left(\frac{\log x - \mu}{\sigma}\Big|0,1\right) \tag{18}$$

Define the parameter vector, $\theta = (\mu,\sigma)$, so that (14) can be used to obtain $f(\theta|n)$. The specification of the prior density $f(\theta)$ is based on the standard use of noninformative improper priors on both parameters, where μ and $\log\sigma$ are assumed to be uniformly distributed. Thus the joint density $f(\theta)$ is proportional to σ^{-1}.[4]

The likelihood function, $f(n|\theta)$, follows from (16) and can be written as:

$$f(n|\theta) \propto \prod_{i=1}^{M} \{\Lambda(x_{U,i}) - \Lambda(x_{L,i})\}^{n_i} \tag{19}$$

---

[4]On the use of a uniform prior for $\log\sigma$, see for example Judge *et al.* (1998, p.150), Box and Tiao (1973) and Zellner (1971, pp.42-44).

The resulting posterior density obtained using Bayes's Theorem, (14), is not analytically tractable. However, a Metropolis-Hastings algorithm can be used to draw observations from it; see, for example, Geweke (1999) and Chotikapanich and Griffiths (2000). Given a drawing of σ^2, a corresponding value of the Gini inequality measure of pre-tax income can be obtained using the fact that, for the lognormal distribution:

$$G_x = 2N\left(\left.\frac{\sigma}{\sqrt{2}}\right| 0,1\right) - 1 \tag{20}$$

and G_x depends only on the variance of logarithms of income.[5] The resulting values can be used to estimate the posterior density for G_x.

The assumption that pre-tax income, x, is lognormally distributed cannot be applied directly to the distributions of tax payments and post-tax income. In these cases the approach proceeds as follows. Each drawing of μ and σ, as part of the Metropolis-Hastings algorithm, can be used to obtain a set of proportions, π_i, corresponding to each group, using the lognormal property in (18). These, by construction, apply also to the distributions of tax payments and post-tax incomes.

In order to apply (9) to the calculation of corresponding values of C_t and C_y, it is necessary to obtain the appropriate values of η_i. These can be obtained by combining the computed π_is with the actual arithmetic means, $\overline{y}_{x,i}$ and $\overline{T}_{x,i}$ defined above. This enables the values of the post-tax Gini, the concentration measures, and hence the progressivity measures, to be obtained for each (μ, σ) combination.[6]

4.2.2   Assumptions About Group Mean Income

If no explicit assumption about the income distribution is made, two assumptions regarding the value of μ_i are examined. First, for the pre-tax income distribution, the μ_i are set equal to the corresponding group arithmetic means, $\overline{x}_i$, as

---

[5]This result is derived in Aitchison and Brown (1957, pp.12-13).

[6]For this reason the computation of the Gini measure of post-tax income is not strictly comparable with the value that would be obtained as the sample statistic, using a grouping of individuals after first ranking by post-tax income.

defined above. Similarly, the corresponding values for the post-tax income and tax concentration measures are taken from the $\overline{y}_{x,i}$ and $\overline{T}_{x,i}$.

The second approach assigns a low probability of the group mean taking values around the end points of each interval and a high probability around the centre of the interval. A class of density functions that is simple and captures this characteristic is that of triangular distributions. Hence assume that, within each group, the mean values follow a triangular distribution over the range defined by the class limits, $x_{L,i}$ and $x_{U,i}$, with the prior for the mode set equal to the sample arithmetic mean, $\overline{x}_i$. The procedure used for each income group is as follows.[7] First draw a random value, $P_i = F(\mu_i)$ from a uniform $(0,1)$ distribution. Check if:

$$P_i < \frac{\overline{x}_i - x_{L,i}}{x_{U,i} - x_{L,i}} \tag{21}$$

which implies that μ_i lies between $x_{L,i}$ and $\overline{x}_i$. If this condition holds, then the range of the distribution for which:

$$F(\mu_i) = \frac{(\mu_i - x_{L,i})^2}{(x_{U,i} - x_{L,i})(\overline{x}_i - x_{L,i})} \tag{22}$$

is appropriate. Hence, substitute for $P_i = F(\mu_i)$ and solve for μ_i to get:

$$\mu_i = x_{L,i} - \{P_i(x_{U,i} - x_{L,i})(\overline{x}_i - x_{L,i})\} \tag{23}$$

If the condition in (21) does not hold, μ_i lies between $x_{U,i}$ and $\overline{x}_i$, and:

$$F(\mu_i) = 1 - \frac{(x_{U,i} - \mu_i)^2}{(x_{U,i} - x_{L,i})(x_{U,i} - \overline{x}_i)} \tag{24}$$

Solving for μ_i gives:

$$\mu_i = x_{U,i} - \{(1 - P_i)(x_{U,i} - x_{L,i})(x_{U,i} - \overline{x}_i)\} \tag{25}$$

The resulting values of μ_i are combined with the p_i from the Dirichlet distribution to obtain the required π_i and η_i from (7) and (8). These are substituted into (9) to generate the posterior density for the Gini inequality measure.

For the post-tax income concentration measure the mode of the triangular distribution is set at the difference between μ_i obtained for the pre-tax distribution

---

[7] See also Chotikapanich and Griffiths (2000).

above and the arithmetic mean tax paid, $\overline{T}_{x,i}$. The limits are $y_{L,i}$ and $\min[y_{U,i}, \mu_i]$, where μ_i is the value obtained in relation to the pre-tax distribution. This procedure ensures consistency between the three distributions and adds precision to the range of post-tax incomes in each group. For the tax concentration measure the value of μ_i is set at the difference between the two values obtained for pre- and post-tax distributions.

5   Numerical Results

With the emphasis on developing methods, the decision was taken to examine the effects of alternative approaches using a simulated data set, rather than a specific cross-sectional survey. This avoids the need to consider features that are specific to a particular application. It is also useful to see how the distributional assumption (of lognormality) performs when the data are in fact known to be sampled from a lognormal population. This section therefore presents numerical results based on a simulated sample of 2000 individuals drawn from a pre-tax income distribution that is assumed to be lognormal. An income tax system, involving six marginal tax rates, was then applied, with individual-specific income thresholds. Finally, each individual was subject to indirect taxation. Post-tax income is defined as equal to the value of expenditure net of indirect tax. The details of the simulation method are described in the Appendix. As discussed above, the pre-tax distribution is based on a lognormal population, but the same assumption cannot apply to tax payments and the post-tax distribution.

The first stage of the analysis involves an investigation of the implications of adopting alternative rules for grouping the incomes. Having decided on an appropriate rule, the full analysis can be carried out. These stages are discussed in the following two subsections.

5.1   Grouping of Pre-tax Incomes

This subsection considers two procedures for grouping the pre-tax incomes. The first method involves the division of the sample into groups containing equal

11

percentiles, and the second method uses a division into groups whose logarithmic class-widths are equal. The use of equal absolute class-widths has little to recommend it in the context of positively skewed distributions since it involves groups with substantially different numbers of observations; preliminary analyses confirmed that it performed badly in comparison with the other two methods. The cost, in terms of computing time, of increasing the number of groups increases substantially. Hence, there is little point in arbitrarily selecting a large number of groups (while retaining non-zero observations in most groups). The question arises of whether there is a optimum number of groups.

In view of the extensive computing demands of the methods described in section 4, the analysis of alternative groupings was restricted to a single measure, the Gini inequality of pre-tax incomes, and a single method of deriving the posterior distribution (the assumption of lognormality). Each grouping procedure was applied to a range of numbers of groups, from 4 to 45. In each case the sample Gini and the arithmetic mean and standard deviation of the posterior distribution were computed. In applying the Metropolis-Hastings algorithm, 85,000 repetitions were used, with the first 10,000 being discarded.

Figure 2 shows the sample Gini and the arithmetic means, using groups of equal logarithmic width and groups containing equal percentiles. In each case these values are compared with the sample value obtained by using all 2,000 individual observations. As expected, the sample values from the grouped data, obtained using equation (9), are much lower than the value from individual incomes when only a few groups are used. They approach the latter as the number of groups increases. However, the estimated arithmetic means of the posterior distributions, as a result of the explicit allowance for the within-group variation, are much closer to the sample value obtained from individual observations. Indeed, in most cases the use of equal logarithmic widths produces values that are slightly higher than that from individual values, for all class widths investigated. The results in Figure 2 show that the use of equal log-widths (combined with the assumption of lognormality) generates mean values of the posterior distributions that are typically closer to the Gini obtained from individual data. Examination

12

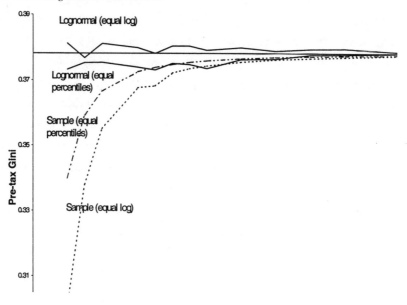

Figure 2: Pre-Tax Gini and Grouping Method

showed that the posteriors are symmetric, so the use of the mean (equal to the median) is consistent with both quadratic and linear loss functions.

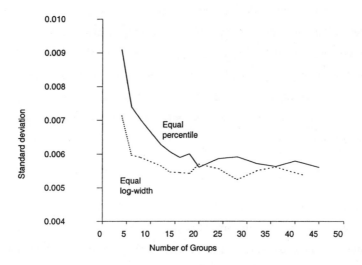

Figure 3: Standard Deviation of Posterior Distributions

Figure 3 shows the standard deviation of the posterior distributions for each combination of number of groups used and grouping method. These results show, in each case, a rapid decline in the standard deviation as the number of groups increases from the minimum value. However, the profiles become relatively flat after about 16 groups. Although there is clearly a penalty resulting from the use of a small number of groups, there is no further advantage to be gained from increasing the number of groups beyond a certain level. Hence, there is not a unique optimal number of groups which minimises the standard deviation. However, the smallest number of groups for which the profile becomes flat can readily be obtained. Figure 3 also shows that using equal logarithmic widths generally produces lower standard deviations. Furthermore, the selection of the smallest

14

value of M for which the standard deviation reaches its minimum imposes, in the case of equal log-widths, no cost in terms of the arithmetic mean being lower than the sample value obtained from individual observations.

These results suggest a preference for the use of income classes of equal log-width. A possible explanation is that the use of equal percentiles involves some very large (wide) income classes in the upper tail of the distribution. Furthermore, the experiments reveal a simple strategy for selecting the number of groups, whereby the number is gradually increased until the standard deviation of the posterior distribution stabilises. There is no further advantage to be gained in using a larger number of groups, whereas there is a substantial cost in terms of computing time.

5.2   The Summary Measures

The results of applying the three methods to obtain the posterior distributions of the various summary measures are shown in Table 1. These were obtained using 18 groups of equal log-width. In the case of the assumption of lognormality, 85,000 repetitions of the Metropolis-Hastings algorithm were used, with the first 10,000 being discarded. In the other two cases, 5,000 draws from the required Dirichlet distribution were used.[8]

The first two columns of results in Table 1 give the sample values obtained using individual observations and the grouped data. The sample values of the Gini inequality measures based on grouped data are, as expected, below the values from individual data. The need to group the data for the analysis of posterior distributions means, as indicated above, that the small amount of reranking between pre-tax and post-tax distributions is concealed by the grouped data.[9] This means that $G_y = C_y$ in all cases, except for individual observations. It can be

---

[8]In the case of the Metropolis-Hastings algorithm, the draws are correlated and it is therefore necessary to take a large number of draws until convergence is reached. This does not apply to the draws from the Dirichlet distribution; experiments showed that the use of more than 5000 did not affect the results.

[9]The sample Atkinson-Plotnick measure from individual observations is equal to 0.00613. This small amount of reranking arises from the fact that the income thresholds differ between individuals, as explained in the Appendix.

Table 1: Alternative Summary Measures: 18 Groups Equal Log-width

Measure	Sample Values		Means of Posteriors		
	Individual	Grouped	Lognormal	Triangular	Group Mean
G_x	0.37816	0.37346	0.38034	0.37638	0.37300
			(0.00535)	(0.01006)	(0.00643)
G_y	0.32186	0.31173	0.31265	0.31684	0.31135
			(0.00450)	(0.01287)	(0.00534)
C_y	0.31573	0.31173	0.31265	0.31684	0.31135
			(0.00450)	(0.01287)	(0.00534)
C_t	0.50686	0.50071	0.50069	0.50017	0.50017
			(0.00566)	(0.00766)	(0.00766)
W_x	17331	17462	17216	17478	17466
			(273.84)	(478.62)	(274.39)
W_y	12727	12917	12834	12932	12920
			(176.71)	(427.33)	(173.86)
K	0.12871	0.12726	0.12035	0.12379	0.12714
			(0.00060)	(0.00782)	(0.00169)
L	0.15630	0.06172	0.06769	0.05954	0.06165
			(0.00090)	(0.00442)	(0.00127)

G_x, G_y pre- and post-tax Gini; C_y, C_t post-tax and tax concentration; W_x, W_y pre- and post-tax welfare; K progressivity; L redistribution.

16

seen that the tax system is progressive. Despite the reduction in inequality, the value of social welfare, W_y is less than W_x because of the reduction in average income arising from the tax.[10]

There is little to choose between the arithmetic means of posterior distributions obtained using the three alternative approaches. In considering the standard deviations of the posterior distributions, the assumption of a triangular distribution produces larger standard deviations than the other approaches. It can be seen that the use of the assumption of lognormality for the pre-tax distribution produces a slightly lower standard deviation than when group arithmetic means are used. This finding is perhaps not surprising in view of the fact that the pre-tax incomes were generated from a lognormal distribution. However, the use of group means produces standard deviations that are very close to those using lognormality.

In a practical case, the form of the pre-tax income distribution is of course not known, and any assumed functional form for the distribution is most unlikely to provide such a good approximation as in the present example. The use of an explicit distributional assumption has been seen to require a very large number of draws when using the Metropolis-Hastings algorithm, whereas the use of group means is much less time consuming, requiring far fewer draws from a Dirichlet distribution. As mentioned above, the results obtained using group means are very close to those using lognormality, which in the present example would obviously be expected to dominate. The use of group means may therefore be suggested as a practical approach, where the sample size is reasonably large. In fact, cross-sectional surveys typically contain many more observations than the present case of 2000 individuals. This avoids any preliminary investigations involving comparisons of alternative functional forms, along with the extensive numerical work.[11]

---

[10]In this context, a measure of the welfare premium from progression could be obtained in terms of the gain in welfare arising from the use of the actual tax structure compared with a proportional tax raising the same revenue; see Lambert (1993).

[11]The use of the lognormal in the present context is able to exploit the convenient analytical expression for the Gini coefficient in terms of the variance of logarithms. This may not be so tractable for alternative functional forms.

17

6   Conclusions

This paper has examined several Bayesian methods of examining posterior distributions of a range of inequality, concentration, tax progressivity and social welfare measures. The approach involves the multinomial distribution and must therefore be applied to grouped distributions. However, individual data are initially required in view of the strong inter-relationships among the three relevant distributions of pre-tax and post-tax income and of tax payments. Use was made of an explicit income distribution assumption and two alternative assumptions regarding the distribution of pre-tax group-mean incomes within each income group.

The methods were applied to a simulated distribution of individual incomes and tax payments. Grouping incomes by selecting classes of equal logarithmic width produced posterior distributions of the Gini measure of pre-tax income having lower standard deviations than obtained using other grouping methods. The arithmetic mean of the posterior distribution is close to the sample value of the Gini based on individual data for all numbers of income classes. However, the standard deviation rapidly falls until it approaches a stable level. This property enables a minimum acceptable number of classes to be selected, which is an advantage given the substantial computing requirements arising from a large number of income groups.

The results showed that there is little to choose between distributional assumptions in terms of the means of posterior distributions for the various measures. The use of groups means was found to produce standard deviations of posteriors that are very close to those obtained using an explicit assumption of lognormality of pre-tax incomes even when, in the present context, the sample is known to be selected from a lognormal population. In view of the extensive computing requirements when using a functional form for incomes, and the difficulty in practice of selecting an appropriate distribution, the results suggest support for the use of group means in practical applications, particularly where large sample sizes are involved. Any loss in precision is likely to be small.

18

Appendix: The Simulated Sample

The computations reported above were carried out on a simulated sample of 2000 individuals. The pre-tax incomes were drawn at random from a lognormal distribution, $\Lambda\left(x|\, 10, 0.5\right)$.

The income tax structure has 6 marginal tax rates: 0.22, 0.28, 0.35, 0.4, 0.45 and 0.5. The basic income thresholds are 8000, 15000, 20000, 25000, 35000, and 42000 (so that a marginal rate of 0.22 applies to income measured in excess of 8000). However, the actual thresholds applying to each individual are individual-specific, since the first threshold is assumed to be lognormally distributed with a variance of logarithms of 2.0 and arithmetic mean of 8000. For each individual, a random draw from this distribution was used to determine the first income threshold, and all higher thresholds were adjusted such that the absolute difference between thresholds is the same as in the basic structure (that is, the second threshold was obtained by adding 7000 to the first threshold, and so on).

In addition, a general consumption tax was applied on the assumption that all income net of income tax is consumed. There is a structure of exemptions such that the proportion of expenditure, q, that attracts a zero consumption tax rate is $r(q) = 200/(q+10000)^{0.65}$. This functional form has been found to provide a good description of actual tax systems, as shown in Creedy (1996). A consumption tax rate of 0.10 is applied to all remaining expenditure. The consumption tax is specified as a tax-exclusive rate, but q is measured in tax-inclusive terms. Hence, the consumption tax paid is equal to $\left(\frac{0.1}{1.0+0.1}\right) q\left(1 - r\left(q\right)\right)$. The post-tax income, y, is obtained as the net-of-tax value of consumption.

19

References

[1] Aigner, D.J. and Goldberger, A.S. (1970) Estimation of Pareto's law from grouped observations. *Journal of the American Statistical Association*, 65, pp. 712-723.

[2] Aitchison, J. and Brown, J.A.C. (1957) *The Lognormal Distribution.* Cambridge: Cambridge University Press.

[3] Atkinson, A.B. (1979) Horizontal equity and the distribution of the tax burden. In *The Economics of Taxation* (ed. by H.J. Aaron and M.J. Boskins). Washington: The Brookings Institution.

[4] Box, G.E.P. and Tiao, G.C. (1973) *Bayesian Inference in Statistical Analysis.* Reading, MA.: Addison-Wesley.

[5] Chotikapanich, D. and Griffiths, W.E. (2000) Posterior distributions for the Gini coefficient using grouped data. *Australian and New Zealand Journal of Statistics*, 4, pp. 901-910. (forthcoming).

[6] Creedy, J. (1996) *Fiscal Policy and Social Welfare: An Analysis of Alternative Tax and Transfer Schemes.* Aldershot: Edward Elgar.

[7] Gelman, A., Carlin, J.B., Stern, H.S. and Rubin, D.S. (1995) *Bayesian Data Analysis.* London: Chapman and Hall.

[8] Geweke, J. (1999) Using simulation methods for Bayesian econometric models: inference, development and communication. *Econometric Reviews,* 18, pp. 1-74.

[9] Judge, G.G., Hill, R.C., Griffiths, W.E., Liitkepohl, H. and Lee, T-C. (1998) *Introduction to the Theory and Practice of Econometrics.* New York: Wiley and Sons.

[10] Kakwani, N.C. (1977) Measurement of tax progressivity: an international comparison. *Economic Journal,* 87, pp. 71-80.

[11] Kakwani, N.C. and Podder, N. (1973) On the estimation of Lorenz curves from grouped observations. *International Economic Review*, 14, 278-292.

[12] Kakwani, N.C. and Podder, N. (1976) Efficient estimation of the Lorenz curve and associated inequality measures from grouped observations. *Econometrica*, 44, pp. 137-148.

[13] Kloek, T. and Van Dijk, H.K. (1978) Efficient estimation of income distribution parameters. *Journal of Econometrics*, 8, pp. 61-74.

[14] Lambert, P.J. (1993) *The Distribution and Redistribution of Income: A Mathematical Analysis.* Manchester: Manchester University Press.

[15] Plotnick, R. (1981) A measure of horizontal inequity. *Review of Economics and Statistics*, 63, pp. 283-87.

[16] Reynolds, M. and Smolensky, E. (1977) *Public Expenditures, Taxes and the Distribution of Income: The United States 1950, 1961, 1970.* New York: Academic Press.

[17] Sen, A.K. (1973) *On Economic Inequality.* Oxford: Clarendon.

[18] Van Dijk, H.K. and Kloek, T. (1980) Inferential procedures in stable distributions for class frequency data on incomes. *Econometrica*, 48, pp. 1139-1148.

[19] Zellner, A. (1971) *An Introduction to Bayesian Inference in Econometrics.* New York: John Wiley.

21

[14]

Bayesian Estimation of Atkinson Inequality Measures

Duangkamon Chotikapanich and John Creedy*

Abstract

This paper examines several methods of obtaining posterior distributions of the Atkinson inequality measure and social welfare function. The methods are compared with asymptotic standard errors and the role of the number of income classes is investigated. If only a small number of groups is available in published data, there is a clear gain from generating the posterior distribution when using an explicit distributional assumption. Even with a small number of groups, the Bayesian approach gives results that are close to the sample values from individual observations.

1 Introduction

This paper provides a Bayesian method of estimating the Atkinson (1970) measure and its associated abbreviated social welfare function, along with their precision, by obtaining the posterior density function. The approach follows that suggested by Chotikapanich and Griffiths (2000) in the context of the Gini measure, which derives the likelihood function from a multinomial distribution.[1] This investigation is warranted in view of the extensive use made of the Atkinson measure.

---

*School of Economics and Finance, Curtin University of Technology, Perth, and Department of Economics, University of Melbourne. This research was supported by a Melbourne University Faculty of Economics and Commerce Research Grant. We have benefited from discussions with Bill Griffiths.

[1]For a Bayesian analysis of tax progressivity and concentration measures, see Chotikapanich and Creedy (2000).

1

The method of analysis is necessarily applied to grouped income distributions rather than individual data, in view of the use of the multinomial distribution.[2] This paper examines the appropriate grouping and the use of alternative assumptions regarding the distribution of income as a whole and the distribution of mean income within each group when the Bayesian methods are used. The methods are also of value when faced with published income distribution data which use a grouping that is largely arbitrary and outside researchers' control.

One advantage of using Bayesian estimation is that it provides a framework for finite sample inference. Therefore, in addition, the results obtained using posterior distributions are compared with those generated for sampling distributions using the methods given by Thistle (1990), which relate to the large sample properties of the Atkinson inequality and social welfare measures.[3]

Section 2 briefly defines the Atkinson measure and gives the asymptotic standard errors relating to the sampling distributions of inequality and associated equally distributed equivalent income. Section 3 describes the Bayesian method. Two basic approaches are used to reflect uncertainty. The first uses an explicit assumption about the form of the income distribution, while the second approach uses two alternative assumptions about the distribution of mean income within each group. Section 4 reports numerical results based on the use of a sample of 2000 individuals. Brief conclusions are in section 5.

---

[2] A multinomial framework for sampling theory estimation of the parameters of a variety of income distributions was used by Kloek and van Dijk (1978) and van Dijk and Kloek (1980), and for the Pareto distribution by Aigner and Goldberger (1970).

[3] For general discussions of the large sample properties of inequality measures, see Cowell (1999) and Giorgi (1999).

2   Atkinson's Measure

Suppose that income, x, follows the continuous density function $f(x)$. Atkinson's inequality measure is linked to a social welfare function. Let W denote the social welfare per capita, for a disinterested judge with $\varepsilon \neq 1$ and where:[4]

$$W = \int_0^\infty \frac{x^{1-\varepsilon}}{1-\varepsilon} f(x)\, dx = \frac{x_{p,e}^{1-\varepsilon}}{1-\varepsilon} \tag{1}$$

The term $x_{p,e}$ is the population equally distributed equivalent income and is that level which, if obtained by everyone, produces the same social welfare as the actual distribution. The coefficient ε is a measure of relative inequality aversion which, as the degree of concavity of $x^{1-\varepsilon}/(1-\varepsilon)$, reflects the judge's view of the 'wastefulness of inequality'.[5] From (1):

$$x_{p,e} = \left\{ \int_0^\infty \frac{x^{1-\varepsilon}}{1-\varepsilon} f(x)\, dx \right\}^{1/(1-\varepsilon)} \tag{2}$$

The Atkinson inequality measure, $A_{p,\varepsilon}$, of the population is the proportional difference between arithmetic mean income, μ, and the equally distributed equivalent level. Hence:[6]

$$A_{p,\varepsilon} = 1 - \frac{x_{p,e}}{\mu} \tag{3}$$

It is required to estimate the Atkinson measure using a random sample, $x_1, ..., x_N$, of size N drawn from the population. Typically, a sample statistic is computed. This can most conveniently be expressed in terms of fractional and negative sample moments about the origin. Let $\alpha = 1 - \varepsilon$, and let m_α denote the sample moment of order α about the origin. Hence:

$$m_\alpha = \frac{1}{N} \sum_{i=1}^N x_i^\alpha \tag{4}$$

---

[4]See Atkinson (1970) for the initial statement, Lambert (1993) for an extensive treatment and Creedy (1996) for an introduction.

[5]For discussion of the 'leaky bucket' experiment which helps to fix ideas about the likely orders of magnitude of ε, see Amiel *et al.* (1999).

[6]Rearrangement of (3) gives, $x_{p,e} = \mu(1 - A_{p,\varepsilon})$ which serves as an abbreviated social welfare function, reflecting the trade-off between equity, $(1 - A_{p,\alpha})$, and efficiency measured in terms of μ. On abbreviated social welfare functions, see Lambert (1993).

Furthermore the sample value of the equally distributed equivalent income is given as $x_e = m_\alpha^{1/\alpha}$, so that the sample Atkinson measure, A_α is expressed as:

$$A_\alpha = 1 - \frac{m_\alpha^{1/\alpha}}{m_1} \tag{5}$$

where the population mean is estimated using the sample value, m_1.

2.1   Asymptotic Standard Errors

The asymptotic standard error of the above estimates of the inequality measure and the equally distributed equivalent income can be obtained as follows. Define the higher-order sample moments about the mean, s_α^2, using:

$$s_\alpha^2 = m_{2\alpha} - m_\alpha^2 \tag{6}$$

and define the sample covariances using:

$$s_{\alpha_1,\alpha_2} = m_{\alpha_1+\alpha_2} - m_{\alpha_1} m_{\alpha_2} \tag{7}$$

Thistle (1990) showed that the asymptotic sampling variance, $V(A_\alpha)$, of the Atkinson measure can be written as follows:

$$V(A_\alpha) = k_\alpha \left[s_\alpha^2 - 2 \left(\frac{\alpha m_\alpha}{m_1} \right) s_{\alpha,1} + \left(\frac{\alpha m_\alpha}{m_1} \right)^2 s_1^2 \right] \tag{8}$$

where:

$$k_\alpha = \left(\frac{1 - A_\alpha}{\alpha m_\alpha} \right)^2 \tag{9}$$

Furthermore, the asymptotic sampling variance, $V(x_e)$, of x_e can be estimated using:

$$V(x_e) = \frac{1}{N} \left(\frac{m_\alpha^{(1-\alpha)/\alpha} s_\alpha}{\alpha} \right)^2 \tag{10}$$

These asymptotic variances are therefore easily computed along with the sample values, A_α and x_e.

4

2.2   Grouped Data

The above results apply to a sample of individual observations. They need to be modified in the case where grouped data are available. Suppose the upper limit of the ith income class is z_i, with $z_0 = 0$. In terms of the population distribution, the probability, p_i, that an individual chosen randomly has income in class i, where $i = 1, ..., M$, is $p_i = \int_{z_{i-1}}^{z_i} f(x) \, dx$. Furthermore the population moments about the origin, of order α, denoted, $\mu_{i,\alpha}$, within the ith class is:

$$\mu_{i,\alpha} = \frac{\int_{z_{i-1}}^{z_i} x^\alpha f(x) \, dx}{\int_{z_{i-1}}^{z_i} f(x) \, dx} \tag{11}$$

Hence:[7]

$$\begin{aligned} \mu_\alpha &= \sum_{i=1}^{M} \left\{ \int_{z_{i-1}}^{z_i} x^\alpha f(x) \, dx \right\} \\ &= \sum_{i=1}^{M} \mu_{i,\alpha} p_i \end{aligned} \tag{12}$$

In practice, the following approach is used. Given a sample of observations drawn from the population, suppose there are n_i observations in the ith income group, with $N = \sum_{i=1}^{M} n_i$. The p_is may be estimated using:

$$p_i = \frac{n_i}{N} \tag{13}$$

The approach to $\mu_{i,\alpha}$ usually depends on the information provided in the observed grouped frequency distribution. If the arithmetic mean income within each group, $\bar{x}_i$, is available, then typically the assumption is made that all values are concentrated at the group mean, and the sample value, $\bar{x}_i^\alpha$ is used as an estimate of $\mu_{i,\alpha}$.[8] Hence the sample moment of order α is estimated using:

$$m_\alpha = \frac{1}{N} \sum_{i=1}^{M} \bar{x}_i^\alpha n_i \tag{14}$$

---

[7]Following standard practice, μ_1 has been written simply as μ.

[8]More generally $\mu_i^\alpha \neq \mu_{i,\alpha}$. When values are assumed to be concentrated at the class midpoints, Sheppard's correction may sometimes be used for integer moments.

5

However, in published data the sample arithmetic mean within each group is not always given. In such cases the class midpoint or, for example, the geometric mean of upper and lower class limits, are instead taken. If the number of groups is small, the resulting estimates of inequality are, as shown below, likely to understate the population values.

3   Posterior Distributions

This section presents two approaches to estimating posterior probability density functions, following Chotikapanich and Griffiths (2000). The first subsection considers the use of an explicit assumption regarding the income distribution. The second subsection considers the situation where no explicit income distribution assumption is made.

3.1   Lognormal Distribution of Income

Suppose that x is distributed lognormally as $\Lambda\left(x|\,\mu_{\log x}, \sigma^2_{\log x}\right)$, where $\mu_{\log x}$ and $\sigma^2_{\log x}$ are respectively the mean and variance of the logarithms of income.[9] Hence $\log x$ follows the normal distribution and:

$$\Lambda\left(x\right) = N\left(\frac{\log x - \mu_{\log x}}{\sigma_{\log x}}\bigg|\, 0, 1\right) \tag{15}$$

There is of course a wide range of distributions which could be used. However, the lognormal distribution was chosen because of its ability to provide a reasonable approximation to many empirical distributions. Furthermore, it has the convenient property that the Atkinson measure can be written as a simple function of the parameter, $\sigma^2_{\log x}$. This result is obtained by first writing $\int x^\alpha d\Lambda\left(x\right)$ as $\int e^{\alpha \log x} dN\left(\log x\right)$. Using the moment generating function for the normal distribution, it can be shown that the population moment of order α is given by:

$$\mu_\alpha = \exp\left(\alpha\mu_{\log x} + \frac{1}{2}\alpha^2\sigma^2_{\log x}\right) \tag{16}$$

---

[9]On the lognormal distribution, see Aitchison and Brown (1957).

Substituting into $A_{p,\alpha}$, as defined in (3), gives:

$$A_{p,\alpha} = 1 - \exp\left(-\frac{\varepsilon}{2}\sigma_{\log x}^2\right) \tag{17}$$

Hence, $A_{p,\alpha}$ depends only on the variance of logarithms of income.

Define the parameter vector, $\theta = (\mu_{\log x}, \sigma_{\log x})$. From Bayes's Theorem:

$$f(\theta|n) \propto f(\theta) f(n|\theta) \tag{18}$$

The specification of the prior density $f(\theta)$ is based on the standard use of noninformative improper priors on both parameters, where $\mu_{\log x}$ and $\log \sigma_{\log x}$ are assumed to be uniformly distributed. Thus the joint density $f(\theta)$ is proportional to $\sigma_{\log x}^{-1}$.[10]

The likelihood function, $f(n|\theta)$, follows the multinomial, $\prod_{i=1}^{M} p_i^{n_i}$. If the lower and upper class limits of group i are $x_{L,i}$ and $x_{U,i}$, the likelihood can be written, for the case of the lognormal distribution, as:

$$f(n|\theta) \propto \prod_{i=1}^{M} \{\Lambda(x_{U,i}) - \Lambda(x_{L,i})\}^{n_i} \tag{19}$$

The resulting posterior density obtained using (18) is not analytically tractable. However, a Metropolis-Hastings algorithm can be used to draw observations from it. For statements of this algorithm see, for example, Geweke (1999) and Chotikapanich and Griffiths (2000).

Given a drawing of $\sigma_{\log x}^2$, a corresponding Atkinson measure can be obtained using (17). The resulting values can be used to estimate the posterior density.

3.2 No Explicit Income Distribution Assumption

If no assumption is made about the income distribution, the Atkinson measure can be expressed in the context of grouped distributions using moments given in section 2 above. This involves finding the posterior distributions for p_i and $\mu_{i,1}$. Using the standard convention, the following defines $\mu_i = \mu_{i,1}$.

---

[10]On the use of a uniform prior for $\log \sigma$, see for example Judge *et al.* (1998, p.150), Box and Tiao (1973) and Zellner (1971, pp.42-44).

3.2.1   Posterior Density For The p_is

Let n and p respectively denote vectors of the observed group frequencies, n_i, and the p_i, for $i = 1, ..., M$. Using Bayes's Theorem, the posterior probability density function for p is:

$$f(p|n) \propto f(p) f(n|p) \tag{20}$$

A possible noninformative form for the prior, $f(p)$, is:[11]

$$f(p) \propto \prod_{i=1}^{M} p_i^{-1} \tag{21}$$

The likelihood function, $f(n|p)$, follows the multinomial distribution, $\prod_{i=1}^{M} p_i^{n_i}$. Hence the posterior probability density function for p is:

$$f(p|n) \propto \prod_{i=1}^{M} p_i^{n_i-1} \tag{22}$$

This is a Dirichlet distribution from which random observations can be drawn and which reflects the uncertainty about the p_is.

3.2.2   Information About The μ_is

Two approaches for reflecting uncertainty about the μ_is are examined here. One approach is simply to set the μ_i equal to the corresponding group arithmetic means, $\bar{x}_i$. The second approach involves the assumption that, within each group, values of μ_i follow a triangular distribution. In each case, given values of μ_i, these are combined with the p_i using the using the usual assumption mentioned above that the group values are concentrated at the mean. Hence the higher-order fractional moments are calculated using $\sum_{i=1}^{M} \mu_i^\alpha p_i$.

Suppose values of μ_i follow a triangular distribution over the range defined by the class limits, $x_{L,i}$ and $x_{U,i}$, with the prior for the mode set equal to the sample arithmetic mean, $\bar{x}_i$. The procedure used for each income group

---

[11]See, for example, Gelman *et al.* (1995, p.399)

is as follows.[12] First draw a random value, $P_i = F(\mu_i)$ from a uniform $(0, 1)$ distribution. Check if:

$$P_i < \frac{\overline{x}_i - x_{L,i}}{x_{U,i} - x_{L,i}} \tag{23}$$

which implies that μ_i lies between $x_{L,i}$ and $\overline{x}_i$. If this condition holds, then the range of the distribution for which:

$$F(\mu_i) = \frac{(\mu_i - x_{L,i})^2}{(x_{U,i} - x_{L,i})(\overline{x}_i - x_{L,i})} \tag{24}$$

is appropriate. Hence, substitute for $P_i = F(\mu_i)$ and solve for μ_i to get:

$$\mu_i = x_{L,i} + \{P_i (x_{U,i} - x_{L,i})(\overline{x}_i - x_{L,i})\}^{1/2} \tag{25}$$

If the condition in (23) does not hold, then μ_i lies between $x_{U,i}$ and $\overline{x}_i$, and:

$$F(\mu_i) = 1 - \frac{(x_{U,i} - \mu_i)^2}{(x_{U,i} - x_{L,i})(x_{U,i} - \overline{x}_i)} \tag{26}$$

Solving for μ_i gives:

$$\mu_i = x_{U,i} - \{(1 - P_i)(x_{U,i} - x_{L,i})(x_{U,i} - \overline{x}_i)\}^{1/2} \tag{27}$$

The resulting values of μ_i are combined with the p_i from the Dirichlet distribution to obtain the required moments.

4 Numerical Results

The numerical results presented in this section are based on a random sample of 2000 individuals drawn from a lognormal distribution with mean and variance of logarithms of 10 and 0.5 respectively. In grouping the individual data, groups of equal logarithmic width were obtained.[13] When obtaining the posterior distributions in the case of lognormality, 85,000 draws from

---

[12] See also Chotikapanich and Griffiths (2000).

[13] Chotikapanich and Creedy (2000) also examined the effects on the Gini measure of using groups containing equal percentiles. The use of equal logarithmic width groups was found to be superior.

9

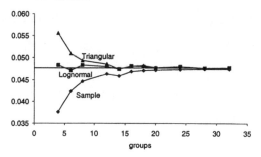

Figure 1: Atkinson Inequality Measure $\varepsilon = 0.2$

the Metropolis-Hastings algorithm were used (the first 10,000 of which were discarded). When applying the other two assumptions (using group means and triangular distribution), the posteriors were based on 5,000 draws from the Dirichlet distribution.

The first issue concerns the effects of increasing the number of groups used. Figures 1 and 2 show the variations in Atkinson measures for ε of 0.2 and 1.4 respectively, which represent low and high values.[14] They also show a horizontal line showing the value of the sample statistic obtained using individual observations. Three sets of curves are shown. The first two are arithmetic means of the posterior distributions under the assumption of lognormality and the assumption that the group means follow a triangular distribution. The third curve gives the sample statistic using sample moments as given in equation (14); hence they are based on the assumption that all values within each group are concentrated at the sample arithmetic mean.[15] It was found that these sample statistics are approximately the same

---

[14]For survey information about attitudes to inequality, see Amiel *et al.* (1999).

[15]The situation where published group data have to be used and athmetic means are not available is discussed below.

10

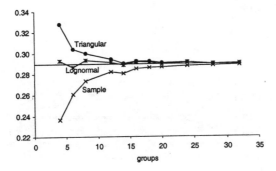

Figure 2: Atkinson Inequality Measure $\varepsilon = 1.4$

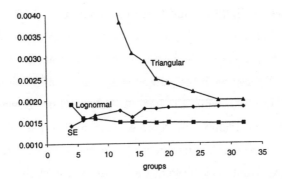

Figure 3: SE and Posterior SD: Atkinson $\varepsilon = 0.2$

11

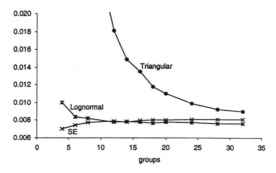

Figure 4: SE and Posterior SD: Atkinson $\varepsilon = 1.4$

as the mean of the posterior in the case where the sample arithmetic mean within each group is assumed to be the true mean.[16] For this reason, only the sample statistics are displayed in the figure.

The profiles in Figures 1 and 2 are very similar, with the only substantial difference being the scale used for the vertical axes. Both the sample statistic, and the mean of the posterior for triangular distributions within groups, gradually approach the sample value based on individual data. The former begins too high while the latter begins too low. However, under an assumption of lognormality (which corresponds in this case to the underlying distribution from which the random sample is drawn), the arithmetic mean of the posterior distribution is close to the sample statistic based on individual data, even where a small number of groups is used to obtain the former.

Figures 3 and 4 show corresponding values of the asymptotic standard error and the standard deviation of the posterior distributions for the inequality measure, again using values of ε of 0.2 and 1.4 respectively. The assumption

---

[16]This is despite the fact that the posterior also considers the existence of uncertainty in the p_i, for which the sample statistic does not allow.

of a triangular distribution (within each income group) appears consistently to give results that exceed those obtained using other approaches. This applies to the inequality measure, as well as to the standard deviation and standard error (except in the case of the inequality measure when a large number of groups is used). The asymptotic standard error increases as the number of groups increases, but it stabilises by about 16 to 18 groups. Conversely, the assumption of lognormality produces a declining standard deviation of the posterior distribution, though this also stabilises at about 16 to 18 groups. The latter two profiles actually intersect, though in absolute terms there is very little difference between the two after they have stabilised.

Figures 5 and 6 show profiles of the equally distributed equivalent income, which serves as an abbreviated welfare measure, obtained as a sample statistic, and the arithmetic mean of the posterior distribution for the assumption of lognormality. The use of a triangular distribution within each income group is not shown in these figures, as the values are substantially different from the other profiles shown. Again, the sample statistic was found to be similar to the mean of the posterior obtained on the assumption that the mean within each group is equal to its sample value, so only the former is shown in the figure. The figures also show, as a horizontal line, the sample statistic obtained using the individual data. As with the inequality measure, the mean of the posterior distribution is little affected by grouping if the assumption of lognormality is used. The sample statistic overstates the welfare measure for a small number of groups, but it approaches the value based on individual observations when about 18 to 20 groups are used.

The asymptotic standard error and standard deviation of the posterior distribution, for the abbreviated social welfare measure, are shown in Figures 7 and 8. These results reflect those obtained for the inequality measure. The two sets of results are seen to converge when the number of groups increases to about 18.

The results given above show that estimates stabilise after about 18 in-

13

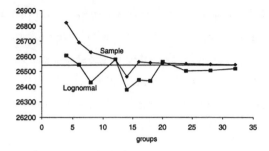

Figure 5: Social Welfare: $\varepsilon = 0.2$

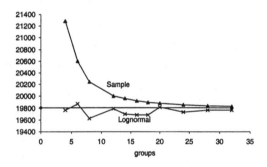

Figure 6: Social Welfare: $\varepsilon = 1.4$

14

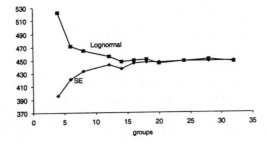

Figure 7: SE and Posterior SD: Social Welfare $\varepsilon = 0.2$

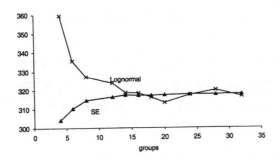

Figure 8: SE and Posterior SD: Social Welfare $\varepsilon = 1.4$

15

Table 1: Summary Measures of Posterior Distributions: 18 Groups

ε		Lognormal A	Lognormal W	Arithmetic Mean A	Arithmetic Mean W	Triangular A	Triangular W
0.2	Mean	0.0480	26438	0.0471	26564	0.0482	26710
	SD	0.0015	450.80	0.0018	449.94	0.0025	680.99
0.5	Mean	0.1158	24556	0.1134	24714	0.1161	24805
	SD	0.0034	400.90	0.0039	396.80	0.0057	622.00
0.8	Mean	0.1787	22808	0.1751	22994	0.1790	23037
	SE	0.0051	362.80	0.0056	358.07	0.0082	573.41
1.1	Mean	0.2371	21185	0.2325	21393	0.2378	21395
	SD	0.0065	335.10	0.0069	331.30	0.0100	533.07
1.4	Mean	0.2914	19677	0.2862	19897	0.2920	19866
	SD	0.0076	316.11	0.0080	315.20	0.0118	499.95

come groups. Hence, numerical result for the alternative methods are given in Tables 1 and 2 for the case of 18 income groups. In these tables, results for five values of the inequality aversion parameter are given. This is because the choice of ε affects the sensitivity of the Atkinson measure to different parts of the distribution and therefore may have been expected to affect comparisons between methods. Table 2 also gives the sample statistics using individual observations, and the associated asymptotic standard errors. The similarity between the results for posterior distributions using arithmetic means (in the middle two columns of Table 1) and the sample statistics and asymptotic standard error (in the final two columns of Table 2) is clear. The results for the grouped data in Table 2 are similar to the use of individual data, which in turn are similar to the Bayesian results using the assumption of lognormality, as shown in Table 1. The results also show that the choice of inequality aversion coefficient does not affect comparisons between alternative estimation methods.

In cases where published grouped income distributions do not report arithmetic means within each income group, it is not possible to use equation (14) as an estimate of (12). For this reason, similar investigations were made

16

Table 2: Sample Statistics and Asymptotic Standard Errors

		Individual		18 Groups	
ε		*A*	*W*	*A*	*W*
0.2	Point	0.0477	26541.01	0.0471	26558.13
	SE	0.0018	449.86	0.0018	446.65
0.5	Point	0.1149	24668.62	0.1134	24708.55
	SE	0.0040	397.42	0.0040	395.25
0.8	Point	0.1772	22930.21	0.1751	22989.79
	SE	0.0057	359.63	0.0056	358.11
1.1	Point	0.2353	21312.82	0.2325	21388.91
	SE	0.0070	333.66	0.0069	332.57
1.4	Point	0.2895	19802.51	0.2862	19892.89
	SE	0.0081	317.97	0.0080	317.20

involving the use of class midpoints and the geometric mean of upper and lower class limits; the results of using the two methods were similar. Furthermore, just as with the use of class arithmetic means, the values were close to those obtained from the corresponding posterior distributions obtained on the assumption that the mean within each group was equal to its sample midpoint or geometric mean.[17]

However, in each case, when using a small number of income groups, the Atkinson inequality measure and its asymptotic standard error (or in the posterior distribution case, the mean and standard deviation of the posterior distribution) were higher than the values obtained from individual observations. This contrasts with the use of group means, where the values were below those computed from individual observations. However, as the number of groups was increased, the sets of estimates converged. These results qualify the broad statement made by Cowell (1999, p. 280) that, 'what is crucial is the availability of data on interval means: k intervals with information about frequencies and interval means gives much more accuracy than

---

[17] Again, this is despite the fact that the posterior distributions allow for the uncertainty regarding the p_is.

17

2k intervals with information about frequencies alone'.[18]

5   Conclusions

This paper has examined several methods of obtaining posterior distributions of the Atkinson inequality measure and its associated abbreviated social welfare function. The results of applying the methods were compared with asymptotic standard errors. The sensitivity of results to variations in the number of income classes was investigated, where the observed distribution was divided into classes of equal logarithmic width.

The comparisons suggest a number of conclusions. First, of the different approaches to the posterior distribution, there seems to be little value in using the assumption of a triangular distribution in order to obtain the μ_is for each income group. When a sufficient number of income groups are used, the mean of the posterior distribution is similar to the other methods, but this assumption produces standard deviations that are too high.[19]

Secondly, setting the μ_is equal to the sample arithmetic mean incomes (or using group midpoints or geometric means of class limits) gives posterior distributions with similar characteristics to the sampling distributions. That is, the means and standard deviations of posterior distributions were very close to the corresponding sample statistics and their asymptotic standard errors, whatever the number of income groups used. This is despite the allowance for uncertainty regarding the p_is that is made in the Bayesian approach. This suggests that if such assumptions are to be made regarding class means, it is not worth going to the extra trouble of obtaining posterior distributions, since the basic sample statistics and asymptotic results are

---

[18] The results mentioned here refer, of course, to groups of equal logarithmic width with a sample drawn from an underlying lognormal distribution. The use of alternative measures of location may not always lead to convergent results as the number of groups increases.

[19] Chotikapanich and Griffiths (2000) found a similar result in the context of the Gini measure, and suggested the possible use of distributions with thinner tails than the triangular.

simple to compute. However, these methods are found to be unreliable for a small number of income groups, though more than about 16 groups produces results that are similar to values obtained from individual observations.

If only a small number of groups is available in published data, there is a clear gain to be obtained from generating the posterior distribution when using an explicit distributional assumption, such as the lognormal. Even with a small number of groups, the Bayesian approach gives results that are close to the sample values that are obtained by using individual observations. Hence, when given few income groups it is useful to devote some energy to investigating the form of the distribution.[20]

Finally, the results suggest that if published data provide a sufficient number of groups, or if individual data are available, there seems to be little difference between results obtained using the Bayesian approach with the assumption of lognormality (even when, as here, this is known to describe the underlying population distribution) and the use of asymptotic standard errors. The latter are of course much easier to compute.

---

[20]It is known that many observed distributions have a fatter upper tail than the lognormal form, but the latter provides a useful approximation over the whole range.

References

[1] Aigner, D.J. and Goldberger, A.S. (1970) Estimation of Pareto's law from grouped observations. *Journal of the American Statistical Association*, 65, pp. 712-723.

[2] Aitchison, J. and Brown, J.A.C. (1957) *The Lognormal Distribution*. Cambridge: Cambridge University Press.

[3] Amiel, Y., Creedy, J. and Hurn, S. (1999) Measuring attitudes towards inequality. *Scandinavian Journal of Economics*, 101, pp. 83-96.

[4] Atkinson, A.B. (1970) On the measurement of inequality. *Journal of Economic Theory*, 2, pp. 244-263.

[5] Box, G.E.P. and Tiao, G.C. (1973) *Bayesian Inference in Statistical Analysis*. Reading, MA.: Addison-Wesley.

[6] Chotikapanich, D. and Creedy, J. (2000) Bayesian estimation of social welfare and tax progressivity measures. *Melbourne University Department of Economics Research Paper, no. 751*.

[7] Chotikapanich, D. and Griffiths, W.E. (2000) Posterior distributions for the Gini coefficient using grouped data. *Australia and New Zealand Journal of Statistics*, 42, pp. 901-910.

[8] Cowell, F.A. (1999) Estimation of inequality indices. In *Handbook of Income Inequality Measurement* (ed. by J. Silber), pp. 269-290. Boston: Kluwer Academic Publishers.

[9] Creedy, J. (1996) *Fiscal Policy and Social Welfare: An Analysis of Alternative Tax and Transfer Schemes*. Aldershot: Edward Elgar.

[10] Gelman, A., Carlin, J.B., Stern, H.S. and Rubin, D.S. (1995) *Bayesian Data Analysis*. London: Chapman and Hall.

20

[11] Geweke, J. (1999) Using simulation methods for Bayesian econometric models: inference, development and communication. *Econometric Reviews,* 18, pp. 1-74.

[12] Giorgi, G.M. (1999) Income inequality measures: the statistical approach. In *Handbook of Income Inequality Measurement* (ed. by J. Silber), pp. 245-268. Boston: Kluwer Academic Publishers.

[13] Judge, G.G., Hill, R.C., Griffiths, W.E., Liitkepohl, H. and Lee, T-C. (1998) *Introduction to the Theory and Practice of Econometrics.* New York: Wiley and Sons.

[14] Kloek, T. and Van Dijk, H.K. (1978) Efficient estimation of income distribution parameters. *Journal of Econometrics,* 8, pp. 61-74.

[15] Lambert, P.J. (1993) *The Distribution and Redistribution of Income: A Mathematical Analysis.* Manchester: Manchester University Press.

[16] Thistle, P.D. (1990) Large sample properties of two inequality indices. *Econometrica,* 58, pp. 725-728.

[17] Van Dijk, H.K. and Kloek, T. (1980) Inferential procedures in stable distributions for class frequency data on incomes. *Econometrica,* 48, pp. 1139-1148.

[18] Zellner, A. (1971) *An Introduction to Bayesian Inference in Econometrics.* New York: John Wiley.

21

Name index